... ...
... AN... BU... ...ONME...

...this book o... ...last dat...

charged... aft...

ACCOUNTING FOR RESOURCES, 1

Accounting for Resources, 1

Economy-Wide Applications of Mass-Balance
Principles to Materials and Waste

Robert U. Ayres

*Sandoz Professor of Environment and Management, Professor of
Economics and director of the Centre for the Management of
Environmental Resources at the European Business School,
INSEAD, France*

Leslie W. Ayres

*Research Associate, Centre for Management of Environmental
Resources, INSEAD, France*

Edward Elgar
Cheltenham, UK • Northampton, MA, USA

Published by
Edward Elgar Publishing Limited
Glensanda House
Montpellier Parade
Cheltenham
Glos GL50 1UA
UK

Edward Elgar Publishing, Inc.
6 Market Street
Northampton
Massachusetts 01060
USA

A catalogue record for this book
is available from the British Library

Library of Congress Cataloguing in Publication Data
Ayres, Robert U.
    Accounting for resources, one : economy-wide applications of mass-balance principles to materials and waste / Robert U. Ayres, Leslie W. Ayres.
    Includes bibliographical references.
    1. Factory and trade waste—Management.   2. Factory and trade waste—Economic aspects.   3. Sustainable development.   4. Industrial management Environmental aspects.   I. Ayres, Leslie. 1933–
II. Title.
TD897.5.A96   1998   98–17085
362.72'8—dc21   CIP

ISBN 1 85898 640 0

Typeset by Manton Typesetters, 5–7 Eastfield Road, Louth, Lincolnshire, LN11 7AJ, UK.
Printed and bound in Great Britain by MPG Books Ltd, Bodmin, Cornwall}

Contents

Figures

Tables

Foreword: Accounting for risk

James Cummings-Saxton

Much of this book is about waste flows in the aggregate. But most people are not really concerned about the 'big battalions', such as mine waste, slag, ash, sewage or trash. More often than not it is the minor, even microscopic, flows that sting most. We care more about subtle environmental pollutants and poisons that can make us sick or – worse still – give us cancer 20 or 30 years from now, cause sterility, or give us defective children or grandchildren. The image of a 'thalidomide baby' must be one of the most frightening of all nightmares.

A great deal has been written and spoken about the dangers of ingesting carcinogenic pesticide residues in our food, of breathing radon gas or formaldehyde leaking from the walls of our own homes or dioxins from the smoke of the municipal incinerator, or of ingesting toxic industrial wastes that have leaked into the groundwater from which we must pump our drinking water. These dangers are especially frightening if only because we cannot see or otherwise sense their presence. Air that smells bad, or water that tastes bad, are not necessarily more polluted than air or water that seems clean and pure. Even the ground our new house or our children's school is built on may turn out to have been an old industrial toxic waste dump.

Some of these fears are certainly excessive. They are based largely on stories in the press, many of them distorted either inadvertently or (in some cases) intentionally. For example, the discovery of an old toxic chemical waste dump site under a real estate development and a school in Niagara Falls – known as Love Canal – led to a series of scary stories in the media based on interviews with public health 'experts' who were willing to talk. This was followed by serious panic, wholesale evacuation of most of the homes, financial disaster for many of the homeowners, whether they moved or remained, a rash of lawsuits, and very adverse publicity and heavy financial penalties on Hooker Chemical Co., the original owner of the site.

Yet, the press, seeking a scapegoat, ignored the fact that Hooker had behaved fairly responsibly, based on current norms. It was actually the local government officials who had wanted the land for a school site (despite documented warnings from Hooker) and then subsequently sold off some of the land at a profit to a developer, contrary to its agreement with Hooker. The developer, in turn, ignored Hooker's warnings and built houses that were sold to unsuspecting people without any mention of the prior use of the land. To this day, however, there is little if any convincing evidence of health damage to the residents attributable to the location of their homes.

This is not to say that Hooker Chemical Co. was totally 'green' in the matter of Love Canal. In the first place, the company could have done a better job, built the disposal site further from human habitation; it could have been built better. Second, Hooker could – and should – have refused to sell that site to the school, regardless of local pressures. Third, Hooker could have bought the land back from the developer, or warned the home-buyers, or taken various other actions.

There are environmental organizations, like Greenpeace, that collect and further disseminate such information – often incomplete and occasionally false – albeit from the best of motives. Having high-minded motives may excuse this practice in the minds of some people. But it is also true that most professional environmental organizations depend on voluntary contributions, which undoubtedly tend to rise when people are worried and frightened and fall when they are not. As organizations, they have a clear motive for presenting only the most negative side of every environmental story.

A case in point here is the current 'Circle of Poison' campaign by Greenpeace. The underlying fact is that some pesticides that are banned in the US are still being exported by US firms to other countries. The 'consumer sovereignty' argument can be made that Americans have no right to decide what pesticides people in other countries should, or should not, use. Apart from this, it is also true that some of the banned pesticides could well be the most cost-effective means of controlling vector-borne diseases, like malaria, sleeping sickness or schistomiasis, that are still scourges in the humid tropics but have long since been eliminated or never were a problem in North America.

To state the moral problem in more provocative form: should we Americans ban exports of DDT and let people die of malaria instead? Actually, that is exactly what we have done, right or wrong. (However, DDT is still produced in India, Indonesia, the former USSR and probably China, certainly under much less safe conditions.) But the current Greenpeace campaign revolves mainly around two other pesticides, chlordane and heptachlor, that are still used extensively for termite control, and very occasionally for other purposes such as locust control, in the tropics.

In the case of termite control, the major alternative in North America is to use wood preservatives. The two possibilities are pentachlorophenol (PCP), which is another banned insecticide. PCP is carcinogenic and usually contains dioxins as a contaminant from the manufacturing process. PCP is now manufactured by several countries in the third world. The other alternative, now preferred in the US, is to pressure-treat the wood by a mixture of highly toxic copper, chromium and arsenic compounds called CCA. Note that, being metals, these compounds are even more long-lived than the organochlorines. The fact is, if the objective is to prevent wood from rotting or being eaten by termites too quickly, there is no choice but to use a nasty toxic chemical of some kind to accomplish that purpose.

Unfortunately, Greenpeace does not discuss alternatives. It simply opposes the export of chlordane and heptachlor. Its campaign argument against this export is entirely based on the fact that very small, but detectable, traces of these compounds have been detected on some tropical products imported from Central America. Thus, the so-called 'circle of poison'. The deliberate implication is that the exported poisons will come back eventually and kill us. The latter threat (only hinted, never quite stated openly) is patent scientific nonsense.

We do not disguise the fact that we find the Greenpeace position on exports of chlordane and heptachlor both ridiculous and, fundamentally, irresponsible. But Greenpeace could not misuse a few nuggets of information – as it has – if more solid and verifiable information about pesticide production, use, toxicity, and dispersion in the environment were available to scientists and regulators. Industry secretiveness on many of the key points is part of the problem, but we will return to that issue later.

Industry is usually blamed automatically, whenever there is a problem, even if the fault actually lies elsewhere. This is because industry, taken as a whole, has a relatively bad record, both in terms of actual pollution and in terms of covering up its mistakes and misstatements (sometimes literally). Members of the public no longer blindly accept the bland assurances of 'environmental friendliness' that regularly emanate from the offices of professional public relations men and even chief executives. It is hard to forget the fact that the tobacco industry has never ceased to assert that 'there is no scientific proof' that smoking causes health problems, despite overwhelming evidence to the contrary. The asbestos industry made similar claims of innocence, found to be false by a jury. Similarly, the nuclear power industry routinely prided itself on its environmental record, before Three Mile Island and Chernobyl created deep skepticism. 'The initial industry response to almost every accident or incident has been evasion or denial. The exceptions (Johnson & Johnson, for one) are still much too rare.

Nowadays some of the larger firms in other industries – especially in the chemical industry – are beginning to try to change their bad reputation by seeking real rather than cosmetic solutions. But, as the nuclear power industry found out, it takes a long time for people to forget having been fooled. At the moment, polls show that environmental groups like Greenpeace are much more trusted by the public than industry.

We do not think that it is a good idea for our society to be manipulated by advertising and clever use of the media by any group, whether on one side or the other. Speaking for ourselves, we are not very trustful. We would rather have the facts.

N.B. James Cummings-Saxton had originally planned to co-author this entire book with us, which is why he uses the word 'we'. We worked together on it during August 1994. Unfortunately, he was prevented from contributing his other planned chapters by a combination of pressure of work and illness in the family. The book we have finally written without him is obviously not the same as the one we would have produced jointly. Nevertheless, we (RUA and LWA) associate ourselves with his views on the need for more reliable and accurate information, especially about chemicals, as he has so eloquently stated above. We hope that he will find time in the future to come back to these important issues.

Preface: Why quantify?

The logical starting point for us is with the question: Why do we need to measure things? The traditional answer is, more or less, as follows: We need physical measures to know what we have, what we have gained, what we have lost, where we are and where we are going. Why do we use numerical measures? Because we need to compare quantities more exactly than 'big' or 'small' or even 'bigger than' or 'smaller than'. This sack of potatoes may be heavier than that one, but how much heavier? This pasture is capable of grazing more sheep than the other one, but how many more?

Quantitative measures are critical for recipes, whether in cooking or chemistry. A little salt – or garlic, or hot pepper – adds savor. Too much makes the dish inedible. How much is enough? A little silicon in the aluminum alloy makes it machinable. Too much makes it brittle. How much is enough? The various constituents of an alloy, or a sauce, or a coloring agent, or a medicament must be present in exactly the right proportions. Much of the training of a chemist, metallurgist, winemaker, baker, cook, apothecary (druggist), or a painter concerns measures and proportions.

Accounting can be defined as the activity of compiling numerical measures of things or actions, in a form that makes comparison and analysis easy, or at least, possible. Accounting, as a profession, is almost exclusively concerned with a single measure, namely money. Accountants keep track of money inflows, outflows, and balances. They perform this function, as a rule, for business and financial enterprises, governments and (increasingly) households. Accountants are essential to the operation of a modem economic system. They allow a businessman to know whether the business is profitable or not in a given period. They are the basis for determining tax liabilities. Comparing accounts over different periods the business man can see trends: he can determine whether the business is growing or shrinking, and how fast. Over longer periods it is possible to see changes in the trends. Is growth accelerating or decelerating? Are profits and/or inventories growing faster or slower than volume? Is the debt/equity ratio increasing or decreasing? This kind of knowledge, in turn, permits the businessman to make rational decisions about market strategy, investment, pricing, wage costs, borrowing, dividend payments and so forth.

The importance of monetary accounting for governments and families is comparable, although the specific questions and issues are different in detail. Governments worry about tax revenues, trade balances, debt, interest rates and the supply of money. Families worry about meeting current bills, credit card balances, mortgage payments, tax liabilities, college costs, and retirement. Small differences can be very important. As Mr. Micawber said[1] 'Annual income twenty pounds, annual expenditure nineteen pounds nineteen six, result happiness. Annual income twenty pounds, annual expenditure twenty pound ought six, result misery.'

Monetary accounts are certainly necessary for modern life. If the number of accountants and the fees of accounting firms are a basis for judgment, the accounting profession is growing in importance. But, as we know all too well, money is not the measure of everything. Some things are literally priceless. There is no way to put a price on life, or liberty, or on human happiness.[2] More relevant to this book, there is no good way to assign monetary values to most of the essential services provided by the environment, ranging from benign climate, breathable air and fresh water to biodiversity, nutrient recycling and waste assimilation.

Yet, many environmental features, can be quantified in terms of other, non-monetary measures. In the absence of reliable monetary measures (that is, prices) such quantification is all the more necessary for making rational policy decisions. Just as the businessman needs to know whether the business that supports him is profitable and growing or unprofitable and declining, and how fast, we as a society need to know how the environment that sustains all life – and, especially, human life – is doing. Is it healthy and stable against perturbations? Is it prospering? Or is it sickening, perhaps to the verge of collapse?

These questions are difficult and deep. In the first place, they can only be answered when we understand very clearly and precisely what we mean by terms like 'healthy' or 'sick' as applied to the environment. Such an understanding requires scientific knowledge, which implies the development of a body of theory based on 'hard' (that is, quantifiable) observational data. Such analysis requires knowledge of the current and changing thermodynamic state of the air, the water, the soil, the weather and climate, and the biota, of course. The thermodynamic state encompasses temperatures, pressures, humidity, wind velocity, chemical and physical composition, and radiation spectrum, at all locations and times.

Yet direct measurement is not enough and never can be enough. The environment is too complex and heterogeneous to understand in terms of direct measurements alone. There can never be enough instruments to make all those measurements. If there were, their very existence would interfere with and modify the system being measured. (This is a version of the Heisenberg 'uncertainty principle'.) Moreover, there can never be a digital computer large enough to record all the data, still less analyze the multiple statistical correlations to ascertain causal relationships and generate accurate forecasts. And if such an all-powerful computer could exist, its programming would be more complex than the world itself, it's operation would require more energy than the sun can produce, and it would be inherently incapable of processing data in 'real time'. For these reasons, 'brute force' science is not the final answer. Data must be gathered, to be sure. But it must be averaged and aggregated over various spatial and time scales, and in other ways.

The essence of real science, therefore, is selection and simplification. Vastly simplified world models are needed, at first. The trick is to build understanding step-by-step by starting with simple models that explain the most fundamental phenomenon, adding complexity (or making changes in the assumptions) only when the existing models are clearly inconsistent with the reality.

Neo-classical economics is a prime example of this evolutionary process in action. It has proved fruitful in explaining certain fundamental social phenomena, namely the operation of exchange markets under various conditions. However insights from this simplified theory tell us nothing about the relationships between man and the natural environment. A new body of theory is needed. It must encompass at least some of the features of neoclassical economics, since economic activity has an important impact on the environment, and vice versa. Human impacts on the environment are, *ipso facto*, caused by land-use changes and by the economic activities of extraction, concentration, reduction, transformation, manufacturing, consumption and disposal of waste materials (and energy). Since man–nature interactions are not pure monetary transactions governed by market mechanisms, in general, they cannot be understood in terms of a pure market model of the world. Other elements must be added, also.

The new elements that must be added to the economic models are material stocks and flows, and physical (that is, thermodynamic) and biological relationships. We have used the term industrial metabolism to convey the flavor of this combination of ingredients.

Endnotes

1. The material in this preface has also been published in a recent symposium volume (Vellinga *et al.* 1998).
2. Charles Dickens, *David Copperfield.*
3. This is a ticklish subject, to be sure. In practice, society makes many political choices that amount to assigning a monetary value to saving a life. This is not done consistently, of course. Society will spend enormous sums to save the life of an astronaut (for instance), or to reduce the cancer risk from some obscure chemical (such as dioxin) while neglecting far more cost-efficient ways of saving lives, such as providing better prenatal care, enforcing speed limits, or prohibiting the sale of cigarettes to minors. Individual choices of careers also imply such valuations. Racing car drivers, motorcyclists, ski racers, boxers, lion tamers and high-wire circus performers take far greater risks than ordinary people; to a lesser extent, so do fire fighters, policemen, divers, coal miners and certain construction workers.

1 Background: Industrial metabolism and materials flow analysis (MFA)[1]

1.1 Definition

The word 'metabolism', as used in its original biological context, connotes the internal processes of a living organism. The organism ingests energy rich, low entropy materials ('food'), to provide for its own maintenance and functions, as well as a surplus to permit growth and/or reproduction. The process also necessarily involves excretion or exhalation of waste outputs, consisting of degraded, high entropy materials. There is a compelling analogy between biological organisms and industrial activities – indeed, the whole economic system – not only because both are materials processing systems driven by a flow of free energy (Georgescu-Roegen 1971), but because both are examples of self-organizing 'dissipative systems' in a stable state, far from thermodynamic equilibrium.[2]

At the most abstract level of description, then, the metabolism of industry is the whole integrated collection of physical processes that convert raw materials and energy, plus labor, into finished products and wastes in a (more or less) steady-state condition. The production (supply) side, by itself, is not self-regulating. The stabilizing controls of the system are provided by its human component. This human role has two aspects: (1) *direct*, as labor input, and (2) *indirect*, as consumer of output (that is, determinant of final demand). The system is stabilized, at least in its decentralized competitive market form, by balancing supply of and demand for both products and labor through the price mechanism. Thus, the economic system is, in essence, the metabolic regulatory mechanism.

Industrial metabolism can be identified and described at a number of levels, the broadest and most encompassing being the global one. Thus, the concept is obviously applicable to nations or regions, especially natural ones such as watersheds or islands. The key to regional analysis is the existence of a well-defined geographical border or boundary across which physical flows of materials and energy can be monitored.

The concept of industrial metabolism is equally applicable to another kind of self-organizing entity, a manufacturing enterprise or firm. A firm is the economic analog of a living organism in biology.[3] Some of the differences are interesting, however. In the first place, biological organisms reproduce themselves. By contrast, firms produce products or services, not other firms (except by accident). In the second place, firms need not be specialized and can change from one product or business to another. By contrast, organisms are highly specialized and cannot change their behavior except over a long (evolutionary) time period.

In fact, the firm (rather than the individual) is generally regarded as the standard unit of analysis in microeconomics. The economic system as a whole is essentially a collection of firms, together with regulatory institutions and households or worker-consumers, using a common currency and governed by a common political structure. A manufacturing firm converts material inputs, including fuels or electric energy, into both marketable products and waste materials. It keeps financial accounts for all its external transactions; it is also relatively easy to track physical stocks and flows across the boundary of the firm and even between its divisions.

1.2 The biogeochemical materials cycle

Another way in which the analogy between biological metabolism and industrial metabolism is useful is to focus attention on the life cycle of individual materials or nutrients. The hydrological cycle, the carbon cycle, and the nitrogen cycle are familiar concepts to earth scientists. The major way in which the industrial metabolic system differs from the natural metabolism of the earth is that many of the natural cycles (for example, water, carbon/ oxygen, nitrogen, sulfur) are *closed*, whereas most industrial cycles are *open*. In other words, the industrial system does not generally recycle its nutrients. Rather, the industrial system starts with high quality materials (fossil fuels, ores) extracted from the earth, and returns them to nature in degraded form.

This point particularly deserves clarification. The materials cycle, in general, can be visualized in terms of a system of compartments containing *stocks* of one or more nutrients, linked by certain *flows*. For instance, in the case of the hydrological cycle, the glaciers, the oceans, the fresh water lakes and the groundwater are stocks while rainfall and rivers are flows. A system is *closed* if there are no external sources or sinks. In this sense, the earth as a whole is essentially a closed system, except for the occasional meteorite.

A closed system becomes a *closed cycle* if the system as a whole is in a steady state, that is, the stocks in each compartment are constant and unchanging, at least on the average. The materials balance condition implies that the material *inputs* to each compartment must be exactly balanced (on the average) by the *outputs*. If this condition is not met for a given compartment, then the stock in one or more compartments must be increasing, while the stocks in one or more other compartments must be decreasing.[4]

It is easy to see that a closed cycle of flows, in the above sense, can only be sustained indefinitely by a continuous flow of *exergy*.[5] This follows immediately from the second law of thermodynamics, which states that global entropy increases in every irreversible process. Exergy is used up at the same time; it is not conserved. Thus, a closed cycle of flows can be sustained as long as its external exergy supply lasts. An open system, on the contrary, is inherently unstable and unsustainable. It must either stabilize or collapse to a thermal equilibrium state in which all flows, that is, all physical and biological processes, cease.

It is sometimes convenient to define a generalized 4-box model to describe materials flows. This model is one of those grand simplifications mentioned in the preface. The biological version of the model is shown in Figure 1.1, while the analogous industrial version is shown in Figure 1.2. Reverting to the point made at the beginning of this section, the natural system is characterized by closed cycles – at least for the major nutrients (carbon, oxygen, nitrogen, sulfur) – in which biological processes play a major role in closing the cycle. By contrast, the industrial system is an open one in which 'nutrients' are transformed into 'wastes', but not significantly recycled. The industrial system, as it exists today, is therefore *ipso facto* unsustainable.

At this stage, it must be acknowledged that nothing can be said about open cycles (on the basis of such simple thermodynamic arguments, at least) with respect to any of the really critical questions. These are as follows: (1) Is there a significant risk that anthropogenic activity, projected into the future, could destabilize the climate? What about the ozone layer? (2) Is there a risk of accelerating global acidification? (3) Are the nutrient cycles (C, N, S)

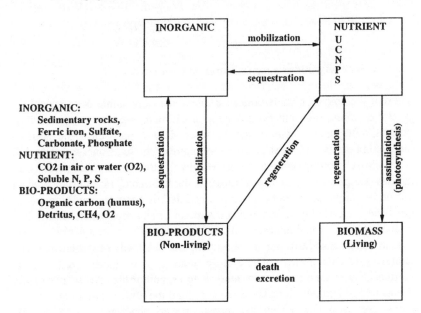

Figure 1.1   4-Box scheme for biogeochemical cycles

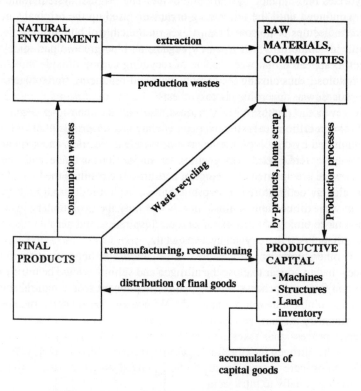

Figure 1.2   4-Box scheme for industrial material cycles

inherently stable or not? If not, does there exist any stable state (that is, a system of closed nutrient cycles) short of ultimate thermodynamic equilibrium? Could such a stable state be reached with the help of a feasible technological 'fix'? (4) If so, what is the nature of the fix, and how costly will it be? (5) If not, how long do we have until the irreversible deterioration of the bio-geosphere system makes the earth uninhabitable? If the timescale is a billion years, we need not be too concerned. If it is a hundred years, civilization, and even the human race, could already be in deep trouble. It is fairly important to try to find answers to these questions.

It should be noted that the bio-geosphere was not always a stable system of closed cycles. Far from it. The earliest living cells on earth obtained their nutrients, by fermentation, from non-living organic molecules whose origin is still not completely understood. At that time the atmosphere contained no free oxygen; it probably consisted mostly of water vapor and carbon dioxide, and possibly ammonia. The fermentation metabolism converted simple carbohydrates into ethanol and carbon dioxide. The original system could only have continued until the fermenting organisms used up the original stock of 'food' molecules or poisoned themselves on the ethanol buildup. The system stabilized temporarily when a new organism (blue-green algae, or cyano-bacteria) appeared that was capable of recycling carbon dioxide into sugars and cellulose, thus closing the carbon cycle and producing free oxygen. This new process was anaerobic photosynthesis.

However, the photosynthesis process also had an open loop. For a long time (over a billion years) the oxygen generated by anaerobic photosynthesis was captured by dissolved ferrous iron or sulfide molecules, and sequestered as insoluble ferric oxide (magnetite), or sulfates. Iron oxide and calcium sulfate were precipitated on the ocean bottoms. The result is the large deposits of high grade iron ore and gypsum that we exploit industrially today. The system was still unstable at this point. It was only the evolutionary invention of two more biological processes, aerobic respiration and aerobic photosynthesis, that closed the oxygen cycle as well.

Still other biological processes – nitrification and denitrification, for instance – had to appear to close the nitrogen and sulfur cycles. The nitrification (nitrogen fixation) process was needed to supplement scarce natural sources of water soluble nitrogen compounds. Without it, the quantity of biomass supportable by the earth would have been very small. But denitrification – the bacterial process that takes oxygen from nitrate (NO_3) molecules and reconverts the nitrogen into the stable gaseous form – is also necessary. Without it the atmosphere would gradually be oxidized and the ocean would be converted gradually to nitric acid.

Evidently biological evolution responded to inherently unstable situations (open cycles) by 'inventing' new processes (organisms) to stabilize the system by closing the cycles. This self-organizing capability is the essence of what James Lovelock called 'Gaia'. However, the instabilities in question were slow to develop, and the evolutionary responses were also slow to evolve. It took several billion years before the biosphere reached its present degree of stability.

In the case of the industrial system, the time scales have been drastically shortened. Human activity already dominates natural processes in many respects. While cumulative anthropogenic changes to most natural nutrient stocks still remain fairly small, in most cases,[6] the rate of nutrient mobilization by human industrial activity is already comparable to the natural rate in many cases. Table 1.1 shows the natural and anthropogenic mobilization (flow) rates for the four major biological nutrients, carbon, nitrogen, phosphorus and sulfur. In all cases, with the possible exception of nitrogen, the anthropogenic contributions exceed the natural flows by a considerable margin. This is the basic reason for concern about long-run stability.

Table 1.1 Anthropogenic nutrient fluxes (teragrams/year)

	Carbon T/yr	%	Nitrogen T/yr	%	Sulfur T/yr	%	Phosphorus T/yr	%
To atmosphere, total	7900	4	55.1	12.5	93	65.5	1.5	12.5
Fossil fuel combustion and smelting	6400		45.0		92			
Land clearing, deforestation	1500		2.6		1		1.5	
Fertilizer volatilization[a]			7.5					
To soil, total			112.5	21	73.3	23.4	15	7.4
Fertilization			67.5		4.0		15	
Waste disposal[b]			5.0		21.0			
Anthropogenic acid deposition			30.0		48.3			
Anthropogenic (NH_3, NH_4) deposition			10.0					
To rivers and oceans, total			72.5	25	52.5	21	5	10.3
Anthropogenic acid deposition			55.0		22.5		5	
Waste disposal			17.5		30.0			

Notes:
a Assuming 10% loss of synthetic ammonia-based fertilizers applied to land surface (75 tg/yr).
b Total production (= use) less fertilizer use, allocated to landfill. The remainder is assumed to be disposed of via waterways.

As indicated in Table 1.1, anthropogenic activities like the use of synthetic fertilizers in agriculture and the combustion of fossil fuels add very significantly to the natural fluxes of these nutrient elements. Figure 2.2 in the next chapter shows the flows of nitrogen and phosphorus in agriculture, for instance. Based on relatively crude materials cycle analyses, at least, it would appear that industrialization has already drastically disturbed, and *ipso facto* destabilized, the natural system.

Table 1.1 and Figure 2.2 illustrate the role of quantitative measurement. The casual reader is likely to glance at the table and figure quickly and – at most – reflect on their implications for policy. The average reader will then pass on, without seriously considering the difficulties underlying the compilation of these numbers. Who gathers them? How are they obtained? How accurate are they? These are questions that should be asked routinely. This book is mostly about these issues. We return to them over and over again in the coming chapters.

1.3 Industrial materials cycles

Returning for the moment to the substantive issues, the industrial metabolic system is not, at present, a closed cycle. It can be described schematically as a sequence of processing stages between extraction and ultimate disposal, with a number of actual or hypothetical intermediate loops that would permit the system to be closed Figure 1.3.

One of the most powerful arguments for closing the cycle is illustrated by the case of zinc (Figure 1.4). When metal ores are extracted from the environment the extraction process itself generates enormous quantities of waste overburden and spoil with no conceivable economic use, but considerable potential for harm. The next stage of processing, concentration, also generates huge quantities of so-called 'tailings' that contain significant quantities of toxic trace elements, such as lead, cadmium and arsenic, as well as chemicals used for the concentration process. (For example, mercury was commonly used – and discarded – in the process of concentrating silver and gold ores in the past. It is still used by illegal gold miners in Brazil, Venezuela and elsewhere. The large-scale industrial mining firms use cyanide instead.) The tailings from most mines are, by definition, too low in grade to be utilized economically. Many tailings heaps constitute an environmental hazard, however, particularly if they are in contact with surface waters that drain into streams and rivers.

The next stage of ore processing is reduction (smelting). This also produces another solid waste, slag, although slag can be used for road paving. Non-ferrous ore processing also typically mobilizes toxic elements like arsenic and cadmium. It also generates significant quantities of sulfur dioxide. In principle, these can be recovered. For instance, the sulfur from roasting

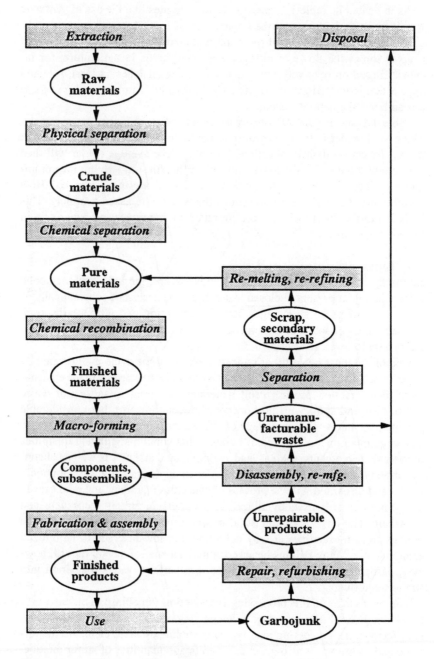

Figure 1.3   The materials cycle

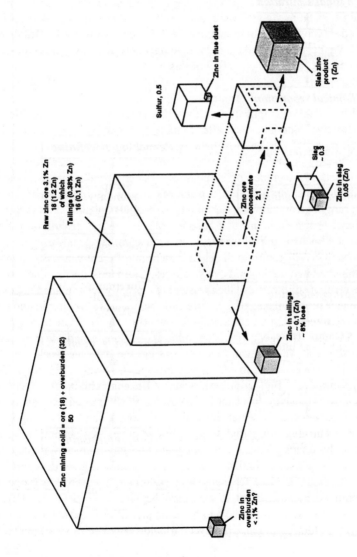

Figure 1.4   Zinc flow in mining and processing of zinc ores per unit slab zinc produced

9

can be used for sulfuric acid production, although in many parts of the world it is simply emitted into the air without treatment.

An interesting insight from the industrial metabolism (IM) perspective is that the ferrous metals sector is much bigger than the non-ferrous sector in terms of the quantity of finished product. But the situation is reversed when we consider energy consumption, waste overburden, mine tailings, and water and air pollution. This would seem to be a powerful a priori argument for sharply increasing recycling in the non-ferrous sector especially (see below).

The industrial materials cycle at the national level was described for the first time, as far as we are aware, in a small and little known book (in French) entitled 'L'écosystème Belgique: Essaie d'écologic industrielle' (Billen *et al.* 1983). We have attempted a similar materials flow analysis (MFA) for the US economy in Chapters 2 through 7 of this book.

1.4   Dissipative uses of materials

Another important implication of the IM perspective is the recognition that *all* extractive materials, even after refining and incorporation into products, are still potential wastes. Most materials return to the environment, generally in chemically or physically degraded form, within a few weeks or months. Fossil fuels are degraded by combustion. The combustion products have no economic value. But they are capable of causing significant environmental harm, ranging from climate warming to acid rain and a number of respiratory and other health problems that arise in polluted areas. Agricultural products eventually become animal wastes, food wastes (garbage) and sewage.

Other materials return to the environment in different ways. Some materials embodied in durable goods, or structures, return to the environment slowly, in the form of solid wastes. Such wastes are normally accumulated in landfills and, under proper management, little damage may result. Other materials are returned to the environment as soluble salts (mainly from chemical processing). Sewage, garbage, ashes, slag, mine spoil, sludges and other categories are visible and well known. Less obvious are the invisible wastes resulting from dissipative uses of materials like lubricants, solvents, pigments, detergents, abrasives, fuel additives, water treatment chemicals, fertilizers, pesticides, explosives, fire retardants, cosmetics, pharmaceuticals and so on.

Yet these categories, which are easily overlooked, can be very important – and very harmful. Tetraethyl lead, a fuel additive, was accumulating hundreds of thousands of tons of lead per year in the environment – mainly in the soil near busy roads – until it was restricted starting a few years ago.[7] This lead will remain in place for many decades, although most of it is (hopefully) immobilized by attachment to clay particles. The case of DDT, PCBs and CFCs are well known. To cite another example, chlorinated solvents, such as methylene chloride (a paint remover), trichloroethylene (a vapor degreaser), perchloroethylene (dry cleaning fluid), and methyl chloroform (also a vapor degreaser) were being used in steadily increasing amounts until it was realized that they could be toxic or carcinogenic to humans with continued exposure, even at low levels. Now they are all being phased out gradually.

Thus, a further contribution of the IM perspective has been to call attention to the fact that many intermediate products of industry are inevitably dissipative. Some of these intermediates are certainly toxic. Chlorine is an interesting example in this context. Based on a recent detailed study of the chlorine industry in Europe it was determined that, based on total chlorine consumed in Europe (1992), two-thirds was 'virgin' (that is, produced by electrolysis of salt) and one third was recycled within the industry, mainly by recovery from waste HCl.

But looking at the outputs, only 46 per cent of the total chlorine flux was embodied in chemical products crossing the 'boundary fence' (that is, sold to downstream users) while 33.7 per cent was recycled back into the industry and 24.7 per cent was lost in waste. Most of this waste was in the form of chlorine salts (mainly NaCl or $CaCl_2$) dumped into rivers. But as much as 1–2 per cent may have been lost in other chemical forms, some of which could be considerably more hazardous. Of the chlorine compounds crossing the fence 60 per cent was embodied in the plastic PVC. Almost all of the rest is used for purposes like water treatment, pulp bleaching (largely phased out in Europe, but still practiced in the US and Canada), solvents, and other products that are dissipated in use.

1.5   Industrial process losses and emissions
As mentioned above, all industrial conversion processes involve some losses. Any chemical engineering textbook provides 'recipes' for the production of major industrial chemicals. A straightforward comparison of mass inputs and outputs shows significant discrepancies. A zero order approximation of these process losses can be derived from the standard recipes by calculating mass loss per tonne of chemical product and multiplying by production. A first order estimate must also consider internal recycling of the kind illustrated (for the chlorine sector) in Chapter 6. A more refined second order estimate is more difficult. It requires the use of process simulation software of the kind (if not the full sophistication) used in process design. We will discuss some examples in a future work (*Accounting for Resources, 2*).

Industrial metabolism involves a much wider selection of elements than natural metabolism. Natural biogeochemical systems have evolved to recycle nutrient elements that are relatively scarce in nature, or at least in chemically available forms. By contrast, industrial systems have developed considerable expertise at extracting and utilizing elements and compounds that are not much utilized in organic substances. This is either because they are too tightly bound with oxygen (for example, silicon, aluminum, magnesium) and/or chlorine (for example, sodium, potassium, calcium) or too rare in nature (for example, the transition and heavy metals). The rare elements and their compounds are much more likely to be biologically hazardous than elements and compounds that are circulated within the natural world. Most heavy metals are in this category. They and their compounds are mostly eco-toxic to some degree. It is likely that this is because they are likely to be disturbing influences in natural environments that evolved without them.

Of course there are many natural toxins, mainly developed by plants as defenses against pests or, in some cases, as weapons used by predators to paralyze or kill their prey. However organic toxins are almost always pro-teins, built from the standard building blocks of all living organisms, namely the 20 amino acids, consisting of the five elements: carbon, hydrogen, oxy-gen, nitrogen and (in three cases) sulfur. Their antidotes can be formed from the same building blocks.

Toxic heavy metals or halocarbons are in a different category. There are no straightforward natural antidotes. Metals cannot be transformed into non metals. At worst they are metabolized and hydrogenated or methylated by anaerobic bacteria, thus becoming volatile or soluble and metabolizable by higher organisms. This process is particularly important in the case of mer-cury and arsenic. The best that can happen in the case of metals is that a soluble or 'mobile' form will eventually be immobilized by some by some natural process (such as adsorption by clay particles) and finally buried or otherwise physically removed from the scene.

One compilation of data on the mobilization of major toxic heavy metals is shown in Table 1.2. Once again, we call attention to the fact that any implica-tions to be drawn from such compilations depend on the accuracy and reliability of the figures. It is important – indeed necessary – to inquire into the sources (and possible sources) of such data.

Halocarbons are also very rare in nature. Only one (methyl chloride) is known to be produced in significant quantities by natural organisms (Gribble 1994). A number of halocarbons are toxic. In the case of halocarbons, there are also two natural processes of importance. One is called bio-accumulation. Some halocarbons are soluble in lipids and can be stored in body fat. When one organism is consumed by another – a grazer or a predator – the halocarbons are accumulated, becoming more and more concentrated. After moving up the food chain several steps in this manner, a very low original concentration in the water or soil can be converted in this manner into a lethally high concentration in so-called 'top predators', such as eagles or gamefish. Ex-actly this process has occurred in the case of DDT and PCBs, for instance. A second natural process is degradation through contact with oxygen, hydroxyl ions, or UV radiation. Degradation eventually reduces complex halocarbons

Table 1.2 Worldwide atmospheric emissions of trace metals (kMT per year)

Element	Energy production	Smelting, refining and manufacturing	Manufacturing processes	Commercial uses, waste incineration and transportation	Total anthropogenic contributions	Total contributions by natural activities
Antimony	1.3	1.5	–	0.7	3.5	2.6
Arsenic	2.2	12.4	2.0	2.3	19.0	12.0
Cadmium	0.8	5.4	0.6	0.8	7.6	1.4
Chromium	12.7	–	17.0	0.8	31.0	43.0
Copper	8.0	23.6	2.0	1.6	35.0	6.1
Lead	12.7	49.1	15.7	254.9	332.0	28.0
Manganese	12.1	3.2	14.7	8.3	38.0	12.0
Mercury	2.3	0.1	–	1.2	3.6	317.0
Nickel	42.0	4.8	4.5	0.4	52.0	2.5
Selenium	3.9	2.3	–	0.1	6.3	3.0
Thallium	1.1	–	4.0	–	5.1	29.0
Tin	3.3	1.1	–	0.8	5.1	10.0
Vanadium	84.0	0.1	0.7	1.2	86.0	28.0
Zinc	16.8	72.5	33.4	9.2	132.0	45.0

Source: Nriagu (1990).

13

to simple compounds like HCl, but intermediate products are not always harmless. Some breakdown products of DDT, for instance, are more toxic than the original.

Of course some halocarbons, especially CFCs, are extremely inert, resistant to breakdown by contact with oxygen and therefore persistent. It is these compounds that eventually diffuse into the stratosphere where they are bro-

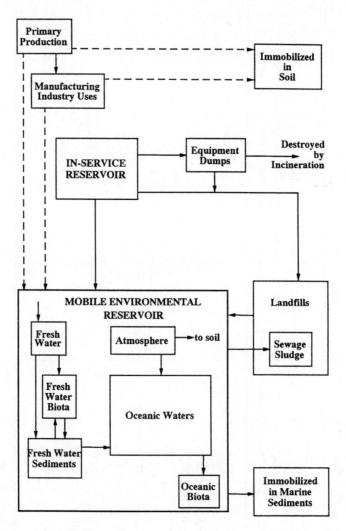

Figure 1.5   Model scheme for assessing risks of environmentally persistent pollutants

ken down by UV radiation. The breakdown products include atomic chlorine, which in turn, catalytically destroys stratospheric ozone. The chlorine itself is not destroyed. A single chlorine atom may destroy a hundred thousand molecules of ozone. This interaction between an industrial product and the natural environment is a good illustration of industrial metabolism 'in action' so to speak.

A point worth emphasizing here is that in the case of dissipative materials that are environmentally persistent, including PCBs, some pesticides, halocarbons and toxic metals, point source measurements are needed. But, point source measurements alone are totally insufficient for purposes of assessing environmental hazards or trends. Figure 1.5 shows, schematically, the sort of model that is needed to assess the risks associated with environmentally persistent pollutants. To quantify such a model it is necessary to keep track of production, use, inventories and reservoirs, and transport mechanisms, over time. Industrial secrecy in the matter of production and consumptive use makes this sort of modelling virtually impossible under present conditions.

1.6 Measures of sustainability/unsustainability

A strong implication of much of the foregoing discussion is that a long term (sustainable) steady-state industrial economy would necessarily be characterized by near total recycling of intrinsically toxic or hazardous materials, as well as a significant degree of recycling of plastics, paper and other materials whose disposal constitutes an environmental problem. Heavy metals are among the materials that would have to be almost totally recycled to satisfy the sustainability criterion. The fraction of current metal supply needed to replace dissipative losses (that is, production from virgin ores needed to maintain a stable level of consumption) is thus a useful surrogate measure of 'distance' from a steady-state condition, that is, a condition of long run sustainability.

Most economic analysis in regard to materials, in the past, has focussed on availability. Data on several categories of reserves (economically recoverable, potential, and so on), production, trade and uses were, until recently, routinely gathered and published by the US Bureau of Mines. However, this activity has been sharply curtailed (for budgetary reasons, apparently, coupled with hostility on the part of industry to government data collection) and shifted to the US Geological Survey (USGS).

In any case, as is well known, figures obtained from industry are a very poor proxy for actual reserves. In most cases the true reserves are much greater than the amounts that are officially documented, even when the documentation is published. The reason, simply, is that most such data are extrapolated from test borings by mining or drilling firms. Because of discounting, it is economically optimal for firms to stop searching for new ore bodies when the reserves in their operational mines or oil/gas fields exceed 20–25 years' supply. Only in the case of petroleum (which has been the subject of worldwide searches for many decades), coal and perhaps phosphate rock is it possible to place much reliance on published data of this kind.[8]

However, a sustainable steady state, as discussed above, is less a question of resource availability than of recycling/re-use efficiency. As commented earlier, a good measure of unsustainability is dissipative usage. The more materials are recycled, the less will be dissipated into the environment, and vice versa. Dissipative losses must be made up by replacement from virgin sources. This raises the distinction between *inherently dissipative* uses and uses where the material could be recycled or re-used, in principle, but is not. The latter could be termed *potentially recyclable*. Thus, there are really three important classes: (1) uses that are economically and technologically compatible with recycling under present prices and regulations; (2) uses that are not economically compatible with recycling but where recycling is technically feasible, for example, if the collection problem were solved; and (3) uses where recycling is inherently not feasible. Admittedly there is some fuzziness in these classifications, but it should be possible for a group of international experts to arrive at some reconciliation.

Generally speaking, it is arguable that most structural metals and industrial catalysts are in the first category; other structural and packaging materials, as well as most refrigerants and solvents, fall into the second category. This leaves coatings, pigments, pesticides, herbicides, germicides, preservatives, flocculants, anti-freezes, explosives, propellants, fire retardants, reagents, detergents, fertilizers, fuels and lubricants in the third category. In fact, it is easy to verify that most chemical products belong in the third category, except those physically embodied in plastics, synthetic rubber or synthetic fibers.

For instance, if one traces the uses of materials from source to final sink, it can be seen that virtually all sulfur mined (or recovered from oil, gas or metallurgical refineries) is ultimately dissipated in use (for example, as fertilizers or pigments) or discarded, as waste acid or as ferric or calcium sulfites or sulfates. Some of these sulfate wastes are classed as hazardous. Sulfur is mostly (75–80 per cent) used, in the first place, to produce sulfuric acid, which in turn is used for many purposes. But in every chemical reaction the sulfur must be accounted for – it must go somewhere. The laws of chemistry guarantee that reactions will tend to continue either until the most stable possible compound is formed or until an insoluble solid is formed. If the sulfur is not embodied in a 'useful' product, it must end up in a waste stream.

There is only one long-lived structural material embodying sulfur: plaster-of-Paris (hydrated calcium sulfate) which is normally made directly from the natural mineral gypsum. In recent years, sulfur recovered from some coal burning power plants in Germany has been converted into synthetic gypsum and used for construction. However this potential recycling loop is currently inhibited by the very low price of natural gypsum and the large 'sunk' investment in the industry. Apart from synthetic gypsum, there are no other durable materials in which sulfur is physically embodied. It follows from materials balance considerations that sulfur is mostly dissipated into the environment of which a major fraction is reactive (for example, as SO_2). Globally, about 52.3 million metric tons of sulfur *qua* sulfur (that is, not including sulfur in gypsum) was produced in 1993. Of this, less than 2 million was recycled (mainly sulfuric acid used for bleaching in the petroleum refining industry).

Except for natural gypsum, very little sulfur (as such) is currently used for structural materials. Thus, most sulfur chemicals belong in class 3 (infeasible to recycle). Following similar logic, it is easy to see that the same is true of most chemicals derived from ammonia (fertilizers, explosives, acrylic fibers), and phosphorus (fertilizers, pesticides, detergents, fire retardants). In the case of chlorine, there is a division between class 2 (solvents, plastics, etc.) and class 3 (hydrochloric acid, chlorine used in water treatment, and so on).

It would be possible, with some research, to devise measures of the inherently dissipative uses of each chemical element, along the lines sketched above. For further discussion, see Chapter 9. Sustainability, in the long run, would imply that such measures should decline. Currently, they are mostly increasing.

With regard to materials that are potentially recyclable (classes 1 and 2) the fraction actually recycled is a useful measure of the approach toward (or away from) sustainability. A reasonable proxy for this, in the case of metals, is the ratio of secondary supply to total supply of final materials: see, for example, Table 1.3. This table shows, incidentally, that the recycling ratio in the United States has been rising consistently in recent years only for lead and iron/steel. In the case of lead, the ban on using tetraethyl lead as a gasoline additive (an inherently dissipative use) is entirely responsible.

Another useful measure of industrial metabolic efficiency is the economic output per unit of material/energy input. This sort of measure can be called *resource productivity*. It can be measured, in principle, not only for the economy as a whole, but for each sector. It can also be measured for each major 'nutrient' element, for example, carbon, oxygen, hydrogen, sulfur, chlorine, iron, phosphorus, and so on.[9] Materials productivity for the economy taken as a whole, however, would not be a reliable indicator of increasing technological efficiency, or progress toward long-term sustainability. The reason is that increasing efficiency – especially in rapidly developing countries – can be masked by structural changes, such as investment in heavy

Table 1.3   US recycling statistics and apparent consumption for selected metals 1987–93

		Quantity (kMT)				
		Recycled metal[1]				Recycle % of
					Apparent	apparent
	Year	New scrap[2]	Old scrap[3]	Total	consumption[4]	consumption
Aluminum[5]	1987	1134	852	1986	6603	30
	1988	1077	1045	2122	6450	33
	1989	1043	1011	2054	6000	34
	1990	1034	1359	2393	6298	38
	1991	979	1522	2501	6012	42
	1992	1144	1612	2756	6869	40
	1993	1312	1632	2944	7852	37
Copper	1987	716	497	1213	2913	42
	1988	788	518	1306	3002	44
	1989	761	537	1298	2945	44
	1990	774	548	1322	2924	45
	1991	682	518	1200	2731	44
	1992	723	555	1278	3028	42
	1993	731	555	1286	3256	39
Lead	1987	52.535	657.532	710.067	1259.029	56
	1988	45.274	691.127	736.401	1274.477	58
	1989	49.612	841.729	891.341	1384.725	64
	1990	48.104	874.093	922.197	1345.381	69
	1991	54.970	829.654	884.624	1283.474	69
	1992	55.424	860.917	916.341	1325.408	69
	1993	60.298	843.262	903.560	1390.464	65
Nickel[6]	1987			32.331	155.781	21
	1988			41.039	159.019	26
	1989			52.131	157.103	33
	1990			57.367	170.042	34
	1991			53.521	156.663	34
	1992			55.871	159.373	35
	1993			54.702	159.313	34
Tin	1987	4.604	11.462	16.066	59.458	27
	1988	3.925	11.350	15.275	60.955	25
	1989	2.795	11.545	14.34	47.285	30
	1990	4.035	13.200	17.235	53.430	32
	1991	5.114	7.982	13.096	39.606	33
	1992	4.894	8.853	13.747	37.321	37
	1993	4.453	7.219	11.672	42.906	27

Table 1.3 (continued)

	Year	New scrap[2]	Old scrap[3]	Total	Apparent consumption[4]	Recycle % of apparent consumption
			Recycled metal[1]			
Zinc	1987	270	82	352	1324	27
	1988	240	97	337	1340	25
	1989	230	117	347	1311	26
	1990	232	109	341	1240	28
	1991	233	120	353	1165	30
	1992	234	132	366	1276	29
	1993	246	109	355	1367	26

Notes:
1. Recycled metal is metal recovered from reported *purchased* new plus old scrap supply.
2. New scrap is scrap resulting from the manufacturing process, including metal and alloy production.
3. Old scrap is scrap resulting from consumer products.
4. Apparent consumption is production plus net imports plus stock change. Apparent consumption is calculated on a contained weight basis.
5. Recycle quantity is the calculated metallic recovery from aluminum-base scrap, estimated for full industry coverage.
6. Nickel scrap is nickel contained in ferrous and non-ferrous scrap receipts.

Source: USBuMines (1993), 'Recycling-Nonferrous Metals', Tables 1 and 2.

industry, which tend to increase the materials (and energy) intensiveness of economic activity. On the other hand, within a given sector, one would expect the efficiency of materials utilization – hence materials productivity – to increase, in general.[10]

Recent work suggests that a useful aggregate measure can be constructed that applies equally well to process inputs (resource flows), process outputs (products and by products) and process wastes. The same measure, called *exergy* applies equally well to fuels, organic materials and inorganic substances. In brief, and oversimplifying for purposes of exposition, exergy can be regarded is the 'useful' fraction of chemical energy. But, equally, it is a measure of the 'distance' from ultimate thermodynamic equilibrium with the environment. It is applicable to, and computable for, all material substances from physical data that are already collected and compiled in reference books.

To derive these aggregates and publish them regularly would provide policy makers with a valuable set of indicators at little cost. Thus, while exergy is not necessarily a good measure of environmental harm in any specific case, it is a very good basis for comparing inputs and outputs, both over time and between sectors, regions or firms in the same line of business.

1.7 Policy implications of the industrial metabolism perspective

It may seem odd to suggest that a mere viewpoint – in contradistinction to empirical analysis – may have policy implications. But it is perfectly possible. In fact, there are two implications that come to mind. First, the industrial metabolism perspective is essentially 'holistic' in that the whole range of interactions between energy, materials and the environment are considered together, not only at a point in time, but through the entire life cycle' of a material, from 'cradle to grave'. The second major implication, which virtually follows from the first, is that from this holistic perspective it is much easier to see that narrowly conceived or short-run (myopic) 'quick fix' policies may be very far from globally optimum. In fact, from the larger perspective, many such narrowly focussed policies can be positively harmful.

The best way to explain the virtues of a holistic view is by contrasting it with narrower perspectives. Consider the problem of waste disposal. It is a consequence of the law of conservation of mass that the total quantity of materials extracted from the environment will ultimately return thence as some sort of waste residuals or 'garbo-junk' (Ayres and Kneese 1969, 1989). Yet environmental protection policy has systematically ignored this fundamental reality by imposing regulations on emissions *by medium*. Typically, one legislative act mandates a bureaucracy that formulates and enforces a set of regulations dealing with emissions by 'point sources' only to the air. Another legislative act creates a bureaucracy that deals only with waterborne emissions, again by 'point sources'. And so forth.

Not surprisingly, one of the things that happened as a result was that some air pollution (for example, fly ash and SO_x from fossil fuel combustion) was eliminated by converting it to another form of waste, such as a sludge to be disposed of on land. Similarly, some forms of waterborne wastes are captured and converted to sludges for land disposal (or, even, for incineration). Air and water pollution were reduced, but largely by resorting to land disposal. But landfills also *cause* water pollution (leachate), and air pollution, due to anaerobic decay processes. In short, narrowly conceived environmental policies over the past 20 years and more have largely shifted waste emissions from one form (and medium) to another, without significantly reducing the totals. In some cases, policy has encouraged changes that merely dilute the waste stream without touching its volume at all. The use of high stacks for coal burning power plants, and the building of longer sewage pipes to carry wastes further offshore exemplify this approach.

To be sure, these shifts may have been beneficial in the aggregate. But the costs have been quite large, and it is only too obvious that the state of the environment 'in the large' is still deteriorating rapidly. One is tempted to think that a more holistic approach, from the beginning, might have achieved considerably more at considerably less cost.

In fact, there is a tendency for suboptimal choices to get 'locked in' by widespread adoption. Large investments in so-called 'clean coal' technology would surely extend the use of coal as a fuel – an eventuality highly desired by the coal industry – but would also guarantee that larger cumulative quantities of sulfur, fly ash (with associated toxic heavy metals) and carbon dioxide would be produced. The adoption of catalytic convertors for automotive engine exhaust is another case in point. This technology is surely not the final answer, since it is not effective in older vehicles. Yet it has also surely deferred the day when internal combustion engines will eventually be replaced by some inherently cleaner automotive propulsion technology. By the time that day comes, the world's automotive fleet will be two or three times bigger than it might have been otherwise, and the cost of substitution will be enormously greater.

The implication of all these points for policy makers, of course, is that the traditional governmental division of responsibility into a large number of independent bureaucratic fiefdoms is dangerously faulty.[11] Yet the way out of this organizational impasse is far from clear. Top down central planning has failed miserably, and is unlikely to be tried again soon. On the other hand, pure 'free market' solutions to environmental problems are limited in cases where there is no convenient mechanism for valuation of environmental resource assets (such as beautiful scenery) or functions (such as the UV protection afforded by the stratospheric ozone layer).

This is primarily a problem of *indivisibility*. Indivisibility means that there is no possibility of subdividing the attribute into 'parcels' suitable for physical exchange or secure and exclusive ownership. In some cases this problem can be finessed by creating exchangeable 'rights' or 'permits', but the creation of a market for such instruments depends on other factors, including the existence of an effective mechanism for allocating such rights, limiting their number, and preventing poaching or illicit use of the resource.

Needless to say, the policy problems have economic and socio-political ramifications well beyond the scope of this book. However, as the Chinese proverb has it, the longest journey begins with a single step.

1.8   Methodology

Our basic approach is to view each industrial sector as a transformation process, where raw material inputs or purchased commodities from 'upstream' sectors, plus 'free goods' from the environment, are converted into products for other 'downstream' sectors, plus wastes. This conversion process is subject to the materials balance constraint, not only in the aggregate, but element by element. In other words, the sum of the weights of all inputs must exactly equal the sum of the weights of all outputs. When both inputs and outputs are known, it is possible to estimate wastes, making due allowance for processes utilizing the free goods (air, water, topsoil).

To avoid unnecessary and distracting biological complications, we treat biomass as a produced good of the agriculture/forestry sectors, even though much of it is arguably free. This leaves us with the problem of accounting for water, both as an input and output, which cannot be done with great precision. Fortunately, great precision is probably not necessary in this case. Labor and capital inputs, such as machinery and fuel or electric power for operating the machinery, are not considered explicitly in this study. However, it should be borne in mind that a considerable fraction of aggregate industrial output is actually destined for the capital (and operating) inputs to other sectors.

Our intention in the next several chapters is to classify outputs into economic commodities and missing mass. The latter is further subdivided into categories, based on level of waste treatment and final disposal medium (air, water, soil). This means it is necessary to be quite careful in accounting for the consumption of oxygen (from air) in oxidation processes, and for the consumption or production of water in hydration, dehydration, dilution, dissolution and so on.

We have selected the year 1993 for analysis, hereafter (with some exceptions) because it is the last year for which we have reasonably good US and international data. Sadly, since the early 1990s a number of formerly useful and reliable data sources in the US have disappeared. Many of these data have never been available in other countries. Thus, the materials flow analysis we present in the following chapters may never be possible to repeat, at least at the same detail and depth.

Endnotes

1. The term 'industrial metabolism' was coined for the first time in the context of preliminary discussions leading to what is now known as the 'Human Dimensions of Environmental Change' program (1987), to call attention to what I thought was a major gap in the program as then envisaged. This led to an article published by the *International Social Science Journal* (UNESCO) (Ayres 1989a), a UNU workshop at Maastricht (1988), a summer 1988 Workshop of the National Academy of Engineering at Woods Hole, the proceedings of which were published as a book by the National Academy Press (Ayres 1989a), and finally a book *Industrial Metabolism* co-edited with Udo Simonis and published by UNU Press (Ayres and Simonis, 1994). Since the early 1990s 'industrial metabolism' has been an explicit part of the program of research on human dimensions of global change of the research directorate (DG XII) of the European Commission.
2. The notion of self-organization in dissipative systems far from thermodynamic equilibrium has been discussed primarily by Ilya Prigogine and his co-workers (for example, Nicolis and Prigogine 1977). The application of this fundamental idea from physics to socio-economic systems is more metaphorical than rigorous (for example, Ayres 1988).
3. This analogy between firms and organisms can be carried further, resulting in the notion of 'industrial ecology'. Just as an ecosystem is a balanced, interdependent quasi-stable

community of organisms living together, so its industrial analog may be described as a balanced, quasi-stable collection of interdependent firms belonging to the same economy. The interactions between organisms in an ecosystem range from predation and/or parasitism to various forms of cooperation and synergy. Much the same can be said of firms in an economy.

4. A moment's thought should convince the reader that if the stock in any compartment changes, the stock in at least one other compartment must also change.

5. Exergy is the term most widely used today. It has been called *available work*, *availability*, and *essergy* (essence of energy).

6. However, this statement is not true for greenhouse gases in the atmosphere. Already, the concentration of carbon dioxide has increased 20 per cent since pre-industrial times, while the concentration of methane is up 50 per cent. The most potent greenhouse gases of all, CFCs, do not exist in nature.

7. TEL was gradually phased out in the US for passenger cars, starting in 1970. Europe did not really start to phase out leaded fuel until 20 years later, and much of the rest of the world still has not done so.

8. Even in this case, the reserve-to-production ratio has remained close to 20 years. For example, this figure was widely published in the 1920s (Graf 1924), cited by Rogner (1987). But the ratio may now be declining.

9. Unfortunately, while collecting and compiling this data is possible, in principle, it is anything but straightforward in practice. Readers will note that we have presented data of this sort in several diagrams for the US in the year 1988. But for a researcher depending on published data to construct the same data sets for other years would require a major effort. Ironically, the task would be relatively straightforward for government statistical agencies with access to more complete data. Why don't they do it?

10. This need not be true for each individual element, however. A major materials substitution *within* a sector can result in the use of one material increasing, at the expense of others, of course. The substitution of plastics for many structural materials, or of synthetic rubber for natural rubber, would exemplify this sort of substitution. Currently, glass fibers are in the process of substituting for copper wire as the major carrier of telephonic communications.

11. The analogous problem is beginning to be recognized in the private sector, as the legacy of Frederick Taylor is finally being challenged by new managerial/organizational forms. The large US firms, which adopted Taylorism first and most enthusiastically at the beginning of the twentieth century, have been the slowest to adapt themselves to the new environment of intense international competition and faster technological change.

2 Agricultural industries

2.1 Introduction to the chapter

This chapter deals with industries based on agricultural products. Our purpose is to construct a materials flow model of the US agriculture sectors, with the capability of accounting for 'missing mass' and estimating waste flows by economic sectors. We refer, where appropriate, to the so-called standard industrial classification, or SIC.[1] The sectors considered in this chapter are as follows:

Major group 01: agricultural production – crops
Major group 02: livestock and animal specialties
Major group 05: fishing, hunting and trapping.

We also consider an important 'downstream' materials processing sector that obtains its material inputs from the sectors listed above, namely:

Major group 20: food and kindred products

Material inputs to agriculture (SIC 01) consist of water, carbon dioxide (from the air), nitrogen fixation (also from the air), minerals and nutrients from topsoil and some supplementary chemicals (fertilizers and pesticides). Energy for photosynthesis comes from sunlight. Fuels are consumed to operate machinery, but fuel mass is not embodied in agricultural products, and is not discussed in this chapter. Commodity outputs, in the first instance, are harvested crops. Animal products, both dairy products and meat, are largely produced from agricultural inputs, although some feeds are recycled (in effect) from SIC 20. They are considered separately, as are the various food and meat processing subsectors.

Missing mass from agriculture in the aggregate, consists mainly of crop wastes, runoff, water vapor carried away by evapotranspiration, and oxygen (a byproduct of photosynthesis). Other losses include soil erosion, nitrogen (and phosphorus) carried away by water sources and gaseous emissions. Missing mass from downstream sectors is less complex, inasmuch as inputs are essentially all some form of biomass, and wastes are similar in composition.

The primary production process in agriculture can be characterized crudely from the following basic equation of photosynthesis, namely:

$$CO_2 + H_2O + \text{photon} \Rightarrow CH_2O + O_2$$

The above equation, with the arrows reversed and ignoring intermediate steps, also crudely describes respiration, which is the basic metabolic process by which plants and animals 'burn' carbohydrates to release energy. Plants fix carbon in daylight and release part of it (about half at night. Thus, net photosynthesis is about 0.5 times gross photosynthesis. Otherwise, water is only utilized by plants as a carrier of nutrients and metabolic products, and for evaporative cooling.

Water is a complicating factor. There is a rough average proportionality between carbon fixation rate (gross photosynthesis) and evapotranspiration, but there is no fixed relationship between water content and metabolic process. Some plant parts are very high in water content, others much less so. In general it seems reasonable to assume that raw biomass contains 50 per cent water, by weight, on average, although refined or processed food or feed commodities are considerably drier.

Unfortunately, government statistics are not informative on the question of water content. Thus our mass balances are clearly artificial insofar as accurate water balances cannot be constructed without much more detailed information. However, we believe that the mass-balance approach illustrated in the following pages (and the next five chapters) is nevertheless quite effective in filling in some of the missing data. To anticipate our conclusions, we believe that mass balances can and should be incorporated explicitly in most statistical tabulations of material stocks and flows.

A note, and a complaint, about units. We are consistent hereafter in expressing all mass flows in either thousands or millions of metric tons (kMT or MMT, respectively). In many instances – indeed, in the case of agriculture, the vast majority – the original sources use other units that have had to be converted into metric. This has been an enormous, and essentially unrewarding, labor for us. We are utterly unable to understand why the US Department of Agriculture, in particular, with plenty of computer power at its disposal, has not long since stopped using miscellaneous volume measures such as bushels, crates, cartons, boxes, sacks, barrels, gallons, and bales. Nor is there any excuse for continued use of miscellaneous mass measures like pounds, hundredweights and short tons.

2.2 Agriculture (SIC 01)[2]
Raw products of US agriculture are classified as grain crops (both food and feed); other field crops (cotton, tobacco, sugar cane and sugar beets); oilseeds (including peanuts); vegetables and melons; fruits and tree nuts; and hay and minor field crops, such as dry edible beans. The total in 1993 was 667.7 MMT, broken down as in Table 2.1.

Table 2.1   US agriculture raw products (MMT)

Grain crops		469.2
Food grains, as grain	49.8	
Feed grains, as grain	145.1	
Other grain use	63.8	
Silage, hay etc.	210.5	
Other field crops (sugar, etc.)		57.9
Oilseeds (soya beans, etc.)		60.6
Vegetables (except dry beans)		50.6
Fruits and nuts (except peanuts)		29.4
Total		667.7

Grass harvested directly by grazing animals from pastures is estimated by the United States Department of Agriculture (USDA) (see SA Table 73) as 183 million (short) tons of 'equivalent feed value of corn', which is unfortunately not defined in weight terms. However, grass certainly has less feed value than grain. We estimate grass consumption as 200 MMT of actual mass. This figure is more likely to be too low than too high. Thus total 'useful' biomass produced by the US agricultural sector was approximately 868 MMT in 1993, which appears to be a relatively average year.

According to one estimate, the average ratio of above ground crop residues remaining on the land to harvest weight is about 1.5 for cereals (straw), 1.0 for legumes such as soya beans (straw), 0.2 for tubers (tops) and sugar cane (bagasse), and 3.0 for cotton (stalks) (Smil 1993). We assume that 'vegetables and melons' are split about 50–50 between root vegetables (potatoes, carrots, beets, turnips, onions) and other plants. The latter are further divided between leafy vegetables (lettuce, spinach, cabbage, chard) and 'fruity' vegetables like tomatoes, peas, beans, melons, and so on. Only the latter leave significant above-ground residues. Fruits are mostly from perennial bushes, vines and trees that shed their leaves annually and require pruning On this basis, total residues left above ground in 1993 would have been around 550 MMT, plus or minus 50 MMT or so. Thus total (above ground) biomass production was about 1200 MMT in 1993. In the US most of the crop residues are left on the land; a small fraction approximately 20 per cent is burned for fuel or used for other purposes (Smil 1993). In China or India, by contrast, as much as two-thirds is burned as household fuel (for cooking).

The composition of this biomass is a mixture of cellulosic fiber, carbohydrates, fats and proteins, plus (50 per cent) water, as explained above. Hence, we estimate that the dry weight of the biomass produced in 1993 was about 600 MMT. For each 100 units of dry output (CH_2O basis), the photosynthetic

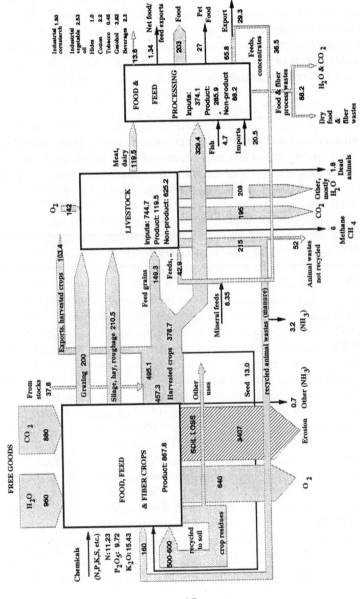

Figure 2.1   Mass flow and C, H and O balances in US agriculture, 1993 (MMT)

process equation implies that 146.7 MMT of CO_2 (containing 40 units of carbon) were initially extracted from the air, while 60 units of water were also consumed, and 106.7 units of oxygen were returned to the atmosphere. Overall, for 1993, water inputs – not including water required for evapotranspiration – were about $600 + 6*60 = 960$ MMT, and carbon dioxide inputs were about $6*146.7 = 880$ MMT. Oxygen produced by the photosynthesis process in agriculture would have been about 640 MMT. The overall flows for US agriculture (1988) are summarized graphically in Figure 2.1.

The above estimates do not take into account the relatively small quantities of other chemical elements embodied in the crops, notably nitrogen, phosphorus and other minerals taken up from the soil or (in the case of nitrogen) fixed by bacteria. It is of interest, however, that the three major chemical elements in (dry) plant tissue are carbon, hydrogen and oxygen These account for 95 per cent of the total mass. Nitrogen accounts for another 2 per cent, phosphorus for 0.5 per cent, potassium for 1 per cent and sulfur 0.4 per cent. These are the major nutrients that are depleted by harvesting and must be replaced by the addition of fertilizers. The remaining 1 per cent of plant mass consists of other mineral elements (see Table 2.2) that are readily

Table 2.2   Chemical composition of plants

Element	% of Plant
Oxygen	45
Carbon	44
Hydrogen	6
Nitrogen	2
Potassium	1
Calcium	0.6
Phosphorus	0.5
Sulfur	0.4
Magnesium	0.3
Manganese	0.05
Iron	0.02
Chlorine	0.015
Zinc	0.01
Boron	0.005
Copper	0.001
Molybdenum	0.001
Total	99.9011

Source: Dictionary of Plant Foods.

Table 2.3 *US grains, 1993 (MMT)*

| | AS table | Production | Exports | Imports | Stock change | Domestic use | | | | Total |
						Seed	Food	Feed	Alcohol	
Total		258.69	77.16	7.03	−34.82	13.04	49.84	145.06	15.45	223.41
wheat a	AS5	65.17	33.40	2.96	1.01	2.61	23.72	6.88	0.52	33.73
rice b	AS26	7.08	3.41	0.31	−0.12	0.19	3.23		0.68	4.11
rye	AS17	0.26	0.00	0.12	−0.01	0.08	0.09	0.18	0.05	0.39
barley c	AS55	8.68	1.44	1.55	−0.28	0.35	0.32	5.25	3.15	9.07
oats d	AS48	3.00	0.04	1.55	−0.10	1.20	1.60	1.81		4.61
sorghum e	AS63	13.56	5.13		−3.23	0.10	0.05	11.46	0.05	11.68
Subtotal except corn		*97.76*	*43.43*	*6.49*	*−2.74*	*4.53*	*29.01*	*25.58*	*4.45*	*63.59*
corn f	AS39	160.93	33.73	0.53	−32.08	8.51	20.83	119.48	11.00	159.82

Notes:

a Detail table gives food, seed, and feed. Alcohol calculated as difference between 'food' in detail table and 'food' in Table 60, but subtracted from 'feed' in AS table 5 (the category said to contain it). AS Table 71 gives feed use as 9.6 MMT.

b Rough basis. Ratio of 'milled' basis to 'rough' basis is 2/3.
   Detail table gives food, seed, brewer's use and residual losses. Feed use assumed to be zero.

c Detail table gives feed and 'food, alcohol and seed'. Seed arbitrarily assumed to be 4 per cent of domestic usage (16 million bushels). Food given in Table 60. Alcohol calculated as difference between detail table and Table 60.

d Detail table gives feed and 'food and seed'. Food given in Table 60. Seed calculated as difference between detail table and Table 60. Alcohol assumed zero.

e Detail table gives 'feed and residual' and 'food, alcohol and seed'. Residual has been adjusted to balance stocks. 'Food, alcohol, seed' has been allocated approximately.

f Detail table gives feed and 'food, alcohol and seed'. Alcohol is assumed to be 11 MMT (see text). Food given in Table 60. Seed calculated as difference between detail table and Table 60.

Table 2.4 US agricultural products, 1993 (MMT)

| Commodity | Production (a) | | | | Exports | | Imports | | Stock Change | Consumption (b) | | | |
	Raw Amt	Raw Ref.	Finished Amt	Finished Ref.	Amt	Ref.	Amt	Ref.	Amt	Disappearance Amt	Disappearance Ref.	Human Amt	Human Ref.
Agriculture–Total	**867.64**				**103.41**		**20.55**			**771.86**		**106.20**	
Grazing on Land	200.00 est									200.00 est			
Total – Field Feeds	**210.46**									**210.46**			
Subtotal – Silage	77.29									77.29			
sorghum for silage	3.55	AS61								3.55			
corn for silage	73.74	AS37								73.74			
Hay and alfalfa	133.17	AS347								133.17			
Total – Grains (see Table 2.3)	**258.69**				**77.16**		**7.03**	1	**–34.82**	**223.41**		**32.10**	AS653
Total – Other Field Crops	**57.94**		**7.82**	AS113	**2.80**		**4.76**		**1.50**	**14.19**		**10.98**	
Subtotal – sugars	52.02		3.67	AS100	0.52		1.83		1.06	8.07	AS113	7.52	AS653
sugar beets	23.81	AS100											
sugar cane	c 28.21	AS105	4.15										
Subtotal – other field crops	5.92						2.93			6.12		3.46	
cotton and cotton lint	3.66	AS77	3.51	AS99	2.29		0.00	AS99	0.44	2.27	AS99		
tobacco	0.73	AS126			1.49	AS99	0.46	AS132		0.45		0.45	AS129
beans, peas, hops	1.53	AS358,367			0.26	AS126	0.06	AS369		1.19		1.12	
coffee, cocoa	d				0.39	AS364–5,369	1.88	SA1123		1.88	SA1123	1.59	AS653
spices	e						0.14	SA1123		0.14	SA1123	0.14	
edible syrups	f				0.14	AS122	0.38	AS119,122		0.19	AS122	0.16	AS653
Total – Oilseeds	**g 60.60**		**39.27**		**16.65**		**0.13**		**–2.99**	**45.49**		**3.28**	**AS188**
Cottonseed	5.75	AS135	3.15		0.12	AS139				5.63			
Flaxseed	0.09	AS142	0.22		0.00	AS142	0.13	AS142		0.23	AS142		
Peanuts	1.54	AS149	0.23	AS153	0.16	AS153				0.33	AS151,154		
Sunflower	2.33	AS170	0.98	AS171	0.34	AS148	0.00	AS153		1.99		0.06	AS153
Soybeans	50.89	AS162	34.70	AS162	16.02	AS162				37.30	AS162		

30

Total – Fruits, Nuts, Vegetables h	**79.95**	**6.80 SA1123**	**8.63 SA1123**	**3.47**	**78.31**	**59.84**
Subtotal – Vegetables	*50.60*				*48.96*	*44.97*
22 commercial vegetables i	30.65 AS191				30.65 AS191	28.94 AS653
potatoes, white and sweet	19.95 AS220				18.31 AS220	16.03 AS653
Subtotal – Fruits and nuts	*29.35*				*29.35*	*14.87*
fruits	28.92 AS247				28.92 AS247	14.60 AS653
nuts j	0.43 AS324				0.43 AS324	0.26 AS653
Miscellaneous (not in grand total) k	*8.05*		*2.57*			*4.45*
Vegetable oils	1.71 SA1123		1.42 SA1123			4.45 AS188
Protein meal	6.34 SA1123		1.15 SA1123			

Notes:

a Finished production denotes crushed weight in the case of oilseeds; sugar weight ('raw value') as opposed to weight of cane or beet in the case of sugars.

b 'Disappearance' represents apparent consumption for all purposes; 'Human' reports total human final consumption as derived from per capita data.

c Finished weight of cane calculated as difference between total sugar (AS Table 113) and beet sugar (AS Table 100).

d Consumption: green bean/liquor equivalent.

e Consumption assumed equal to imports.

f Corn, maple, molasses and honey (corn consumption included in corn).

g Human consumption: salad and cooking oil + soap.

h Imports include bananas.

i Excluding dry beans and dry peas and hops.

j Shelled nuts, excluding peanuts.

k Human consumption: margarine, shortening, edible tallow.

31

available from the soil. The flows of nutrients (N, P) in US agriculture is discussed in more detail later.

Exports in 1993 amounted to 103.4 MMT of harvested crops (food grain, feedgrain, oilseeds, vegetables, fruits and nuts, cotton and tobacco) not including byproduct feeds, sugar, vegetable oils or animal products. Obviously there were also significant imports, notably tomatoes, bananas, and other fruits and nuts, plus coffee, tea and cocoa beans, 20.5 MMT. Net exports of raw unprocessed products were therefore 103.4 − 20.5 = 82.9 MMT. The remainder of the agricultural output was consumed directly or indirectly within the US. Final consumption of all food products (not including beverages) for 1993 was 203 MMT, plus 2.3 MMT for alcoholic beverages and 11.5 MMT for various industrial products (cotton, wool, hides, tobacco, alcohol, soaps, and so on) consumed domestically. In addition, there was 65.8 MMT of byproduct feedstuffs, of which 29.3 MMT was exported and 36.3 MMT was consumed by domestic livestock. Flows of US grain in 1993 are shown in Table 2.3; those of agricultural products in full in Table 2.4.

According to the US Department of Agriculture livestock in the US in 1993 were fed 149.3 MMT of grain plus byproduct feeds amounting to 42.9 MMT (AS Table 71) plus 210 MMT of harvested roughage (hay and silage) (AS Tables 41, 65, 354).[3] We attempt to account for the byproducts later.

Assuming the animal intake of pasturage (mainly by cattle) to be about 200 MMT, we can thus account for total animal feed consumption in 1993 amounting to 602.7 MMT, not including water, but including mineral supplements such as salt, urea and other minor inputs.

2.3   Mass balances for major crops
The food/feed processing sector consists of a number of activities, including grain and oilseed milling, meat and dairy processing, cotton processing, oil products, sugar production, fermentation industries, plus canning and freezing. Unfortunately, the major statistical agencies do not clearly separate these activities or clearly identify their inputs and outputs. We attempt to construct mass balances for corn, wheat and soybeans in the following pages, beginning with grain milling.

Domestic food products (flour, prepared cereals, packaged rice, baby foods, and so on) consumed from *all* grain mills in the US in 1993 amounted to 24.4 MMT. This estimate is taken from data on food consumption (AS Table 653).[4] However, it does not include grain consumed by the fermentation industries, which produce both alcoholic beverages and fuel alcohol. We estimate (below) that 15.5 MMT of grains – mostly corn – were used for fermentation products in 1993.

Inputs to the domestic grain and oilseed milling sectors are not reported as such. In principle they can be estimated indirectly as gross production plus net stock drawdowns, less net exports, less grain fed directly to animals, and less unmilled grain consumed for seed or alcohol (that is, by the fermentation industry). This data is available for most individual grains, but not all. We can begin with corn (see Table 2.5). So all the corn (for grain) appears to be accounted for in the aggregated statistics shown in the table. For wheat see Table 2.6.

Table 2.5   US corn 1993

			million bushels	MMT
Gross production	AS Table 39		6336	160.9
Net stock drawdowns		2113 – 850 =	1263	32.1
Subtotal (supply)		6336 + 1263 =	7599	193.0
Net exports	AS Table 39	1328 – 21 =	1307	33.2
Fed to animals	AS Table 39		4704	119.5
Food, seed and alcohol	AS Table 39		1588	40.3
Residual	7599 – (1307 + 4704 + 1588) =		0	0.0

Table 2.6   US wheat 1993

			million bushels	MMT
Gross production	AS Table 5		2396	65.2
Net stock drawdowns		531 – 568 =	–37	1.0
Subtotal (supply)		2396 – 37 =	2359	64.2
Net exports	AS Table 5	1228 – 109 =	1119	30.4
Fed to animals	AS Table 5		272	7.4
Seed	AS Table 5		96	2.6
Food and alcohol	AS Table 5		873	23.7
Residual	2359 – (1119 + 272 + 96 + 873) =		–1	0.0

Again, the residual is obviously a rounding error. Only the food category involves milling. However, AS Table 60 accounts for only 853 million bushels (21.6 MMT) of wheat destined for food, but explicitly excludes wheat used in alcoholic beverages. It would appear that the difference between AS Table 5 and AS Table 60, 19 million bushels (0.48 MMT), must have been used by brewers and distillers.

The third major crop is soybeans (see Table 2.7). The balancing procedure is the same. The discrepancy in this case is also a bit more than rounding error, but not too serious.

Table 2.7   US soybeans 1993

		million bushels	MMT
Gross production	AS Table 162	1871	50.9
Net stock drawdowns	292 – 209 =	83	2.3
Subtotal (disappearance)	=	1954	53.1
Net exports	AS Table 162 =	589	16.0
Seed and 'residual'	AS Table 162	96	2.6
To mill for crushing	AS Table 162	1276	34.7
Residual	1954 – (589 + 96 + 1276) =	–7	–0.2

2.4   Mass balances for grain/oilseed/sugar milling and alcohol

In this section, and the next, we consider several major subsectors of the food processing industry, SIC 20. Grain mill products constitute SIC 204; sugar and confectionery products are in SIC 206, fats and oils are SIC 207. Beverages are SIC 208; malt beverages (beer) are SIC 2082–3, distilleries are SIC 2085. An overall summary is presented in Figure 2.2, which shows how the numbers fit together. The reader can refer to this diagram for help.

We begin with grain milling, in which wheat and corn are by far the most important. In the case of wheat it appears that 872 million bu (23.72 MMT) were processed (milled) for food in 1993 (AS Table 5). The USDA states that 2.3 bushels produce 100 lb of flour (AS p. ix). This implies a flour yield of 70.7 per cent. Converting to metric units, domestic flour (and cereal) production would have been 16.76 MMT. This is remarkable, because it exactly matches – to three decimals – the annual consumption figures (148 lb/capita) given in AS Table 60, when multiplied by a 1993 population of 258 million persons. Almost too good to be true. We suspect that one of these figures was derived from the other. It is noteworthy that there was a 'lost mass' of 6.96 MMT in the milling process. However this was used for animal feed. This is a fairly close match with the figure for 'wheat millfeeds', fed to livestock, namely 6.74 MMT (AS Table 69).

Corn is more complicated, because USDA lumps 'food, feed and alcohol' together in its table linking supply and disappearance of the grain (AS Table 39). However, according to AS Table 60 (cited in the previous paragraph, corn products consumed for food (corn meal and flour, hominy grits, syrup, sugar and starch, but excluding corn oil) amount to 102.1 lb/capita or (multiplying by population and converting to metric units) 11.94 MMT. But Table 60 also allocates 820 million bushels of corn to 'food'. At 56 lb/bushel this comes to 20.83 MMT for milling, 8.9 MMT more than accounted for by per

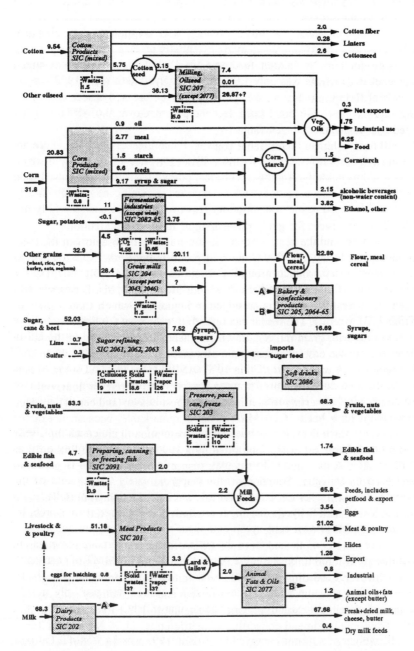

Figure 2.2   Mass balances in US food processing sectors, 1993 (MMT)

capita consumption. We cannot find any explanation of this discrepancy in the USDA statistics.

In the case of wheat, the mill byproducts were all accounted for as wheat millfeeds, and fed to animals, leaving essentially no loss. The corresponding category for corn is 'gluten feed and meal', but the quantity consumed domestically in 1993 was only 1.095 MMT (AS Table 69) and 1993 was an exceptional year in this regard. Other years, before and since, consumed significantly less. We are forced to conclude that over 9.6 MMT is truly missing, at least from the statistics.

We cannot explain this missing mass with confidence. However, there are not many possibilities. One is that the USDA statistics are seriously in error, which seems unlikely. Another theoretical possibility is that corn-based food products (cornmeal, cereals, syrup) are exported in significant amounts, nearly comparable to domestic consumption. However, this also seems highly unlikely.

A third possibility is that some of the missing mass consists of other products that are not mentioned in the agricultural statistics. There are two, as it happens: corn oil and cornstarch. Corn oil constitutes 3–4.5 per cent of the kernel, whence potential production is 0.6 MMT to 0.9 MMT. It happens that corn oil is also the cheapest of all the vegetable oils except palm oil (AS Table 190), which is a further indication of its wide usage. In fact, we believe that as much as 0.9 MMT of corn oil may have been produced in the US in 1993 (more than any other vegetable oil except soybean oil); the lower limit is probably 0.4 MMT. Part of this oil is used in salad oils and some of it is certainly used commercially by mass food processors for deep frying (for example, chicken). However, at most, this would only reduce the missing mass from 9.6 MMT to 8.7 MMT.

A further possible explanation is that quite a lot of corn gluten and millfeeds are produced and exported. This possibility is consistent with other data, as will be seen. A fifth possibility is that quite a lot of cornstarch is produced and used by industry. Starch constitutes approximately 72 per cent of the weight of the corn kernel. Thus potential starch production from milled corn was about 15 MMT. Syrup and sugar are both manufactured from starch, by hydrolysis. But known corn syrup and sugar production do not account for anywhere near all of the starch in the grain. Cornmeal contains some starch, but there is still room for more. We suspect that about 1.5 MMT of cornstarch is produced for industrial purposes (such as wallpaper paste and adhesives). The remainder of the missing mass (7.2–7.7 MMT) was probably mostly exported corn millfeeds, except for some unavoidable waste (perhaps 0.5 MMT).

The weight of soybeans shipped to mills in 1993 was 34.7 MMT. Outputs of milling include oil and cake and meal. Domestic production of cake and meal was 27.7 MMT (AS 164). Domestic production of soybean oil was 6.34 MMT (AS 164). The total weight of products was therefore 34.04 MMT. The mass disappearance of 0.66 MMT (2 per cent) is probably true waste (husks, hulls, dirt, and water).

From AS Table 164 it can be calculated that domestic consumption of soybean cake and meal for animal feeding (allowing for exports and stock changes) was 22.9 MMT. According to AS Table 69, consumption of soybean cake and meal for animal feeding was 23.9 MMT, a close enough match. In the same way, using AS Table 164 we estimate domestic soybean oil consumption as 5.84 MMT and exports as 0.694 MMT, respectively. Unfortunately there are no independent data on oil consumption, but AS Table 185 gives exports as 0.691 MMT, also a good match.

The total domestic disappearance of fats and oils, including animal fats and oils (lard and tallow), comes to 10.67 MMT (AS Table 188). Consumption of all fats and oils for industrial purposes – such as soaps and detergents, paints and plastics – was 2.65 MMT (AS Table 188). This implies that consumption of fats and oils in food must have been 8.0 MMT. Based on consumption data (AS Table 653),[5] we estimate that domestic consumption of all vegetable oils for food was 6.5 MMT, while animal fats in food amounted to 1.5 MMT. (This division is not precise, due to composites such as margarine and shortening.) From SA Table 1123, imports of vegetable oils were 1.4 MMT, exports were 1.7 MMT, so net exports were 0.3 MMT. Net exports of animal fats were 1.28 MMT.

Thus, total US production of fats and oils, both animal and vegetable, in 1993 must have been 10.67 + 0.3 + 1.3 = 12.3 MMT. If domestic production of vegetable oils was 8.3 MMT and net exports were 0.3 MMT, industrial use must have been approximately 1.5 MMT. Given domestic consumption of animal fats for food of 1.5 MMT (of which 0.55 MMT was butter), industrial use of 1.05 MMT plus exports of 1.28 MMT, implies lard, tallow and grease production of 3.28 MMT (including fish oils). Note that if vegetable oil production were smaller, animal production would have to be larger, and vice versa. It happens that according to the UN (1993), animal fats produced in the US in 1991 amounted to 3.8 MMT. If this figure were also correct for 1993, then vegetable oil production would have been lower by 0.5 MMT, and this subtraction would have to come out of corn oil.

However USDA only accounts for production from sources of oilseeds adding up to less than 7.4 MMT, mostly from soybeans.[6] We think that a good part of the difference between known sources and total disappearance must have been corn oil. As noted earlier, we estimate that up to 0.9 MMT of corn oil may have been produced. (This is about the maximum possible, given the oil content of the corn.)

Per capita grain-based beverage alcohol (excluding wine) consumed in the US in 1993 by persons over the age of 18 amounted to 32.4 gallons of beer and 1.9 gallons of distilled spirits (SA Table 227). Assuming beer is 5 per cent alcohol, by volume, and distilled spirits are 40 per cent (typical of whiskey), each person consumed 8.9 liters (or 7 kg) of ethanol, mostly (65 per cent) in beer. The adult population was 191 million, whence alcohol consumption in beverages was approximately 1.34 MMT (100 per cent ethanol basis). Of this, 0.46 MMT of ethanol was in distilled spirits, and 0.88 MMT was in beer. Beer also contains about 0.9 MMT of carbohydrates (dry weight).

Beer is made almost exclusively from barley malt, which we have already noted. In 1993 3.65 MMT of barley was malted. Assuming 90 per cent yield, malt production was about 3.28 MMT. On average this would generate 0.59 MMT of spent grain (for feed) plus 0.1 MMT of dust and sludge. Fermentation yielded about 0.8 MMT of carbon dioxide.

Whiskey made in the US is about half based on corn, the remainder being made from rye, wheat and small amounts of other grains. It follows that corn accounted for 0.23 MMT of the alcohol in spirits, plus or minus 0.05 or so. On a weight basis, about 2.5 units of grain are required per unit of ethyl alcohol produced (with an (approximately) equal production of carbon dioxide).[7] So, the production of distilled spirits required of the order of 0.6 MMT of corn, and an equal quantity of other grains (for example, rye).

However, we also know that much larger amounts of corn are used to produce ethyl alcohol for 'gasohol', supported by government subsidy of $0.14 per liter.[8] As it happens, this lucrative business is largely monopolized by one firm, Archer Daniels Midland, whose alcohol output is secret. However we can make an intelligent guess, based on available statistics, simple chemistry and the mass balance methodology. As it turns out, we can also find the answer elsewhere (in the energy statistics.)

In 1993, subtracting corn used for 'food', in AS Table 60 from corn used for 'seed, food and alcohol' (AS Table 39) the difference was 19.5 MMT, for seed and alcohol. We do not have specific data for corn used as seed, and USDA does not provide it. One approach to estimation might be to make some plausible assumption. For instance, one might guess that no more than 2.5 per cent of the crop would suffice for seed (as for rice), or 4 per cent as for wheat. As it happens, however, we were able to deduce the missing number in another way. (We think the details are worth recounting for the light they shed on how mass balance methodology can be used.)

The International Energy Agency of the OECD publishes an annual compendium of energy statistics, including an energy balance (IEA 1995). For 1993 this balance showed 11 487 TJ (terajoules) of 'gas/liquids from biomass' as inputs to petroleum refineries. This can only refer to ethanol destined for blending with gasoline as 'gasohol'. Converting from energy to mass units, using standard thermodynamic enthalpy tables, this corresponds to 3.82 MMT of ethanol for gasohol. To this must be added the alcohol in whiskey (0.23 MMT) for a total of 4.05 MMT. Converting back into corn equivalent, this implies 433 million bu, or 11 MMT of corn for alcohol, leaving 335 million bu or 5.3 per cent of the crop, for seed. (This 5.3 per cent figure for seed corn is higher than wheat, which works out at 3.9 per cent, and much higher than rice, at 2.54 per cent.)

By a very curious coincidence we found another source just before finalizing this manuscript. It is the article 'Nitrogen' in the US Bureau of Mines *Minerals Yearbook 1993* (p. 720). In that article a consulting firm in Washington DC, Information Resources, Inc. is cited as having estimated that 1.1 billion gallons of ethanol 'may be required to meet projected US oxygenated fuel demand created by the Clean Air Act in 1993'. This amounts to 419 million bu of corn equivalent; a close match to the 433 million bushel estimate above. We have no idea why an article on nitrogen (and ammonia) should discuss ethanol from corn, but we are happy that it did.

Elsewhere in the same article, it is stated that only cornstarch, 72 per cent of the kernel, is fermented for alcohol, while the remaining 28 per cent of fiber, protein and oil is currently sold as 'distillers' dried grains and solubles' (DDGS).[9] From all this it can be deduced that the fermentation process in distilleries using 11 MMT of corn as 'feed' would have yielded – in addition to the 4.05 MMT of alcohol – about 3.73 MMT of CO_2 and 3.08 MMT of byproducts, mostly water vapor and DDGS that can be used for high protein animal feed.

Cotton is a major agricultural product that contributes little to feed and nothing to food. Unfortunately 1993 data are incomplete. In 1988 the US produced 9.2 MMT (net weight) of raw cotton. This was ginned to yield 3.36 MMT of cotton fiber (lint), 5.50 MMT of cottonseed, plus 0.27 MMT of linters. Linters is a fibrous material used for felting and cellulosic chemical manufacturing, so it is not a waste. The cottonseed was allocated to mills and 'other uses' including exports. The sale to mills was 4.38 MMT; 3.38 MMT was actually crushed (USDA 1992, Table 141 p. 107). The mill product was 0.56 MMT of oil and 1.53 MMT of high protein cottonseed oilcake, used for animal feed, plus 1.29 MMT of milling waste.

Data for 1993 are similar, except that USDA did not report the raw production or linters. However, cotton fiber production in 1993 was 3.51 MMT, and cottonseed production was 5.75 MMT, more or less in the same proportion. Of this, 3.15 MMT was crushed, yielding nearly 1 MMT of oil and 1.42 MMT of cake and meal, plus 0.73 MMT of mill waste. Linters production has not been reported since 1989, but if the proportions held, it should have been 0.28 MMT, which implies an original total raw cotton input of 9.54 MMT. Linters are used in the manufacture of chemical cellulose.

Sugar cane weighing 28.2 MMT and sugar beets weighing 23.8 MMT yielded 7.52 MMT of refined sugar in 1993 (AS Table 113). (About 0.69 MMT of lime was also used in the latter process.) Sugar cane and beet refining also yielded about 1.022 MMT and 0.692 MMT of animal feed, respectively, plus 0.113 MMT of 'blackstrap' molasses, for a total of 1.830 MMT of feeds (AS Table 121). To this was added another 0.785 MMT of imported sugar-based animal feeds, for a grand total of 2.615 MMT. The mass unaccounted for from domestic sugar refining, altogether, amounted to about 43 MMT. Since the final products are dry, or nearly so, most of this mass loss – probably 26 MMT or so – is surely water vapor from the various evaporation stages in sugar production. About 3 per cent of the input mass of cane – about 0.85 MMT – is organic filter sludge.[10] A similar percentage is probably applicable to beets, giving a total of 1.6 MMT.

The remainder of the dry cane waste was fibrous 'bagasse' (approx. 9 MMT), which can be burned as boiler fuel, but is also commonly used in the manufacture of hardboard, plastic fillers and as a source of the chemical furfural (Shreve 1956 p. 650). The beet sugar process involves some use of sulfur dioxide to bleach the sugar, leaving a solid residue containing calcium sulfite ($CaSO_3$) amounting to 7 MMT or so. This may be used as a soil conditioner. All of these figures are somewhat uncertain, of course.

In addition, truck crops (vegetables and berries) and tree crops (fruits and nuts) accounted for a harvest weight of 79.9 MMT. Exports took 6.2 MMT and imports added 8.6 MMT, for a total domestic supply of 83.3 MMT. Final consumption (on an 'as purchased' basis) accounted for 68.3 MMT. The difference, 15 MMT was presumably waste, divided between food processing plants and retail stores. We estimate that two-thirds of this mass loss (10 MMT) was evaporative water loss from freeze drying (for example, of orange juice) and other processing. The rest was husks, shells, stems, seeds, and other unwanted plants parts. The bulk of the food process waste goes into waterways or municipal wastes from thousands of point sources, including retail shops. Some is recovered for other uses. A small amount may be composted or burned for energy recovery.

2.5 Mass balances for animal products (SIC 201) and fish (SIC 091-2)

Animal products in the US can be subdivided into red meats, poultry, eggs and dairy products. The live weight of animals slaughtered for red meat in 1993 was 29.60 MMT (AS Tables 378, 417, 399). Salable weight of red meat, after processing, was 18.94 MMT, a reduction of 10.66 MMT (AS Table 433). The difference – missing mass to be accounted for – consisted of heads, hides, internal organs, blood and entrails. Byproducts of meat processing include lard and tallow, hides, dog and cat food, glue, bone meal, blood meal, meat meal and 'tankage'. We have no estimates of meat byproducts used in pet foods (see below).

Domestic consumption of lard and edible tallow in food, both direct and in shortening, amounted to about 1.75 MMT according to our estimate above. Industrial consumption (for soap, fatty acids, and so on) was probably 0.8 MMT and exports were 1.28 MMT, for a grand total of 3.3 MMT (AS Tables 187, 188). Other sources suggest a higher figure, of the order of 3.8 MMT, albeit for a different year.[11] Blood meal, bone meal and tankage (2.22 MMT) are utilized in animal feed concentrates used domestically (AS Table 69). The raw weight of hides is not given by USDA, but other evidence suggests that the weight of undressed hides in 1988 (mostly for export to foreign tanneries) was about 1 MMT. It could not have changed much by 1993. This figure reflects some weight loss from drying but it still may be too low.[12]

We have explicitly accounted for 6.5–7 MMT of the 'missing mass'. Evidently, 3.5–4 MMT remains unaccounted for. It is tempting to assume this must be waste. However, this assumption would be too hasty. Part of it is probably meat meal for export; total exports of protein meal (from various sources) amounted to 6.344 MMT (SA Table 1123). Some of the 'missing mass' may be pet food, for which we have no explicit data. We conjecture that up to 2 MMT is evaporative water loss in the production of meals and concentrates. There is little true waste at this stage of processing.

Exports of red meat products in 1993 amounted to 0.78 MMT and imports (mostly of beef) amounted to 1.45 MMT. Thus domestic disappearance of red meat was 19.61 MMT. However, final consumption of meat ('as purchased') was only 13.70 MMT. The difference of 5.9 MMT is mainly waste fat and bone, largely generated by meatcutters in retail shops. Some of this waste goes back to renderers, who recover lard, tallow and bone meal, but much of it ends up in municipal refuse and, finally, in landfills. We do not know how much.

In the case of poultry, live weight of broilers, chickens and turkeys in 1993 was 17.32 MMT (SA Table 1146, AS Tables 500 501). The above figures include an allowance for roosters and pullets too old for egg laying, but not other types of poultry (ducks, geese). Dressed carcass weight of poultry produced in the US was 12.4 MMT (AS Table 499). This implies a byproduct and waste flow at the processing plant of 4.92 MMT, much of which is probably recycled as pet food or meat meal for animal feed. Some was water vapor. Some (mostly feathers, beaks and claws) is dumped or burned, although even feathers are now being converted into feather meal. Exports of poultry were 1.03 MMT. Final consumption of poultry ('as purchased') was 7.32 MMT in 1993. Thus, a further loss of 4 MMT presumably occurred at the retail level, including restaurants. Some of this may be recovered for pet food. Part of it surely ends up in garbage as municipal refuse or in waterways (as BOD).

Egg production in 1993 was 4.26 MMT, while consumption was 3.54 MMT (AS Table 521). The differential was partly exports (0.11 MMT), but mainly for hatching. Raw milk production in 1993 was 68.30 MMT, and 67.47 MMT was marketed. Exports (0.26 MMT) and imports (0.28 MMT) were nearly equal. Final consumption of milk products 'equivalent' (including butter) was 67.68 MMT (AS Table 653). Some dried milk is used for animal feeding (0.4 MMT). The statistical discrepancy between production and consumption statistics is very small (less than 2 per cent) and probably insignificant (AS Table 481). There is a mass reduction in cheese manufacturing, but it is entirely due to evaporative losses of water. The water loss in cheese making and milk drying was about 26 MMT in 1988, and would have been slightly larger – perhaps 28 MMT – in 1993.

Domestic landings of raw fish in 1993 were 4.75 MMT, of which 1.02 MMT was classified as inedible (AS Table 684). Exports were (0.98 MMT) – mostly edible (salmon fillets) and imports were 1.66 MMT, of which 1.32 MMT was edible (AS Table 686). Thus the domestic supply was 5.42 MMT. Of this, 1.25 MMT was classified as inedible and converted into fish meal or oil for animal feed. Yet, only 0.654 MMT of fish meal was consumed as fish meal by animals in the US (AS Table 69). The difference (0.6 MMT) was probably water evaporated in the process. Only 4.04 MMT of fish was designated as being for human consumption, and only 1.74 MMT was finally consumed by humans (AS Table 653). We conjecture that at least 2 MMT of this 3.3 MMT missing mass was converted to dog and cat food. The rest was presumably fish heads, tails, fins, guts and bones that are discarded during commercial fish dressing, especially at the retail level. (Much of this is doubtless also consumed by domestic or feral cats.)

Altogether, feed concentrates and mill byproducts amounting to 36.8 MMT were fed to domestic livestock in 1993 (AS Table 69). An additional 11.73 MMT of feeds and fodders was exported, plus 6.344 MMT of high protein feeds (SA Table 1123). The total comes to 54.9 MMT. To confuse matters worse, if we compare total exports of wheat and products (SA Table 1123) with exports of wheat grain (AS Table 5) there is a difference of 3.326 MMT, which we cannot explain, since we have specifically accounted for wheat millfeeds of 6.74 MMT and obtained a satisfactory balance. However comparing exports of feed grains and products from (SA Table 1123) with individual export totals from SA tables (cited earlier in the text) there is a much bigger difference of 7.941 MMT, which is difficult to account for. Either there is a major statistical error or exports of corn, in particular, are much greater than stated in AS Table 39. (Possibly this is the explanation for the 'missing mass' in corn-for-food, discussed earlier.)

In any case, we can now account for a number of components of the byproduct aggregate. These include wheat millfeeds of 6.74 MMT, corn gluten millfeeds of 1.09 MMT, cake and meal from soybeans (27.7 MMT), cottonseed meal (1.53 MMT) and other oilseed meals (0.70 MMT). Sugar mills generated 1.83 MMT of feeds and another 0.79 MMT of sugar-based feeds was imported. Brewers and distillers spent grains or DDGS contributed 3.75 MMT; meat processing added 2.2 MMT and fish meal 0.65 MMT. Dried milk was 0.4 MMT. All of these add up to 47.38 MMT.

An additional 7.5 MMT is needed to account for the total of 54.5 MMT. As mentioned above, we had 9.6 MMT missing from the corn balance. We tentatively allocated it partly to oil (0.9 MMT), partly to cornstarch for industry (1.5 MMT) and the rest (7.2 MMT) to millfeed. Performing a mass balance on oilseed milling we also find a discrepancy. We can account for inputs of 39.28 MMT, but USDA statistics on outputs gave us 7.4 MMT of oil and 26.87 MMT of cake and meal, leaving a missing mass of 4.3 MMT. We estimate that 0.8 is true solid waste, and the rest (3.5 MMT) is meal. Added to the 47.4 MMT we could account for before, the new total comes to 58.1 MMT, slightly too much but well within the uncertainties of our calculations. Needless to say, if corn exports were understated in AS Table 39, the missing mass would be reduced and so would the difference between figures in *Statistical Abstract* and *Agricultural Statistics*.

Of course things may not be so simple. In fact, there is also another major unknown 'sink'. It is obvious that substantial quantities of specialized canned meat products are consumed by dogs and cats. We lack data, but on the basis of body weight, the amount of feedstuff involved must be at least a few percent of the human consumption. We have already tentatively allocated 2 MMT of fish to pet food. It is not implausible to suppose that meat and poultry byproducts, and grain byproducts for pets might be produced and consumed in comparable quantities.

But recall that 5 MMT of mass was still unaccounted for from red meat processing (though 2 MMT is probably water vapor) and nearly another 5 MMT from poultry processing. We also noted the further disappearance of nearly 10 MMT of meat and poultry at the retail level some of which could certainly be recovered and rendered for lard, tallow, bonemeal or used for pet food. All in all, we can see possible utilization routes for at least a few MMT of the 20 MMT 'unaccounted for' above. It is very difficult to identify any large unutilized waste flows in the food processing sector, except for sugar, fruits and vegetables.

2.6 Nutrient and mineral flows[13]

Large tonnages of chemical inputs (fertilizers, pesticides) are used in the agricultural sector. The nitrogen content of ammonia used for fertilizer consumed domestically was 11 226 MMT in 1993, which was 86.5 per cent of all the synthetic ammonia consumed in the US (MY, 'Nitrogen', Table 2).

Domestic phosphate rock production in 1993 was 11.94 MMT (P_2O_5 content) of which 1.018 MMT was exported and 1.092 was converted into elemental phosphorus and thence into other phosphorus chemicals (MY 'Phosphates', Table 4, p. 822). Most of the rest (9.724 MMT) was used for domestic agricultural purposes, mainly fertilizers (ibid., Table 5).

A third major plant nutrient is potassium. It is produced from several different salts, but statistics are given in terms of K_2O equivalent. US domestic production in 1993 was 1.506 MMT (K_2O equivalent) but apparent consumption was 5.432 MMT in the same units (MY, 'Potash', Table 1, p. 848). Non-fertilizer (that is, chemical) use is negligible.

The fourth critical nutrient is sulfur, which is low in some soils. However, sulfur deposition from air pollution ameliorates this problem. For the rest, sulfur is normally supplied in combination with nitrogen, as ammonium sulfate and, in elemental form, as lime-sulfur (0.914 MMT S).

Apart from plant nutrients, significant quantities of minerals are used as feed supplements for animals. An approximate total can be deduced by comparing two tables in *Agricultural Statistics*, namely Tables 69 and 71. The former table gives the 'disappearance' of commercial byproducts feeds in all categories, adding up to 37.55 MMT for 1993; the latter table gives feed concentrates fed to livestock and poultry, for the same year, of 43.85 MMT, including mineral supplements. It is logical to suppose that mineral supplements therefore amounted to 6.3 MMT.

No further data on the subject are to be found in *Agricultural Statistics* (AS), but there are some data in *Minerals Yearbook* (MY). For instance, urea, a fertilizer material, is also used in fairly large tonnages (about 0.115 MMT N-content) for animal feed supplements (MY 'Nitrogen', Table 5). Defluorinated phosphates (as dicalcium phosphate) are used for this purpose (MY 'Phosphates', p. 813). We have no recent data on consumption, but annual capacity was about 250 kMT in 1955 (Shreve 1956, p. 349). Current levels might exceed 400 kMT.

Sulfur, also, is utilized for this purpose, mainly as sodium sulfate (MY 'Sodium sulfate', Table 5, footnote 5). It is quite likely that potash (probably as potassium chloride or 'muriate of potash') is used also, since potassium is essential for all animals. Calcined magnesium and magnesium sulfate are both fed to animals, probably to the extent of at least 100 kMT, perhaps more. Most important, in 1993 2.704 MMT of salt (sodium chloride) was used in agriculture, entirely for animal feeding. The other large mineral supplement – especially for poultry grit – is crushed stone (mainly limestone) of which 2.054 MMT was consumed in 1993 (MY 'Stone', Table 13). Thus we can explicitly account for 4.87 MMT of the 6.3 MMT imputed. Phosphates, potash and a few minor minerals undoubtedly account for the rest.

Many of these nutrient substances find their way, either directly, or via animal excreta, into surface waters and ground waters. Much of the nitrogen, phosphorus and salt content of animal feed ends up in urine, either on pastures or at feedlots. Some of this excreted nitrogen pollutes ground water and some is volatilized as ammonia, resulting in air pollution. Ammonia in the atmosphere reacts either with sulfuric or nitric acid, producing ammonium sulfate or ammonium nitrate. Phosphates and potash are lost from plants in litter or wood ash. Phosphates in animals are concentrated in bones and teeth. These materials are mostly recycled to the land (as bone meal), except to the extent they are contained in human food and lost in sewage. These chemicals act as fertilizers in forests, lakes and streams (which are said to be eutrophic).

Animal feed concentrates in the US average 79 per cent digestibility. From this we can conclude that 21 per cent of the mass of animal feed concentrates (192.2 MMT) fed to dairy cattle, beef cattle in feedlots, hogs and poultry is passed through immediately as feces. Harvested roughage, silage and hay (210.5 MMT) has lower digestibility, probably around 60 per cent. This implies 40 per cent waste as feces. The two together imply manure output from on-farm and industrial animal feeding operations, amounting to roughly 125 MMT, give or take 10. In addition USDA estimates that animal intake from pastures is about 200 MMT. Assuming 60 per cent digestibility, roughly 80 MMT of manure is probably left on pastures. This figure could be too low; the digestibility of pasturage may be as low as 40 per cent.[14]

Of the total manure (approx. 205 MMT), it appears that 125 MMT is generated by animals in confinement, and of this, 75 per cent (83 MMT) is probably recycled to croplands (Smil 1993). The remainder of the manure from feedlots (42 MMT, about 50 per cent solid) is lost to runoff or otherwise. Manure left on pastures (80 MMT) is returned directly to the soil – but not to croplands *per se* – and does not constitute a waste. The chemical composition of manure is summarized in Table 2.8.

As regards outputs of the livestock 'sector', a total of 119.48 MMT can be accounted for as the gross weight of animal carcasses, eggs and dairy products produced for the market (see above). Thus total feed inputs of 593 MMT and manure outputs (50 per cent moisture basis) of 205 MMT can be accounted for, leaving 593 – 205 – 119.5 = 268.5 MMT for animal metabolism (respiration) and all other losses. 'Other' losses include spoilage, dead animals not harvested, feed for horses and mules, domestic consumption by farmers, ammonia and methane emissions. Note that dead animals account for about 4 per cent of live weight, or roughly 2 MMT, but if they are disposed of by burial we can reasonably assume that the mass in question is another form of excreta. Methane emissions from animals (discussed later) total 0.68 MMT, and go directly to the air. Ammonia is also emitted, but from manure and urine. Part of the mineral supplements, especially salt and grit,

Table 2.8   Composition of manures (per cent)

	Cattle	Horse	Sheep	Swine	Chicken
Moisture	81.33	68.85	64.82	77.56	64.82
Organic	16.74	27.06	30.70	15.50	30.70
Ash	2.06	6.70	4.72	6.02	4.72
N	0.53	0.55	0.89	0.63	0.89
K_2O	0.48	0.57	0.83	0.41	0.83
P_2O_5	0.29	0.27	0.48	0.46	0.48
Ca	0.29	0.27	0.21	0.19	0.38
Mg	0.11	0.11	0.13	0.03	0.13
Cl	0.03	0.08	0.08	0.03	0.08
S	0.036	0.036	0.06	0.03	0.06
B	0.016	0.016	0.016	0.0005	0.016
Mn	0.003	0.003	0.003	0.0008	0.003
Zn	0.0016	0.002	0.002	0.0006	0.0021
Cu	0.0008	0.0008	0.0008	0.0002	0.0006

Note: Totals add to more than 100% due to double counting.

Source: Dictionary of Plant Foods.

are certainly excreted – say 4 MMT – but these can also be assumed to be incorporated in the manure. The remainder of the items can be treated as metabolic requirements.

A rough cut at the mass balance suffices: consider a 'lost mass' of 268.5 MMT, as suggested above. Subtract 2.5 MMT for dead animals and airborne emissions of methane. Assume that 50 per cent of the remainder (133 MMT) is carbohydrate (CH_2O) metabolized for energy by the reverse of the photosynthesis reaction noted at the beginning of the chapter. The other 50 per cent is assumed to be water. The oxidation of 133 MMT of carbohydrate implies oxygen consumption by the animals of 142 MMT and generates 195 MMT of CO_2 as respiratory output. The oxidation process itself also generates 80 MMT of water (vapor), to be added to the 133 MMT of water already identified. Thus we calculate a minimal water output of 80 + 133 = 213 MMT. Adding up all the inputs, then, we get 593 (feeds) + 142 (oxygen) = 735. Adding up the outputs, we get 205 + 195 + 213 + 119.5 + 2.5 = 735. Given the uncertainty of some of the numbers, especially the water, this is a reasonable balance. We have cheated, of course, by neglecting the nitrogen, sulfur and other nutrient elements that contribute to metabolism (see Figure 2.1).

The minor components of metabolic wastes (nitrogen, phosphorus, sulfur, and so on) pass largely through the kidneys. However one other pollutant is worth mentioning, namely methane. All animals have anaerobic organisms in their guts that convert a small amount of food intake into methane, typically 1–2 per cent on an energy basis. However for cattle and sheep the percentage is larger, ranging from 5.5–7.5 per cent, depending on quality and quantity of feed. Taking these factors into account, Crutzen *et al.* have estimated annual methane output of 60 kg per head of cattle and 8 kg per head of sheep (Crutzen *et al.* 1986). Cattle population in 1993 was 99.2 million, while sheep population was 10.2 million (SA Table 1140). Methane emissions from these sources therefore amounted to 6.03 MMT.

Nitrogen and phosphorus flows for US agriculture have been estimated, as shown in Figure 2.3 (Smil 1993). Note that Smil's figures do not exactly match ours, partly because they represent averages rather than data for a specific year.

Schlesinger and Hartley have estimated annual ammonia (NH_3 emissions per head) from animals as follows: 15.5 kg from cattle and horses, 2.4 kg from sheep, 2.35 kg from pigs and 0.21 kg from poultry (Schlesinger and Hartley 1992, Table 4). Based on 1993 populations of cattle and sheep as above, plus 58.2 million pigs and 7 billion chickens and turkeys (SA Table 1145), this comes to a total of 3.18 MMT.

Fertilizer itself is also a source of ammonia emissions; the emission factors for urea and ammonium sulfate spread on the soil surface are estimated at 0.2 and 0.1 respectively; for other fertilizers – including anhydrous ammonia injected directly into the soil – the emission rate is lower (around 3 per cent) (Schlesinger and Hartley 1992, Table 6). In 1993 2.46 MMT of urea (N-content) was used as fertilizer in the US, along with 0.5 MMT (N-content) of ammonium sulfate (MY 'Nitrogen', Table 6, p. 737). But total fertilizer consumption in the US (including imported fertilizers) was 10.31 MMT (N-content) (ibid. Table 6). Apparently most of the imported fertilizers were in the 'other type' category. On this basis, fertilizer use apparently generated total ammonia emissions of 0.2*2.46 + 0.1*0.5 + 0.03*(10.31 – 2.96) = 0.76 MMT (N). Combining the two sources (animal excretion and fertilizer), we can account for airborne ammonia emissions of 3.18 + 0.76 = 3.94 MMT (N) or 38 per cent of the N-content of applied fertilizer.

According to one independent estimate, of 100 units of N in fertilizer, roughly 50 is taken up by harvested crops, of which 47 is subsequently consumed by animals and 42 is eventually excreted in animal urine (Crutzen 1976). Most of this nitrogenous waste is generated at feedlots, since fertilizer is seldom used on grazing land, and the nitrogen uptake by grazing animals is largely left behind as manure or urine. About 24 units of fertilizer N find their way to rivers, lakes and groundwater, of which ten units are direct runoff

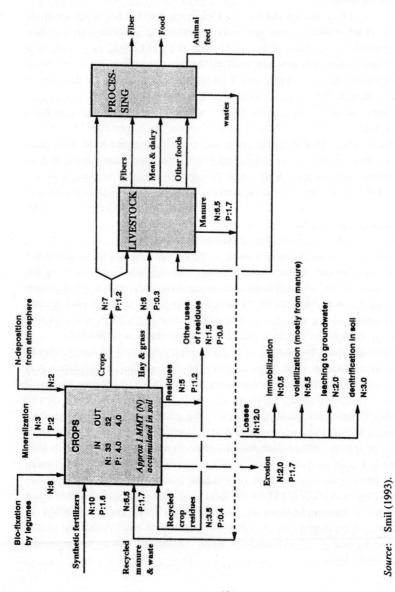

Source: Smil (1993).

Figure 2.3 N and P balances in US agriculture, 1988 (MMT)

from the soil, eight are from animal excreta at feeding stations, and six are from human sewage reflecting downstream consumption of food. Thus about 18 per cent of agricultural nitrogen fertilizer use (N-content) reappears within a few weeks or months as waterborne pollution, although only 10 per cent is direct fertilizer loss. Since 10.43 MMT (N) was used for fertilizer and feed supplements in 1993, this implies an overall waterborne N-waste flow of 2.5 MMT (N-content).

The rest of the unaccounted for nitrogen in the applied fertilizer (about 32 per cent) is embodied in root and stem material that is unharvested or harvested directly by animals and remains with the soil (20–25 per cent), or is reconverted to nitrogen gas and returned to the atmosphere by denitrifying bacteria in the soil (5–10 per cent). This would suggest denitrification losses (from fertilizer alone) of 0.5–1.0 MMT.

However, denitrification applies to the whole nitrogen cycle, of which the use of synthetic nitrogen fertilizer only accounts for 30 per cent (10 units N of 33 total flux). Total denitrification losses for US agriculture have been estimated at 3.0 MMT (Smil 1993). For every 16 units of nitrogen emitted as N_2, it seems that roughly 1 unit (on average) is emitted as N_2O, a potent greenhouse gas, but these emissions tend to be episodic and associated mostly with transitional periods. Based on Smil's figures, total N_2O emissions from US agriculture would be about 0.19 MMT/y, but only a third of this would be 'excess' to the natural cycle, thus contributing to buildup.

Nitrogenous fertilizer use has come to be recognized as one of the major sources of global atmospheric N_2O buildup, with 0.7 MMT of N_2O being the current 'best guess' of worldwide emissions from this source (Schlesinger 1991). The US was responsible for roughly one-eighth of worldwide nitrogenous fertilizer use in 1993 (MY 'Nitrogen', Table 14, p. 743), and probably a similar proportion of fertilizer-based N_2O emissions – or 0.09 MMT.

The greatest mass movement from agriculture is the loss of topsoil due to wind or water erosion. A detailed study of topsoil loss due to agriculture was carried out by the US Soil Conservation Service in 1982 (Brown and Wolf 1984, p. 17). It was found that 44 per cent of US cropland was losing topsoil at an unsustainable rate (that is, faster than the natural rate of soil formation). The topsoil loss in 1982 was estimated at 1.53 billion metric tons. A different survey, the United States *Natural Resource Inventory*, gives much higher numbers (cited in Adriaanse *et al.* 1997). According to the latter, the erosion loss rate from wind and water on non-federal land in the US (79 per cent of the total area) was 5525 MMT in 1975, 5267 in 1980, and has declined since then monotonically ever since to 3543 MMT in 1993 and 3407 MMT in 1994. Erosion is largely due to agriculture, although road construction and logging do contribute significantly in some watersheds. We do not have any detailed breakdown.

The long-term declining trend appears to be a consequence of various erosion control policies, including 'soil banks' and increasing use of 'no-till' methods of cultivation. Also, it must be pointed out that eroded material is not immediately carried out to sea; much of it is later redeposited on the same field, or in the bed or bank of a nearby stream. It is worthwhile remembering that the annual flood of the Nile is actually the major source of fertility for all the lands along the valley of the Nile, from Aswan to the Delta. Erosion is a threat to the fertility of the slopes near the headwaters of a river, but it is also a source of fertility further down the valley. It may take many years for a particle of soil from a field in Montana or Minnesota to reach the Gulf of Mexico. On the other hand, the natural cycle of erosion and redeposition no longer functions naturally in valleys where the river is confined between dikes and dams. When major floods occur (as they do), enormous amounts of material are carried downstream and out to sea in a few days or weeks.

The overall 1993 losses from US agriculture can be summarized as follows. First in magnitude is topsoil erosion of 3530 MMT (although much of this is from non-agricultural areas and activities). Next, the difference between gross biomass production by crop plants (neglecting pastures) and gross harvested biomass was between 500 and 600 MMT. This material was mostly returned to the soil where it serves an important function, so it would probably not be called a waste by most biologists and soil scientists. However some of this biomass could have been burned directly for fuel (as in India or China) while retaining much of the mineral nutrient value; or, still better, it could be converted into biogas and/or compost,[15] thus recovering energy but retaining most of the nutrients and soil conditioning value. In that sense, this material was used somewhat less efficiently than it might have been.

The next category of agricultural waste is the difference between gross inputs to animal husbandry and gross outputs of animal products (including dairy products). Biomass consumed by animals (including pasturage) was about 593 MMT (50 per cent dry), while raw output, before processing, was 52.4 MMT (50 per cent dry equivalent) plus manure production of 125 MMT (50 per cent dry) in confined spaces (not including 80 MMT left on pastures).

The manure could, in principle, have been recovered and utilized more efficiently (via the biogas/compost route) for energy recovery, more efficient recycling of nutrients and reduced pollution of groundwater and air. Instead, most of the manure from large-scale animal feeding operations is either wasted or treated like sewage, resulting in a sludge that is landfilled but leaving most of the nutrients and soluble organics in the water. An additional 268 MMT (50 per cent dry) was lost mass consumed by the animals themselves for metabolic purposes and ultimately converted into CO_2 (195 MMT) and water vapor (213 MMT). This loss could only be avoided if people consumed less meat and milk.

Ammonia emissions to the atmosphere, direct from fertilizer use, seem to be about 0.7 MMT (N), or 7 per cent of fertilizer inputs, but volatilization losses from manure and urine add another 3.2 MMT. Methane emissions to the atmosphere from grazing animals in the US were apparently about 0.68 MMT.

We have estimated mass losses from the domestic food processing sector as follows: grain and oilseed milling 0.8 MMT; fermentation wastes 4.85 MMT of CO_2 plus 1.95 MMT of solid wastes; cottonseed milling 1.5 MMT solid wastes; sugar milling 30 MMT water vapor, 8 MMT bagasse, 6 MMT soil conditioner and 1 MMT solid waste (for example, filter sludge); vegetable and fruit canning, freezing and distribution 15 MMT (of which 10 MMT is water vapor), meat and poultry packing 10 MMT unaccounted for (but probably not lost), plus about 10 MMT unaccounted for downstream (mostly waste); dairy processing 26.1 MMT (entirely water), and fish packing and retailing 3.3 MMT (unaccounted for but mostly pet food).

For the food processing sector as a whole (including losses in retail shops) this adds up to about 5 MMT CO_2 from fermentation and around 30 MMT (plus or minus 3) of dry organic mass losses, of which at least 8 MMT and possibly as much as 12 MMT can be burned for energy recovery. Other organic waste of plant origin consists of fruit/vegetable skins and stems, nut shells, pits and seeds, inedible leaves, spoilage, and so forth, that could be composted (5 MMT), plus filter sludges and the like (3–4 MMT) and up to 10 MMT of meat/fish waste (skin, bones, fat, feathers) lost along the retail chain. In practice, most of the unburned mill wastes, plus animal wastes – formerly fed to pigs – are either dumped into waterways or sent to landfills. In the long run they mostly oxidize, generating CO_2 although some fraction will decay in anaerobic conditions producing methane instead.

The material losses that we have identified as likely waste streams are 'dry' in the sense that they do not include the weight of washing, cooking, or process water. The also do not assume a priori mass reduction by combustion of biomass for energy recovery. In this connection, a survey by Science Applications Inc. (SAI) commissioned by EPA, attempted to identify dry wastes from the industrial sectors (SAI 1985). The SAI estimate of dry weight of wastes from food and feed processing was 6.3 MMT (based on 1976 data). This strongly suggests that combustible dry wastes such as bagasse were, in fact, mostly burned for mass reduction and energy recovery. A significant fraction of the missing mass was actually downstream in the retail sector. Thus, our analysis is qualitatively consistent with SAI's results.

Endnotes

1. The standard source is *Standard Industrial Classification Manual 1987*, published by the Office of Management and Budget, Executive Office of the President, Washington DC. It

is available from the National Technical Information Service (NTIS), Springfield, Va
(USOMB 1987).

2. Unless otherwise specified, all data in this section refers to the year 1993 and is taken
    from one of two US government publications, namely *Statistical Abstract of the United
    States 1995* (US Bureau of the Census) or *Agricultural Statistics 1995–1996* (Department
    of Agriculture). Where appropriate, we refer to specific tables by number, as SA Table
    xxx or AS Table yyy. The latter (AS) contains far more detail but is much more difficult to
    use, due to the extreme proliferation of volume and weight units. In fact, conversion
    factors are listed for 80 different measures in the front of the volume, and some others are
    defined in footnotes or not at all. We have converted all units to metric tons or million
    metric tons (MMT). Despite the overwhelming detail in *Agricultural Statistics* there are
    numerous omissions. We have been forced to make our own estimates in several cases,
    using indirect evidence, due to the fact that data for certain commodities has been
    suppressed or aggregated inappropriately in order to 'avoid disclosure' of certain
    monopoly operations, especially with respect to uses of grain.

3. The statistics on animal feeding in AS Table 71 do not exactly match the statistics in AS
    Table 2.2. The discrepancy is mainly for wheat. We cannot account for it.

4. AS Table 653 disagrees with AS Table 60 in the case of oats; we have used the latter
    (larger) figure.

5. The calculation is not straightforward, since fat consumption is given in pounds of fat per
    capita, with one category (shortening) that includes both animal and vegetable fats.
    However the contents of shortening are given in AS Table 182. Shortening accounted for
    about 700 million lbs of lard and edible tallow, or 2.7 lb/capita for the 1993 US popula-
    tion of 258 million.

6. See AS Chapter III, Tables 137, 147, 151, 164, 171. Note that oil production from
    sunflower seeds is not given, but the quantity of sunflower seeds crushed for oil was
    approximately 1 MMT. The oil content of different oilseeds varies from 30 per cent to 40
    per cent. So the maximum quantity of sunflower oil produced in 1993 was 0.4 MMT.

7. The basic equation for fermentation of sugar is $C_6H_{12}O_6 \rightarrow 2(C_2H_5OH) + 2CO_2$ from
    which it follows that 100 mass units of corn sugar (or starch) yields 51 mass units of
    ethanol and 49 mass units of carbon dioxide.

8. The subsidy in question was the brainchild of Senator and later Presidential aspirant
    Robert Dole. The US government paid out $6.3 billion from the outset of the program
    (1983) through 1995, and the drain continues (Roodman 1996). The major beneficiary has
    been Archer Daniels Midland (ABM), which controls the market. It would seem to be no
    coincidence that Dole has received at least $255 000 in campaign contributions from
    ADM (ibid.). (Bush and Clinton have also received substantial donations.)

9. In fact, cornstarch is only 60–65 per cent of the kernel. Proteins constitute 8–10 per cent,
    other complex carbohydrates (pentosans) constitute 7–7.5 per cent, oil is 3–4.5 per cent,
    fiber 1.2–1.5 per cent and ash 1.2–1.3 per cent (Shreve 1956, p. 657).

10. Sugarcane has a high water content, which is mostly lost in the refining process. Accord-
    ing to one source, 1000 units of cane yields 100 units of sugar, 270 units of bagasse (dry
    cellulosic fibrous material) and 34 units of filter cake, known as chacaza, which consists
    of insoluble sugars (Nemerow 1995). Typically it is not worthwhile to crystallize all of
    the soluble sugars; a portion is retained in the form of a thick syrup (molasses) that is used
    in the manufacture of rum and other fermentation products, or fed to animals. It is worth
    noting that the industry actually has a higher recovery rate than the above suggests.

11. See UN *Industrial Statistics* 'lard' (ISIC 3111–31, p. 112) and 'Oils and fats of animals,
    unprocessed' (ISIC 3115–07, p. 156) (UN 1991).

12. See UN *Industrial Statistics Yearbook 1988*, 'Hides, cattle and horses, undressed – total
    production' ISIC 3111–311, p. 115. This refers to fresh weight, prior to tanning. Another
    source suggests that the mass of undressed cattle hides is about 16 per cent of the mass of
    processed red meat (Nemerow 1995, Fig. 5.4). Since beef production in 1993 was 10.58
    MMT (AS Table 443), this would imply total weight of raw cattle hides as 1.6 MMT. Hog
    and sheepskins would add something to this figure.

13. Up to now we have used a simplified citation, namely AS when referring to *Agricultural*

Statistics for 1995 or SA for *Statistical Abstract, 1995*. In this section we will also frequently refer to two publications of the US Bureau of Mines, *Minerals Yearbook 1993* and *Minerals Yearbook 1989*. The first will be cited simply MY with chapter, table and page number as appropriate. The earlier one is cited as MY 1989. All other references are given in full, of course.

14. The above estimates do not represent either the 'fresh' weight of manure – which is relatively wet – nor the 'dry' weight of its solid content. Being based on inputs, the wastes are assumed to have the same water content as the feeds, that is about 50 per cent. Actual 'fresh' weight of animal manure is about 3 times higher in the case of cattle and pigs, and at least double in the case of other animals. See Table 2.8.

15. Composting is well-understood in principle but little practiced except in small farms and gardens. It is, of course, rather labor intensive, since the organic materials – plant parts with or without animal manure – must be collected, shredded, and turned over several times for efficient composting. Normal composting is accomplished by aerobic bacteria and it can be accelerated by facilitating airflow through the mass. However anaerobic bacteria can also accomplish the same purpose in an enclosed space, with the production of methane gas that, in turn, can be utilized as fuel.

3 Forest industries

3.1 Introduction to the chapter
This chapter also deals with industries based on biomass, namely forest products. The SIC sectors considered in this chapter are

Major group 04: forest products
Major group 24: lumber and wood products, except furniture
Major group 26: paper and allied products

Material inputs to forestry (SIC 04) consist of water, carbon dioxide (from the air), nitrogen fixation (also from the air), minerals and nutrients from topsoil. Energy for photosynthesis comes from sunlight. Fuels are consumed to operate machinery, but fuel mass is not embodied in wood or paper products, and is not discussed in detail in this chapter.

Missing mass from forestry, in the aggregate, consists mainly of logging wastes, runoff, water vapor carried away by evapotranspiration, and oxygen (a byproduct of photosynthesis). Missing mass from downstream sectors is less complex, inasmuch as inputs are essentially all some form of biomass, and wastes are similar in composition.

Water is a complicating factor. There is a rough average proportionality between carbon fixation rate (gross photosynthesis) and evapotranspiration, but there is no fixed relationship between water content and metabolic process. Some plant parts are very high in water content, others much less so. In general it seems reasonable to assume that raw wood biomass contains 48 per cent water, by weight, on average (Ulrich 1990, Table 7).

3.2 Lumber and wood products other than paper (SIC 24)[1]
Wood products are mostly derived from managed timber tracts, except for regulated harvesting from national forests. But, of course, timber is not a cultivated crop. As in the case of agriculture, the primary inputs are land, water and carbon dioxide from the air. Major outputs are timber and oxygen; minor outputs include gums, barks, maple syrup and – in tropical countries – tree products harvested from the jungle, such as natural rubber, gutta percha and some nuts. Several important natural resins and solvents (for example, turpentine, 'naval stores') are derived from gums. Downstream chemical products based on wood distillates include acetone, methyl alcohol, pine oil (pinenes), terpenes, tall oil, and tanning extracts.

Neglecting the minor products of the forestry sector, we can construct a rough mass balance for US timber tracts.[2] The data given below implies that the total mass of raw product that was harvested in 1993 was 520 MMT. In addition, timber residues of 144.6 MMT were left in the forests. All of this material had a moisture content of approximately 48 per cent, as already noted. The harvested timber (roundwood) amounted to 318.3 MMT on an air dried (15 per cent moisture) basis (ibid.). Subtracting the water, this implies a bone dry weight of 270 MM. About 2 per cent of this dry weight (5.4 MMT) is mineral ash, leaving 265.6 MMT for cellulose, hemicellulose and lignin, and a carbon content of approximately 44 per cent by weight,[3] or 117.5 MMT. Allowing for the harvest residues, forests required a carbon dioxide input of 552 MMT of carbon dioxide from the air, plus 507.5 MMT of water, some of which was used for photosynthesis. Oxygen generated thereby was 401 MMT. Emissions of water vapor from air drying would have been about 202 MMT.

The nutrient balance of wood products is comparable to the case of agriculture, although no synthetic fertilizers are used on forest lands. Nitrogen and phosphorus are mostly recycled through litter and humus, with some nitrogen input from NOx from fossil fuel combustion, deposited via acid rain. Terrestrial vegetation has an estimated carbon–nitrogen–phosphorus ratio of 800:10:1 (Deevey 1970). Assuming this were roughly accurate for harvested wood, the nitrogen content of the wood removed from the forests would be of the order of 1.5 MMT, while the phosphorus content would be of the order of 0.15 MMT. However, most of the N, P nutrients are embodied in the living tissues (leaves, bark), and the bulk of this is left in the forest. The ash content of harvested wood, as noted above, is roughly 0.54 MMT, of which 1 per cent (0.05 MMT) was presumably phosphorus.

Harvested forest products consist of logs ('roundwood') in three sub-categories, namely softwood (from conifer trees), hardwood, and fuel wood. The structure of this sector is shown in Figure 3.1. Published US statistics on industrial roundwood production and lumber/wood products are normally given in volumetric terms (cords, cubic feet) or area (board feet) terms. These must be converted to common volumetric terms (cubic feet) and finally, where appropriate, to mass terms. These conversions are obviously subject to some uncertainty. We cannot understand why the US Forest Service does not at least provide consistent mass equivalents in all its tables in metric units.

Reported domestic US production of wood in 1993 was 18 046 million cubic feet, 'roundwood equivalent' (mcfre), of which 3083 mcfre was fuelwood (Howard 1997, Table 4). Apparent consumption was 19 497 mcfre (ibid.). Apparent domestic consumption of all industrial roundwood (not including fuelwood) was 16 413 mcfre, including net imports of 1491 mcfre (ibid.). According to this source, lumber products accounted for somewhat over half

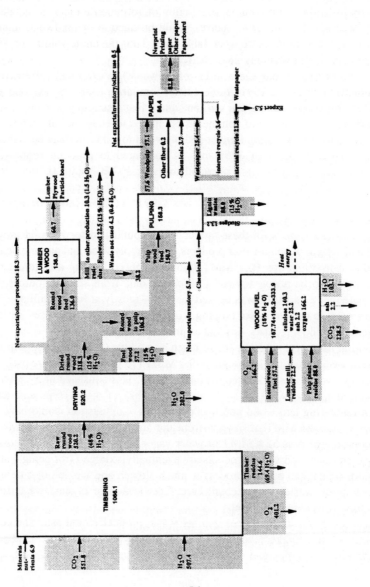

Figure 3.1 Wood, pulp and paper sectors in the US, 1993 (MMT)

of total consumption, or 8826 mcfre, or approximately 136 MMT. Pulpwood accounted for 5757 mcfre of which 5391 (106.8 MMT) was produced domestically. The remainder of the industrial roundwood consumption was for plywood and veneer, 1293 mcfre, other uses (miscellaneous products, net exports of logs and net exports of pulpwood and chips), 1207 mcfre.

Lumber is measured in board feet, where 1 cf is practically equivalent to 16 board feet (bf, or 1000 board feet = 62.15 cubic feet (Darr 1994). Converting board feet to solid volume, production of softwood lumber in the US in 1993 was 33 346 mbf (2083 mcfre), while production of hardwood lumber was 11 771 mbf (736 mcfre) (AS Table 646). Thus the cubic volume of 1993 cut lumber output was only 2819 mcfre.

US production of particle board (from sawdust) in 1988 was 239 mcfre in volumetric terms (SA 1991, Table 1191). Similarly, 1988 US plywood and veneer production was 23 336 million square feet (assuming ⅜ inch), which converted to 729 mcf solid volume, as compared to 1630 mcf of roundwood inputs (ibid.). Thus, taking lumber and plywood together, we can account for useful wood products of 3751 mcf as compared to reported roundwood consumption by lumber and plywood mills of 10 120 mcfre (Ulrich 1990, Table 4). In addition, 3000 mcfre of woodchips were exported to the pulp sector, as noted above. The remainder was 3369 mcf (33 per cent of roundwood inputs), which we assume to have been largely used as fuel within the sector.

No separate figures for these products were published for 1993. However, the total weight of salable mill products (lumber, plywood and particle board) produced in 1993 was 60.7 MMT (Howard 1997), leaving a difference of 75.3 MMT to be accounted for. Combining data from several sources, we estimate that 22.5 MMT was burned for fuel – mostly at lumber mills – 38.2 MMT went to pulp mills for pulping, 10.3 MMT went to 'other uses' including exports, and 4.3 MMT was lost as process waste.

Within the forest products sector taken as a whole (but excluding pulp and paper), we can account for roughly 79.7 MMT (15 per cent moisture basis) of wood and wood wastes burned for fuel in 1993. This consisted of 57.2 MMT harvested for fuelwood, as such, and 22.5 MMT of wood chips and scrap from lumbering and wood products operations. Combustion would have required about 94 MMT of oxygen from the air and generated 129 MMT of carbon dioxide plus 52.8 MMT of water vapor and some NO_x (not discussed here). Of course all wood products are eventually oxidized (rot being a slow form of oxidation) but the process is much slower, and we do not take final consumption wastes into account here. Combustion of organic waste from pulping is discussed separately.

Wood combustion produces another waste product, wood ash. The combustion of undebarked wood chips and scrap yields 1–2.5 per cent ash; debarked wood chips and sawdust yield 0.5–1.4 per cent ash (Obernberger

1994, Table 2). We can assume fuelwood (including bark) averages 2 per cent ash (or a total of 1.1 MMT), while industrial wood and pulp average 1 per cent ash content. This implies 0.2 MMT ash from the combustion of scrap industrial wood. Altogether, in addition to wastes already mentioned, we must add 1.3 MMT wood ash. Much of this ash is emitted into the air.

The chemical composition of wood ash is about 45 per cent oxygen and the remainder mostly light metals, especially calcium (29 per cent), silicon (8.3 per cent), potassium (5.4 per cent), magnesium (3.2 per cent), iron (2.3 per cent), manganese (2.0 per cent), phosphorus (1.0 per cent) and sulfur (0.9 per cent) (Obernberger 1994, Table 3). Most of these metals are not scarce, and their slow removal from the forest soil constitutes no problem. Nor are these oxides toxic. However potassium, phosphorus and sulfur are essential nutrients, and their removal does constitute a potential problem of depletion over long periods of time. Sulfur and nitrogen are being replaced (by atmospheric deposition) faster than they are being removed. Phosphorus contained in wood ash amounts to the order of 0.013 MMT. Wood ash does also contain trace quantities of some toxic heavy metals, especially zinc (2ppm). This is not known to be a problem at present, however.

3.3   Pulp and paper (SIC 26), overview
Pulpwood feed for US domestic woodpulp production in 1993 was 150.7 MMT (15 per cent moisture), of which 5.7 MMT was imported pulpwood and 38.2 MMT came from domestic lumber mills, as noted above (Howard 1997). The pulpwood input (but not the chips) includes some bark, which constitutes about 11.5 per cent of the raw weight of roundwood (USOTA 1984, Table 5), but a smaller fraction – we assume half, lacking any firm data – of the mass of pulpwood actually shipped to pulp mills. Apparently some debarking operations are not located near potential fuel users and disposal is becoming a problem (Nemerow 1995, p. 114). Assuming the same weight percentage for air dried pulpwood, this assumption implies that about 7 MMT of bark (15 per cent moisture) would be produced by debarking operations near or at the pulp mill. (This bark is burned as 'hog fuel'). The pulpwood consists of 50 per cent cellulose, 15–18 per cent hemicellulose, 30 per cent lignin and 2–5 per cent 'extractives' such as turpentine.

In addition, we note that 25.4 MMT of repulped wastepaper was utilized in paper production. Given an industry output of 82.8 MMT, this implies a recovered paper utilization rate of 30.6 per cent.[4] Not all of this recovered paper was post-consumption waste; some was internal scrap recycling within the paper production sector. To obtain a match between total mass inputs and outputs of the paper sector, we calculate that internal recycle must have been 3.6 MMT, which seems reasonable. Thus 21.8 MMT of repulped post-consumption wastepaper was utilized. To obtain 21.8 MMT of usable pulp, about

24.2 MMT of wastepaper must have been pulped, since about 10 per cent (2.4 MMT) of the original mass would have been lost in the repulping process. The lost mass consists mostly of inorganic fillers and coatings, plus short cellulose fibers (USOTA 1984, figure 24). Thus total domestic pulp supply (excluding internal recycle) was 57.1 + 25.4 = 82.5 MMT in 1993. Adding 3.7 MMT of fillers, fixatives, pigments (mainly titanium dioxide) and other chemicals,[5] and subtracting 3.6 MMT for internal recycle, the domestic output of paper and paper products was 82.8 MMT.

Other inputs to the pulping process – including secondary pulp – included at least 8.1 MMT of miscellaneous makeup chemicals (Table 3.1). Since these chemicals are not embodied in the pulp product, it follows from materials balance considerations that the annual discharges of chemical wastes from the pulp and paper industry must be roughly equal to the annual chemical inputs to pulping, element by element. Total mass inputs to the pulp and paper sector in 1993 were 162.2 MMT, not including recycled paper or process water.

Woodpulp produced by domestic pulpmills in 1993 was 57.6 MMT of which 0.5 MMT was diverted to net exports, inventory changes and 'dissolving grade' cellulose for the chemical industry. The rest went to paper production. Waste outputs amounted altogether to 100.7 MMT. Since the pulp (10 per cent moisture) is slightly drier than the pulpwood, the waste outputs are slightly wetter. Based on air dried inputs, 17.9 MMT of this mass was presumably water. This would have left 82.8 MMT (bone dry weight) of which 8.1 MMT was pulping chemicals and bleaches. The organic remainder (74.7 MMT, approximately) consisted of lignin, hemicelluloses, and resins. Small amounts of lignin are recovered for use as lignosulfonates; virtually none of the hemicelluloses are currently recovered for chemical use.[6]

These pulping chemicals and organic residues are carried in an intermediate stream called 'black liquor' which is partially dehydrated and subsequently burned for chemicals (mainly sodium sulfate) and energy recovery. It must be remembered that, even though chemical recovery is reasonably efficient, the annual chemicals input of 8.1 MMT represents makeup for chemicals *lost* in various processes along the way. Most of the mass loss is in the form of water soluble salts (primarily NaCl) but some is lost as gases that escape with combustion wastes, and some is lost in the sludges from water treatment.

We do not have exact figures for 1993, but in 1991 the American Forest and Paper Association (AFPA) estimated that 83 170 million (short) tons, or 75.3 MMT of waste organic material was used as fuel. This apparently did not include the bark ('hog fuel') that is also burned for heat recovery (we have assumed 7 MMT). These two add up to 82 MMT, roughly. The energy recycling figure in 1993 was presumably about 3 per cent larger, in proportion to pulp production, or about 84.5 MMT.

Table 3.1 Chemicals used in US paper manufacturing, 1988 and 1993 (kMT)

Chemical		1988	Source	1993	Source
Sulfuric acid	H_2SO_4	826	MY 1989 'Sulfur'	304	MY 1993 'Sulfur'
Sulfur	S	8	MY 1989 'Sulfur'	27	MY 1993 'Sulfur'
Lime	CaO	1140	MY 1989 'Lime'	1190	MY 1993 'Lime'
Magnesium hydroxide	MgO	150	est. authors	253	MY 1993 'Magnesium'
Caustic soda	NaOH	2400	MY 1989 'Salt'	2390	MEB 1995
Chlorine	Cl_2	1500	MY 1989 'Salt'	950	MEB 1995
Oxygen	O_2	neg.	–	290	MEB 1995
Hydrogen peroxide	H_2O_2	neg.	–	120	MEB 1995
Sodium chlorate	$NaClO_3$	200	est. by authors	828	MEB 1995
Sodium chloride	NaCl	340	MY 1989 'Salt'	115	MY 1989 'Salt'
Sodium carbonate	Na_2CO_3	110	MY 1989 'Soda Ash'	140	MY 1993 'Soda Ash'
Sodium sulfate	Na_2SO_4	240	MY 1989 'Sodium sulfate'	180	MY 1993 'Sodium sulfate'
Kaolin	Kaolin	3960	MY 1989 'Clays'	3460	MY 1993 'Clays'
Titanium dioxide	TiO_2	243	MY 1989 'Titanium'	350	MY 1993 'Titanium'
Aluminum sulfate	Al_2SO_4	300	est. authors	300	est. authors
Total		11417		10897	

Evidently the AFPA figures are inconsistent with ours, if their numbers refer to bone dry organic material. We were unable to obtain an unequivocal answer on this point, but we conjecture that the AFPA numbers must refer to organic material with some nominal moisture content, probably the same as air dried wood, namely 15 per cent. In that case, the (extrapolated) AFPA figure on material burned for energy recovery in 1993 would be adjusted downward to 72 MMT, more or less. This is quite close to our estimate for 1993 (75.3 MMT bone dry), based on the mass balance arguments summarized above. It also allows room for the mineral ash content of the wood (2 per cent, or 1.5 MMT) which must be part of the sludge waste from the water treatment plant, or the combustion wastes from the boiler. Obviously these numbers depend on how much bark is burned at the pulp mill.

The heat value of the organic waste is apparently about 11 500 million BTU per short ton, only about half of the heating value of oil. Recycling for energy and chemical recovery yielded 1.02 quadrillion BTUs of heat energy in 1991. This was 40 per cent of the total energy consumption of the US pulp and paper industry. Combustion byproducts include water vapor, carbon dioxide and ash. The latter is captured by scrubbers and eventually disposed of in sludge from the water treatment process.

Final waste streams from pulping therefore consist of airborne combustion wastes from the energy recovery operations, mineral ash, soluble salts (mostly NaCl) and insoluble sludges from water treatment operations.[7] Carbon dioxide emissions from the chemical recovery operations must have amounted to roughly 122 MMT (not including CO_2 from other fuels). Sludges containing roughly 2 MMT of mineral ash, plus some insoluble calcium compounds and traces of organochlorines, along with some fiber, constitute the major waste.

According to the US Forest Service (Howard 1997), 82.8 MMT of paper and paperboard was produced in the US in 1993, of which 30.6 per cent was from repulped waste (SA Table 1160). In that year 31.7 MMT of waste paper (38.2 per cent) was recovered for use, and 5.34 MMT was exported [ibid.]. The 'unrecycled' fraction of final paper consumption, amounting to 51.3 MMT, was either burned or disposed of in landfills. At least 2.5 MMT of this was inorganic fillers, much of which is converted into fly ash during combustion. Ultimately, all of the organic remainder (cellulose) is either oxidized to CO_2 or reduced to methane (from anaerobic decay in landfills). Assuming only CO_2 were produced, production would have been 78.5 MMT. Figure 3.1 summarizes the major mass flows.

3.4 Pulping processes and chemicals

All of the pulping processes except the mechanical ones (for newsprint) use chemical reagents – notably sodium hydroxide or sulfurous acid – to 'digest' (that is, dissolve) the lignin and separate it from the cellulose fibers in the wood. In principle, these chemical reagents are mostly recovered and recycled internally, as summarized in Table 3.1. In practice, of course, recovery is incomplete and some makeup chemicals are required. In fact, makeup requirements and imputed overall losses and wastes are quite considerable.

The sulfate (kraft) process is used for 85 per cent of US production of chemical pulp because it yields strong fibers of pure cellulose[8] and because it is the only process that can be used on southern pine woods, which have a high resin content. The process is based on the use of caustic soda (sodium hydroxide, NaOH) and sodium sulfide (Na_2S) to dissolve the lignin. The resulting 'black liquor' is dried and burned to recover sodium sulfate (and heat energy), to the maximum extent possible. Makeup chemicals are caustic soda, or sodium hydroxide (NaOH), 'salt cake' or sodium sulfate (Na_2SO_4) and limestone (calcium carbonate). The latter is typically calcined on site to produce lime (CaO), but lime can be purchased directly. Older plants (pre-1970) apparently recovered about 95 per cent of the reagents in the black liquor, per batch. But newer plants are said to achieve as much as 99–99.5 per cent recovery, by utilizing electrostatic precipitators on the recovery furnace. However, these claims are impossible to reconcile with the very large requirements for makeup chemicals.

Unfortunately, published descriptions of the pulping processes are rare and appear to be highly idealized. One of the most widely cited (Sittig 1977), as quoted in Tellus Institute (1992) states that 65 kg of sodium sulfate and 15.5 kg of lime are required per metric ton of pulp with 10 per cent moisture content. Based on roughly 45 MMT of kraft pulp, this would imply a national total consumption of nearly 3 MMT of sodium sulfate and 0.7 MMT of lime for kraft pulping alone. Sodium carbonate is a possible substitute for caustic soda, since the hydroxide can be produced from the carbonate by reacting with lime. However, even allowing for this possibility, the Sittig numbers apparently assumed much lower recovery rates than modern practice.

The sulfite process is used for a small fraction of US pulp. It is the process of choice for higher quality white papers. The active reagent in the sulfite process is calcium or sodium bisulfite which reacts with lignin to form calcium or sodium lignosulfonates.[9] Lignin and hemicelluloses are dissolved, but not resins. Thus, the sulfite process is only suitable for low resin woods, such as spruce, fir and hemlock. Also, the resulting fibers are less strong than kraft fibers, although they are used for certain special papers. The other (semi-chemical) process is less severe than the others and removes less of the lignin and hemicellulose. The main active agent is sodium sulfite (Na_2SO_3), which can be made from soda ash (sodium carbonate) and sulfur dioxide, also from elemental sulfur. Sittig (1977) states that requirements for the neutral sulfite semi-chemical (NSSC) process are 122 kg of soda ash (sodium carbonate) and 70 kg of sodium sulfite, per metric ton (10 per cent moisture) pulp. Given 4 MMT of NSSC pulp production in the US, this implies total requirements of 0.6 MMT for soda ash. Again, these figures appear to be far too high.

Sodium sulfite is made on site by burning elemental sulfur and absorbing the SO_2 in soda ash (generating CO_2 in the process). The needed soda ash is presumably already included in Sittig's per ton estimate above. To produce 85 kg of sodium sulfite takes at least 71.5 kg of soda ash and 21.6 kg of sulfur (disregarding conversion process losses), so to produce 4 MMT of NSSC pulp there would be a gross elemental sulfur requirement of 86.4 kMT. Again, this is much higher than actual apparent consumption. Table 3.1 summarizes our estimate of total chemical use in the US pulp and paper industry.

Other chemical inputs to the pulp and paper industry were used primarily in bleaching. Most virgin chemical pulps for paper are bleached. In 1988 the primary bleaching agents were elemental chlorine (Cl_2), caustic soda and chlorine dioxide. The latter is manufactured in-house from sodium chlorate, because chlorine dioxide is explosive and too dangerous to ship. In 1988 the paper and pulp industry was still the second largest user of chlorine, taking 1.5 MMT or 14 per cent of total US chlorine output (MY 1989, p. 849). By 1993 chlorine use for this purpose had declined sharply, to 0.95 MMT according to the American Forest and Paper Association (MEB *c*. 1995, p. 33). Meanwhile, use of other bleaches, notably oxygen (0.29 MMT), hydrogen peroxide (0.12 MMT) and chlorine dioxide from sodium chlorate (0.828 MMT), has been rising (MEB *c*. 1995, p. 33).

The major route for conversion of sodium chlorate to chlorine dioxide utilizes sulfuric acid and soda ash and yields chlorine dioxide and sodium sulfate. The sodium chloride used by the US paper and pulp industry was probably used for regenerating zeolite ion exchange water-softeners.

Bleaching wastes are currently mostly (90 per cent) sodium chloride (salt). But it is the residue that matters. It has been estimated that 10 per cent of the chlorine used is chemically bound to lignins and other organic materials in the pulp. This organo-chlorine material constitutes a significant part of the process waste. Roughly 6 per cent of the mass of the raw pulp is lost during bleaching. The bleaching effluent contains significant quantities of chlorinated organic compounds with very high molecular weights. In fact, from 70–95 per cent of spent chlorination and alkali extraction liquors have molecular weights greater than 1000. Such compounds cannot be separated, quantified or identified by present means. However measurable traces of dioxins and furans are found among these wastes (Holmbom 1991).

The kraft process emissions of greatest environmental concern are non-condensible sulfur containing gases (hydrogen sulfide, methyl and ethyl mercaptans, dimethyl sulfide, and so on). These are generated at the rate of about 2.5 kg/MT of pulp (IBRD 1980). For sulfate pulp in toto, uncontrolled emissions of sulfur containing gases would have been about 0.1 MMT. EPA has estimated airborne effluents (excluding CO_2) from the sector to be about 1.15 MMT (USEPA 1991).

As a matter of interest, we show some recent unpublished data for Finland, courtesy of the Finnish Environmental Institute. In 1994 Finnish requirements per 1000 kg (metric ton) of pulp in 1994 are shown in Table 3.2. At US output levels, this would imply 1.73 MMT of sulfuric acid, 0.125 MMT of magnesium sulfate, 0.1 MMT of sulfur dioxide (or 0.05 MMT of sulfur), 0.4 MMT of lime, 1.02 MMT of caustic soda, 0.58 MMT of oxygen, 0.175 MMT of hydrogen peroxide, 1.27 MMT of sodium chlorate, 0.023 MMT of sodium chloride and 0.107 MMT of methylamine, for a total of 5.48 MMT.

Table 3.2   Chemical use for pulpmaking in Finland, 1994

Chemical	kg/MT of pulp	Total at US pulp production level (MMT)
Sulfuric acid (H_2SO_4)	30.433	1.73
Magnesium sulfate ($MgSO_4$)	2.216	0.125
Sulfur dioxide (SO_2)	1.699	0.1
Lime (CaO)	7.000	0.4
Caustic soda (NaOH)	17.760	1.02
Oxygen (O_2)	10.737	0.58
Ozone (O_3)	0.180	
Hydrogen peroxide (H_2O_2)	2.997	0.175
Sodium chlorate ($NaClO_3$)	22.452	1.27
Sodium chloride (NaCl)	0.392	0.023
Methylamine (CH_3NH_2)	1.880	0.107

The two patterns are remarkably different. The Finns use magnesium sulfate instead of sodium sulfate or soda ash; they use much less caustic soda and less lime but much more sulfuric acid in the pulping process. Other major differences are in bleaching. The most common sequence of bleaching operations in the US consists of five steps: it begins with a vapor-phase chlorination, followed by caustic extraction and chlorine dioxide, the latter two stages being repeated a second time. The pulp is washed at each stage.

The Finns (and Swedes) have eliminated all direct use of elemental chlorine, replacing it by elemental oxygen, ozone, hydrogen peroxide and chlorine dioxide (from sodium chlorate). We do not know the reason for using methylamine, but presumably it is also connected with the bleaching process. As regards bleaching, at least, seems likely that the US pulp sector will gradually approach the Finnish pattern over the next decade.

The chemicals used in pulping and bleaching are not embodied in the product. They are recycled within the plant, insofar as practical, but the annual inputs, as shown in the above tables, are for *makeup* purposes. They – or various transformed compounds of the same elements – are ultimately discarded. The wastewater that leaves the pulping complex carries these materials in some form, hopefully a fairly harmless one. Sodium and calcium chlorides and sulfates are the major wastes, along with some trace elements, mineral ash and organics. See Figure 3.1.

Additional materials are used in the US paper industry and embodied in the product. The most important of these is clay (kaolin) which is used both for filling and coating fine papers. Another is titanium dioxide, used for whiteness. A third is aluminum sulfate ('alum') which is a fixative for dyes and colors. Alum improves the ink absorbing quality of printing paper. There are no published data on the uses of alum, but it is produced in large quantities – about 1 MMT per year – and we conjecture that the paper industry is the biggest consumer. At least 3.7 MMT of fillers and other chemicals, and possibly as much as 4.5 MMT, were embodied in US paper products in 1993.

These materials do enter the waste stream at the time waste paper is recovered for re-pulping. In fact, such materials constitute a significant percentage of the weight of high quality printing papers. Inks, colors and coatings, at least, must be largely removed before the pulp can be re-used. The process of de-inking is a particularly dirty one, which itself generates a significant waste stream.

Endnotes

1. Up to now we have used a simplified citation, namely AS when referring to *Agricultural Statistics* for 1995 or SA for *Statistical Abstract of the United States, 1995*. In this section we will also frequently refer to two publications of the US Bureau of Mines, *Minerals Yearbook 1993* and *Minerals Yearbook 1989*. The first will be cited simply MY with chapter, table and page number as appropriate. The earlier one is cited as MY 1989. All other references are given in full, of course.

2. Virtually all US data are published in volumetric units, such as cubic feet and board feet. In the annual statistical publication of the US Forest Service, *Forest Statistics of the United States, 19xx* only one of 38 tables gives data in mass units, and that one table refers only to residues. Moreover, the publication provides no mass to volume conversion factors. The standard annual publication *Agricultural Statistics* includes a chapter on forest products, but only in volume units or monetary units. No conversion factors are given for wood or wood products in that publication either. Our data comes from another publication *US Timber Production, Trade, Consumption and Price Statistics, 1965–94* (Howard 1997) in which mass (weight) units were used for one summary table, Table 7. However, while we have used the most recent volumetric data, courtesy of Howard (ibid.), the final report was not yet in print when we did our mass balance analysis and we have had to construct our own version of his Table 7, using volume to mass conversion coefficients derived from an

earlier Forest Service publication (Ulrich 1990). We understand that Howard was in the process of revising those conversion factors, but we have not yet seen the revised version.

3. Cellulose has the approximate formula $C_6H_{10}O_5$, which means that it has a composition of 44.4 per cent C, 6.2 per cent H and 49.4 per cent O.

4. This is somewhat less than the figure of 32.4 per cent published in *Statistical Abstract* for 1993 (SA Table 1160). However, it is based on more accurate data.

5. Actually this is a lower limit, since it includes only inorganic materials (kaolin, alum, and so on) that we have been able to account for explicitly from published sources.

6. There are several products that are, or can be, recovered from spent kraft process liquor in small quantities, including artificial vanillin (flavoring agent), turpentine, tall oil and tannin (Nemerow 1995, Fig. 5.2). An attractive possibility is to ferment or otherwise convert the hemicellulosics (sugars) to ethanol. Until now, all known fermenting agents produce an enzyme, lactate dehydrogenase, that breaks down the hemicellulosics into a mixture of ethanol and lactic acid. Fortunately, a new discovery at Imperial College, London, may change this situation. It is a mutant strain of the fermenting bacterium, *Bacillus stearothermophilus*, which lacks the enzyme and thus converts hemicellulosics directly to ethanol, without the usual mixture of lactic acid. Unfortunately, the mutation appears unstable and the organism reverts back to the original form which produce the enzyme. Thus, the current challenge is to bioengineer a strain that lacks the gene.

7. As it happens, net dry wastes (for example, sludges) of 8.5 million short tons (7.7 MMT were reported by an EPA contractor for the early 1980s (SAI 1985). This is somewhat smaller than our estimate of 17 MMT (which, however, includes 15 per cent water).

8. The word kraft here is not a proper name; it is simply German for 'strong'.

9. A small percentage of the lignosulfates is recovered for use in a number of industries as water reducers (for example, in concrete), emulsifiers, sequestrants, binders, dispersants and copolymerizing agents.

4 Extractive materials: Fuels

4.1 Introduction to the chapter

This chapter deals with industries that extract non-renewable fossil fuels and process them into finished fuels. We also discuss fuel and energy consumption. As before, the focus is on materials accounting, with an emphasis on emissions and wastes.

There are two types of waste associated with extraction *per se*. These are (i) earth displaced in the process of searching for and removing ore (overburden) and (ii) unwanted contaminants removed by physical methods, such as screening, washing, settling, flotation, centrifuging and so on. The next stage of processing is refining (mainly applicable to petroleum) followed by combustion. For convenience, all combustion-related wastes are discussed together in one section where electric power generation is also considered briefly.

4.2 Coal mining and drilling (SIC 12)[1]

Coal mined in the US in 1993 amounted to 857.7 MMT, of which 53 per cent was bituminous and 29 per cent was subbituminous. The rest was lignite. Exports took 68.3 MMT. Coking accounted for 28.4 MMT, yielding 21 MMT of coke from domestic coal and 7.4 MMT of other products, mainly coke oven gas consumed for electric power production or combined heat and power (CHP).

Coal mining is the largest single source of solid waste materials. The actual numbers are 'proprietary' and unpublished. The waste from underground mines is comparatively low, possibly around 10 per cent of the mass of coal mined. For open pit mines the amount of overburden is extremely variable and depends on the depth. One publication compared four western mines with an average overburden to coal ratio of 4.8:1 to an eastern mine with a ratio of nearly 27:1.[2] Partitioning the country into 'eastern' and 'western' zones, and using these multipliers, yields an average overburden ratio of 6.56:1. This is similar to an estimate we received several years ago from an anonymous source at the US Department of Energy. Since national coal production in 1993 was 858 MMT (IEA 1995), total materials handled in coal mining, exclusive of the coal itself, was apparently of the order of 5600 MMT. However, these estimates are obviously crude and depend very sensitively on the particular mines examined.[3]

Coal mining is also a source of methane, since methane is trapped in the coal seams and is released when the coal is pulverized. Coal mining releases methane as a function of the depth of the mine. The most recent estimates set these emissions at 1.5 m^3 (= 1 kg) per metric ton for surface mines (60 per cent of US production) and 8.5 m^3 (= 5.55 kg) per metric ton for underground mines (40 per cent of output) (Dones *et al.* 1996, Table 4.1.III). For the US, this comes to 2.4 MMT of methane emissions from coal mining. Total global emissions from coal mining have been recently estimated at 25 MMT/y, of which 7 per cent is recovered (IEA 1995). We have no information on methane recovery in the US.

In addition, some utility coal is washed to remove pyrites and ash, resulting in a significant further production of waste refuse. In 1975 a Department of Energy 'factbook' stated that about 41 per cent of soft coal produced was cleaned, resulting in 16 tons of coal refuse (ash and pyrites) for every 100 tons of coal shipped. No data on the amount of sulfur actually removed was given, but the combined ash and sulfur content of the coal could not have been reduced by more than half. If the high sulfur coal originally had 4 per cent sulfur (probably an overestimate) and 10 per cent ash, the weight reduction in cleaned coal could not have been more than 7 per cent, and given that only 40 per cent of the coal was washed, the overall weight reduction could not have been more than 3 per cent. Thus the weight of coal refuse must have been mostly water.

In any case, by 1993, however, this figure – if accurate – had probably declined somewhat due to the closure of some high sulfur coal mines and restructuring of the coal industry to exploit more cheap low sulfur western coals. (Also, coal cleaning refuse poses its own disposal problem, being a significant cause of acid mine drainage.) As of 1993, we estimate that only about 30 per cent of the coal that is mined needs to be cleaned – mainly in the Midwest – and that the dry weight of coal washing refuse (equal to the weight reduction for clean coal) was somewhat less than 3 per cent of the total mined, or less than 25 MMT. A more plausible number might be 20 MMT (dry). Since this is the assumed weight reduction, it follows that the weight of coal mined prior to cleaning must have been about 20 MMT larger than the reported amount, or 878 MMT.

We do not have specific data, but for consistency with EPA emission data (discussed later) it appears that in 1993 roughly 2.4 or 2.5 MMT of elemental sulfur (in the form of pyrites) was removed from utility coal before burning. If the refuse had a 10 per cent sulfur content, some 25 MMT (dry weight) of refuse would have been generated by the coal cleaning process. If the refuse was 12.5 per cent sulfur, only 20 MMT would have been generated. Obviously this estimate is very crude, but it is more or less consistent with other information. Combustion emissions are discussed later. An overview of the coal 'system' (including electric power generation, discussed later in this chapter) is shown in Figure 4.1.

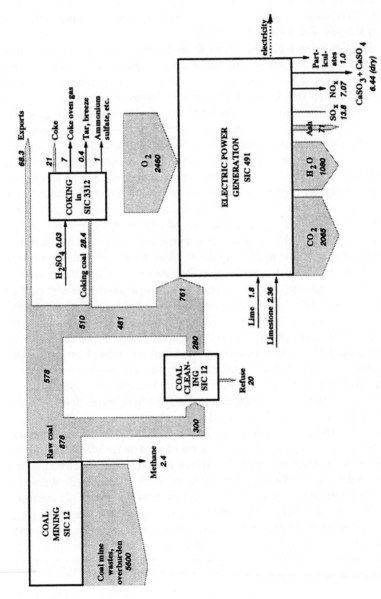

Figure 4.1   US coal system, 1993 (MMT)

69

4.3   Petroleum and natural gas production (SIC 13)

Petroleum and natural gas production involve relatively little solid waste; the major waste is 'produced water' (often saline), which is typically contaminated by drilling muds and materials removed from the holes and some hydrogen sulfide (H_2S). For instance, during 1993 the US oil and gas industry drilled 24 900 wells and drilled 42.3 million meters of holes (MY 'Barium', p. 129). Assuming 6 inch pipe for the holes, the material actually removed from the holes would have been 18 liters per linear meter, or 750 million liters. Recalling that a liter of water weighs 1kg, by definition, and assuming an average specific gravity of 3 for drilling wastes displaced by pipe, or about 2.25 MMT, plus (roughly) another 4–5 MMT or so of material that was removed and displaced by the drilling mud (allowing for water content). We therefore estimate a total of 6–7 MMT for earth and rock displaced by drilling.

Drilling muds constitute a much larger waste category. Drilling muds are, on average, 86 per cent water (much of which is taken from the wells themselves), plus 3 per cent oil, 2 per cent polymers and 9 per cent other materials (USOTA 1992). The latter include clay, barite, chrome lignin sulfonates, and so on. EPA has estimated that drilling fluids used in 1985 weighed 63 million tons, or 55 MMT (USOTA 1992). Additional 'associated wastes' amounted to 2 MMT. Most of these wastes are stored in ponds, where the water gradually evaporates. In 1985 1.85 MMT of barite was consumed for well drilling in the US (MY 1988 'Barium', Table 7). Equally detailed data for 1993 are not given, but it appears that petroleum and gas well drilling accounted for 0.944 MMT in that year (MY 'Barium', Table 4). Assuming that the total weight of drilling mud is proportional to the barite content, it follows that drilling fluids used in 1993 must have weighed close to 27 MMT.[4] Material removed at domestic barite mines or in processing plants accounted for another 1 MMT of waste.

A much larger estimate of 'hidden flows' is worth mentioning. According to the recent World Resources Institute study of material flows, 'hidden flows' of materials associated with oil and gas production in 1993 were 34 MMT for domestic oil production and 101 MMT from domestic gas production (Adriaanse *et al.* 1997, p. 63). It is not clear how the WRI estimates for petroleum were obtained, except that they were based on unpublished calculations by the Wuppertal Institute in Germany (ibid.). (We think the Wuppertal estimates for oil *per se* are too high; in fact they roughly match our estimates for both oil and gas drilling.) In the case of gas, the WRI figure was taken to be 'the difference between gross and net production of dry natural gas' (ibid.) but no effort was made to account for the difference.[5]

Total output of crude oil in the US in 1993 was 338.152 MMT. Exports were 0.158 MMT and imports were 360.102 MMT, for an apparent consumption of 698.096. However, 0.493 MMT was consumed directly in the extraction process, and not sent to refineries. (This was probably used for drilling muds.) Refinery inputs were 692.59 MMT, leaving 5 MMT unaccounted for.

Statistics on natural gas are collected in volumetric terms (million cubic feet, or mcf) by the US Department of Energy (USDOE). Based on data for the years 1967–85, from 5–10 per cent of gross production (depending on the year) is used for repressurization (of oil wells), non-hydrocarbon gases (H_2S, CO_2) accounted for 1–1.5 per cent; venting and/or flaring now accounts for about 0.5 per cent (down from 2.4 per cent in the 1960s), 'extraction loss' (NGL removal) accounted for 3.8–4.2 per cent, and 'unaccounted for' ranged from 0.2–3.5 per cent; thus final 'dry production' was typically 85–88 per cent of the gross (Barns and Edmonds 1990, Appendix Table C2.1). Figures for 1993 were not at hand when this was written, but we accept Barns and Edmonds' estimate of 0.5 per cent venting and flaring loss for current practice, of which less than 0.1 per cent was probably vented (ibid.). Disregarding gas pumped back into the ground at the well for repressurization, we assume that the difference between gross production and net consumption (including 'unaccounted for') was about 10 per cent in volume terms, though considerably more in mass terms.

Assuming purified gas to be 100 per cent methane, the quantity produced in the US in 1993 was 361.97 MMT (Table 4.1).[6] Natural gas liquids (NGL) recovered in 1993 from natural gas in the US amounted to 51.332 MMT (IEA 1995). Most of this (33.926 MMT) went to the petrochemical industry as feedstocks; most of the rest was used as fuel by the electric power industry or as LPG for rural households and a few buses. Elemental sulfur is recovered from crude natural gas by the Claus process: the total for 1992 was reported to be 2.525 MMT; the 1993 figure was probably about 2.450 MMT.[7] Natural gas from certain fields in the US is also nearly the only commercial source of helium in the world, although the mass involved was insignificant (17 kMT).[8] Thus, useful products added up to about 416 MMT. The waste component of crude gas (consisting mostly of CO_2 N_2 and H_2O) was approximately 8 MMT.

Natural gas output in the US in 1993 was reported by the US Department of Energy to the International Energy Agency as 20 087 petajoules (PJ) or 362 MMT methane equivalent; an additional 2529 PJ (45.6 MMT) was imported and 150 PJ (2.7 MMT) was exported.[9] Stocks of natural gas were depleted in the US by 306 PJ (5.3 MMT). Total domestic supply in 1993 was therefore 22 772 PJ or 410 MMT. On the other hand, conversion uses (mainly electric power production) accounted for 2893 PJ (52 MMT); oil and gas extraction consumed 1280 PJ (23 MMT) and petroleum refineries (below) took 798 PJ (14.4 MMT). So-called 'final consumption' took 17 029 PJ or 313 MMT. These consumption categories add up to exactly 22 000 PJ (396

Table 4.1 US energy statistics, 1993 (MMT)

Commodity	Production		Exports		Imports		Consumption[a]	
	raw	finished	raw	finished	raw	finished	raw	finished
Refinery inputs								
Crude oil	338.152		0.158		360.102		692.591	
Feedstocks		51.332		1.407		26.635		34.384
NGL		6.544				5.604	6.079	
Additives						0.870		
Total refinery input	**338.152**	**57.876**	**0.158**	**1.407**	**360.102**	**33.109**	**733.054**	
Refinery products								
LPG		17.921				0.445		54.823
Motor Gas		316.957		4.789		9.697		322.185
Av gas		0.874				0.011		0.863
Jet fuel		67.530		2.632		3.364		68.844
Kerosene		2.334		0.164		0.040		2.402
Diesel		157.330		13.563		7.308		143.965
Residual fuel oil		50.958		6.857		19.057		40.026
Naphtha		7.122				0.896		7.997
Petroleum coke		41.048		17.121		0.125		24.219
Other		55.148		1.566		7.868		55.221
Total refinery output		**717.222**		**46.692**		**48.811**		**720.545**

Coal						
coking	73.282	45.044			28.416	21.030
bituminous	453.769	20.627		6.631	438.833	
subbituminous	249.386	1.932			260.684	
lignite	81.238				75.620	
Natural gas (b)	422.000	2.700	362.000	45.600	410.000	37.853
Total other fuel	**1279.675**	**70.303**	**362.000**	**52.231**	**1213.553**	**58.883**

Notes:
[a] IEA computes as Apparent Consumption including energy sector 'Transformation' = Production – Exports + Imports + Transfers – Statistical Differences.
[b] 0.1802 kg/TJ.

Source: IEA 1995 pp. 251–3.

MMT) leaving a fairly large statistical discrepancy between supply and consumption of 772 M (13.9 MMT or 3.5 per cent) between the two totals. On the other hand (unlike earlier editions of the OECD/IEA, tables), no allowance is made for gas consumed in gas processing, transmission (to drive turbo-compressors) or gas lost in the system through leakage. An overview of the oil and gas system in the US is shown in Figure 4.2.

Some comments on the 'missing gas' are in order here. It is difficult to allocate the losses precisely between the two possible sinks. In fairness, the gas transmission companies themselves have difficulty in doing this with absolute precision, although they presumably know quite accurately how much gas goes into one end of a pipe and how much is received at the other end, and they can calculate the gas consumption of their compressors. Compressors are mostly run by standardized 10 MWe gas turbines, with known characteristics. However, the transmission systems are complex and the large pipelines are a storage system whose contents are variable in time. The USDOE methane study referred to earlier estimates transmission and leakage losses for the US as 1.5 per cent of dry gas production, which would be 5.4 MMT (Barns and Edmonds 1990, p. 3.20).

A recent European study provides comparative estimates of data on gas processing and transmission losses: 0.1 per cent for processing, 1 per cent for turbo-compressor power (for transmission) and 0.13 per cent loss from transmission leakage (Frischknecht *et al.* 1994, cited by van Liere 1995 p. 33). Apparently on-shore flaring also accounted for 0.96 per cent of Dutch gas output.[10] A still more recent European study updates some of the earlier data and estimates gas transmission leakage losses of western European pipelines at only 0.02 per cent, in the long distance part of the system. However, there are additional leakages in the distribution grid, which also has high pressure and low pressure components. In the high pressure part of the grid the leakage rate in Europe is estimated to be 0.07 per cent while in the low pressure part of the grid, which serves local homes and runs under the street, it is 0.9 per cent (Dones *et al.* 1996, p. 34).

Unfortunately the Dutch and European data cannot be applied directly. The European gas distribution system in general is both newer and more compact than the US system. By contrast, transmission losses and leakage for Russian gas (from the Urals) have been estimated as high as 10 per cent by some experts, although the consensus estimate is lower. See article on Gazprom (*Economist*) Nov 29, 1997 p. 73. A leakage rate of 2 per cent for Russian gas was assumed in a life cycle study of greenhouse gas emissions commissioned by the International Energy Agency (Dones *et al.* 1994). Of course, the Russian system is notoriously leaky and has been badly maintained for many years.

There are no specific data on these loss categories for the US, because the gas transmission companies do not publish any details of their operations. But a

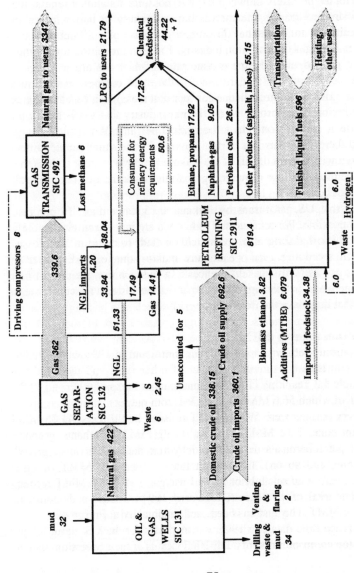

Source: IEA (1995) pp. 251–3.

Figure 4.2 US oil and gas system, 1993 (MMT)

75

range can be estimated on the basis of the OECD/IEA energy balance (IEA 1995) and the European data. In the case of the US, it seems not unreasonable to assume that the use of gas as fuel for turbo-compressors may account for 2 per cent or so (8 MMT) while leakage – mostly local – accounts for another 1.5 per cent of the gas flowing through the system (that is, 5.4 MMT). This agrees exactly with the Barns and Edmonds (1990) estimate cited earlier.

We harbor a suspicion that the US Department of Energy, which provides the basic data to the International Energy Agency for its annual tabulations, recently reclassified the 3.5 per cent missing gas from 'distribution losses' (as in earlier editions) to 'statistical differences' because of political pressures from the domestic gas transmission industry. The obvious reason for nervousness on the part of the industry is that natural gas leaks are a source of 'greenhouse' emissions. In fact, methane – the main component of natural gas – is a far more potent greenhouse gas (per unit mass) than carbon dioxide. In fact, the notion being promoted by the gas industry that gas is a 'benign' fuel, because it contains only half the *carbon* per unit of chemical energy content and therefore emits less carbon dioxide for the same output of heat, must be taken with a grain of salt. If the leakage problem is more serious than we think, the increased use of natural gas would make the greenhouse problem worse, not better.

We doubt that US gas losses by leakage are greater than 1.5 per cent, though it is possible. We applaud the industry's attempts to minimize them. But we also think that serious efforts should be made to monitor these losses, as the Dutch are doing. And we deplore making the leaks disappear by relabelling them as 'statistical differences'. In this context, we cannot help but note that when people appear to be trying to hide the facts, it raises suspicions that they have something nasty to hide.

4.4 Petroleum refining (SIC 2911)[11]

Reported domestic refinery inputs of crude petroleum in 1993 were 692.098 MMT. US refineries consumed a number of other fuels and feedstocks as shown in Table 4.2, resulting in a total input in mass terms of 692.6 + 132.8 = 825.4 MMT of which 56.6 MMT is recycled from outputs.

Net refinery outputs were 595.97 MMT finished liquid fuels, 41.05 MMT of petroleum coke, 7.12 MMT naphtha, 17.92 MMT of ethane, propane, butane, and petrochemicals derived by dehydrogenation (ethylene, propylene, butadiene, and so on). In addition there were 55.15 MMT of other products (asphalt, road oil, lubricants and waxes), and 32.76 MMT refinery off-gases. The total of all outputs, including recycled fuels and hydrogen, comes to 756 MMT. The system is depicted graphically in Figure 4.2.

The difference (lost mass) in 1993 was 69.5 MMT, which is about 8.5 per cent of net inputs. In other words, the efficiency of mass conversion appears

Table 4.2   Reported US domestic refinery inputs, other than crude oil, 1993 (MMT)

Fuel product	MMT
Refinery off-gases as fuel	31.704
Imported feedstocks (BTX)	34.384
Natural gas liquids (NGL)	17.494
Natural gas @ 18.02 MMT/PJ	14.410
Petroleum coke	15.581
Heavy fuel oil	1.963
LPG + ethane	0.870
Other refinery products	0.513
Hydrogen (approximate)	6.0
Ethanol from corn[a]	3.82
Other additives (MTBE)	6.079
Total	132.82

Note: [a]   In the OECD statistics there is an entry for 'gas/liquids from biomass' to petroleum refineries (OECD 1995 p. 253). Since we know that ethanol from corn is indeed used for 'gasohol', and that the quantities involved are consistent with our estimate based on 'missing' corn (see discussion in Chapter 2), it is virtually certain that this entry refers to ethanol.

to be 91.5 per cent. However, all of the lost mass (69.5 MMT), plus the recycled fuels (50.6 MMT) – a total of 120.1 MMT – were either burned for heat within the refinery or lost in some other way. Thus the refining process consumes 120 MMT of hydrocarbons to produce a net output of 700 MMT. The thermodynamic efficiency of the refining process, from this perspective, is only 85 per cent. Assuming petroleum products average 87 per cent C, this also resulted in 384 MMT of CO_2 emissions. In addition, there would be significant quantities of water vapor, plus some carbon monoxide and hydrocarbons, including fugitive volatile organic compounds (VOCs) and SO_2. Refineries are certainly one of the major sources of VOCs, of which 12.75 MMT were emitted by stationary sources in the US in 1993. A 1985 US Environmental Protection Agency (USEPA) compilation of emission factors estimated VOC emissions from petroleum refineries as 0.05 per cent of throughput (US EPA 1985), which would imply VOC emissions of 0.4 MMT. VOCs from petroleum refining include significant quantities of benzene, toluene, xylene and other aromatics, many of which are carcinogenic.[12] EPA estimated airborne effluents from the sector as 2 MMT (USEPA 1991).

Crude oil contains small quantities of sulfur and mineral ash, depending on its origin. (For example, Venezuelan oil is particularly high in sulfur.) The petroleum refining industry recovers sulfur from crude oil and produces some sulfuric acid as a byproduct (2.4 MMT H_2SO_4, or 0.786 MMT S). Most of this sulfuric acid is used, initially, within the refinery, for bleaching. However, over half of the spent acid is later recovered and sold as a byproduct (1.3 MMT). Most of the ash in crude oil probably remains with the refinery solid wastes and sludges. Assuming 0.1 per cent ash in the crude oil would imply 0.7 MMT of solid waste. (The actual figure may be higher or lower). The spent sulfuric acid (2.1 MMT) is presumably neutralized, either by reaction with some of the alkaline minerals (NaO, KO, MgO, CaO) in the ash content of crude oil, or by added lime. Refineries also utilize purchased materials from other sectors in the refining process, including salt (0.72 MMT) and kaolin (used to manufacture zeolite catalysts, 0.122 MMT) which subsequently reappear in (mostly solid or liquid) wastes. Since these materials do not appear in products, they must be part of the waste stream. The use of salt is unclear, but it may be used for regenerating catalysts or water softeners (Gaines and Wolsky 1981).

A US EPA contractor, Science Applications Inc. (SAI) estimated dry solid wastes from petroleum refining as 1.27 MMT (1981 data) (Allen and Behmanesh 1992, Table III). However a survey of US refineries by the American Petroleum Institute for the years 1987–88 estimated total solid and liquid waste for these years as 14.6 MMT and 14.5 MMT, respectively, of which roughly 75 per cent was aqueous (Bush and Levine 1992, Table V). The aqueous wastes were unspecified as to composition, but some mineral content can be presumed. Given that mineral ash content of crude oil must have ended up somewhere, it is clear that SAI's estimate was considerably too low. On the other hand, US EPA has estimated non-hazardous (wet) wastes by the petroleum refining sector for 1985 as 152 MMT (US EPA 1988; Allen and Behmanesh 1992, Table II). Presumably most of this was water.

The 1983 US Census of Manufactures reported water withdrawals by SIC 29 of 2900 MMT (2100 mgd), of which 91 per cent was used for cooling purposes and 9 per cent for processing. Processing wastes are nevertheless significant. Crude oil is desalted before refining. Water pollution from this process contains emulsified oil as well as salts, ammonia, sulfides and phenols. Also, this process involves considerable water use. The sector reports a very high internal recycling ratio of 7.5, which is reasonable for cooling water allowing for evaporative losses. Wastewater discharges were therefore of the order of 260 MMT, which is not too far out of line with the EPA estimate of 152 MMT, mentioned above.

4.5 Fuel combustion and electric power (SIC 491), wastes and losses[13]

Earlier in this chapter we discussed fossil fuels extraction and primary fuel processing. The ultimate fate of all fuels, of course, is combustion for purposes of generating heat or mechanical power. The power, in turn, produces electricity, drives vehicles, or performs other sorts of mechanical work. However it is easy to get bogged down in detail, looking at fuel consumption in every industry and activity. As a matter of interest, we have included Table 4.3 giving energy consumption by fuel for the major industrial subsectors considered in this book as reported in SA Table 945. The letter D indicates suppressed data. Numbers appearing in boxes with a D are our own estimates. Luckily the column and row totals are known, so a single estimate based on information from another source enables us to fill in four blanks arranged symmetrically. For instance, according to the American Forest Products Association (AFPA) 40 per cent of the energy used in the pulp and paper sector (c. 1993) was from lignin waste (MEB 1995). If this was true in 1991, then 40 per cent of the row total is 1000 trillion BTU. This enables us to fill in the remaining blank in that row for natural gas consumption (838 trillion BTU). Similarly we can now fill in two blanks in row 20, using the row and column totals. There are still 24 missing numbers, but only six would enable us to deduce the rest, by the same method. We have made estimates for all of them; the Greek letters α, β, γ, δ, ϵ, and ξ are error terms.

The crucial fact is that when fossil fuels are burned, no matter how or where, there are combustion products that must be counted as wastes. Some of these wastes are very dangerous to health, if not to the environment. This is particularly true for coal. In 1993 the US consumed 840 MMT of coal. This included 28.4 MMT of coking coal, which yielded 21 MMT of coke (for metallurgy) and approximately 7 MMT of coke oven gas, plus small amounts of byproducts. Most of the coal and coke oven gas were used for electricity generation. On the average, US coal 'as mined' has a sulfur content ranging from 0.4–4.8 per cent. The average sulfur and ash contents of US bituminous coal are 1.85 per cent and 10.55 per cent respectively; for subbituminous (western) coal the figures are 0.43 per cent and 7.2 per cent; for lignite the averages are 0.92 per cent and 14 per cent (WEC 1992, Table 1.5), but these characteristics vary by location.[14] Sulfur and ash content can be significantly reduced by washing.[15] (We have noted that large quantities of high sulfur coal refuse are generated by this process.) The overall average sulfur content of all coals burned in the US in 1993, therefore, is shown in Table 4.4. Total embodied sulfur was therefore approximately 11 MMT. The sulfur in coking coal is mostly recovered as ammonium sulfate (about 1 MMT) and sold as fertilizer. Based on this calculation, the utility coal burned in the US in 1993 contained about 10.5 MMT of sulfur, while heavy fuel oils and other fuels might have contributed another 0.5 MMT, for a total of 11 MMT (22 MMT of SO_2). None was recovered for use. However, some was captured by scrubbers.

There are two desulfurization technologies, 'wet' and 'dry'. The wet scrubber uses a spray of lime (CaO) and water to 'scrub' the flue gases after most

Table 4.3 US energy consumption by industry, 1991 (trillion BTU)

SIC	Net electr.	Residual fuel oil	Distilled fuel oil	Natural gas	LPG	Coal	Coke + breeze	Other	Σ=D+ S+Z	Total	Total −Σ
20	169	27	17	D 226	5	154	D 1	D 357	584	956	372
21+23+25	39	2+S	2+Z	42	3+Z	21	–	27+Z	1	136	135
22	101	12	6	108	2	31	–	13	–	274	274
24	61	2	16	41	4	2	–	325	–	451	451
26	201	156	9	D 838	5	296	D 1	D 1000[a]	1839	2506	667
27+31	56	1+Z	3	53	1+Z	1+S	–	5+S	1	120	119
28	440	D 112−β	14	2227	D 1440+β+γ	D 282−γ	10	526	1834	5051	3217
29	105	65	21	838	D 70−δ−γ	D 2+γ	D 2+δ	4864	74	5967	5893
30	116	8	3	96	3	7	–	6	–	238	238
32	105	9	20	381	D 18+δ	293	D 2−δ+ε	D 52−ε	72	880	808
33	499	D 34+β	11	708	D 12−β	853	278	72	46	2467	2421
34	102	3	6	175	4	5	D 6−ε	D 6+ε	12	307	295
35	101	3	4	109	2	11	1	6	–	237	237
36	102	4	2	79	1	D 12+α+ξ	D 3−ξ	D 9−α	24	212	188
37	118	12	7	133	2	D 31−ξ	3+ξ	17	34	323	289
38+39	54	4	D 5	41	2+S+Z	D 6−α	–	18+α+S	30	130	100
Total	2370	454	146	6095	1574	2006	308	7304	4551	20255	15704

Notes:

Range of parameter values: $-12 < \alpha < 5$; $-33 < \beta < 111$; $-1 < \gamma < 70$; $-2 < \delta < 2$; $-6 < \varepsilon < 6$; $-3 < \xi < 3$.

Rows and columns may not add to totals due to rounding error plus '−' and 'Z' entries. However, all agree within 1 unit.

D (SA Table 945) 'Withheld to avoid disclosing data for individual establishments'. Authors' estimates given subject to uncertainties as shown.

S (SA Table 945) 'Withheld because Relative Standard Error is greater than 50 per cent'. Authors' estimates given.

Z (SA Table 945) 'Less than 0.5 trillion BTU'.

[a]   If lignin waste accounted for 40 per cent of the total (AFPA) then we can fix 'other' for SIC 26 at 1000.

80

Table 4.4   Sulfur and ash content of US coals, 1993 (MMT)

Coal type	Quantity	Sulfur content		Ash content	
		%	MMT	%	MMT
Bituminous	453.779	1.85	8.39	10.56	47.9
Sub-bituminous	249.386	0.43	1.07	7.2	18.0
Lignite	81.238	0.92	0.75	14	11.4
Coking coal	28.416	1.85	0.53	10.55	3.0
Total	812.819		10.74		80.3

Source: IEA (1995).

of the particulates (fly ash) have already been removed by electrostatic precipitators. This yields a fairly clean mixture of wet calcium sulfite ($CaSO_3$) and calcium sulfate ($CaSO_4$). In 1993 1.8 MMT of lime (CaO) was sold for purposes of sulfur removal from flue gases, up from 1.4 MMT in 1988. Since CaO has a molecular weight of 56 and SO_2 has a molecular weight of 64, 7 units of lime will neutralize 8 units of SO_2 (or 4 units of S). It follows that wet scrubbers in 1993 removed 1.6 MMT of SO_2 from the flue gases and generated 3.4 MMT of solid waste (dry weight). In principle, this waste material can be used in place of natural gypsum for the production of wallboard. This is already being done in Europe, to some extent. It is one of the features of the well-known industrial ecosystem in Kalundborg, Denmark (Ehrenfeld and Gertler 1997). However in the US this waste is not utilized and is normally disposed of in ponds. (Calcium sulfite and sulfate are both hygroscopic or 'water-loving'. The mineral gypsum has the formula $CaSO_4.2H_2O$.)

The other method is to inject dry powdered limestone ($CaCO_3$) into a fluidized bed furnace. The calcium carbonate calcines and reacts at high temperatures with the sulfur oxides to produce CO_2 and dry sulfite and sulfate particles, but mixed with the fly ash. Both types of particulates are then removed electrostatically together, yielding a dry mixture that is easier to dispose of but has no potential uses at present. The sale of limestone for this purpose was 1.035 MMT in 1988 and 2.361 MMT in 1993. Obviously the second approach is growing much faster. Based on molecular weights, it can be verified that 100 units of $CaCO_3$ combine with and remove 64 units of sulfur dioxide, and emit 44 units of carbon dioxide. Thus dry scrubbers using limestone presumably removed 1.52 MMT of SO_2, emitted 1.04 MMT of CO_2 and generated 2.84 MMT of dry waste, not counting the weight of ash with which it is mixed, in 1993.

Taken together, both types of flue gas desulfurization (FGD) removed 1.6 + 1.52 = 3.12 MMT of SO_2, generated 1.04 MMT of CO_2 and also 3.4 + 2.84 = 6.24 MMT of solid waste (dry weight), not counting fly ash. For comparison, EPA estimated that flue gas desulfurization (FGD) by electrical utilities produced 16 million tons (14.4 MMT) of wet and dry solid wastes in 1984 (USEPA 1988, 1991). This certainly included both water and ash.

At first glance the data appear contradictory. According to EPA, total emissions of SO_2 within the US in 1993 were 19.518 MMT, of which 0.721 MMT was released by motor vehicles (mainly diesel engines) and 18.797 MMT was released by stationary sources, of which the electric power sector was responsible for 13.781 MMT (IEA 1995, Table p. 19). But according to the input data, SO_2 emissions to the atmosphere from the electric power sector alone should have been nearly 22 MMT (based on sulfur in the fuel) less the amount removed by flue-gas desulfurization (3.12 MMT) leaving about 18.9 MMT in the air. Yet EPA reports only 13.8 MMT. The gap is large (5.1 MMT). To account for the 'disappearance' of 5.1 MMT of SO_2 requires the elimination of 2.55 MMT of elemental sulfur from the coal. The most probable reconciliation of these figures is that the difference was largely attributable to coal washing, although some high sulfur coals (and possibly some coal washing refuse) was probably used by the cement industry. A plausible allocation would be 0.15 MMT (S) in coal consumed by the cement industry and 2.4 MMT (S) removed by cleaning (discussed earlier). However, this allocation is speculative. Coal also contains significant quantities of mineral ash (roughly equivalent to the mineral shale). The average ash content of US coal, noted a few paragraphs above, as burned, is approximately 10 per cent. It amounted to 82.8 MMT for the nation, in 1993. About 2.8 MMT was associated with coking coal; most of this remains with the coke and finds its way eventually into blast furnace slag. About 1 MMT was embodied in coal consumed by the cement industry (see above). The ash content of coal used as a fuel in the cement industry ends up as part of the cement itself. (In fact, as we have noted, the cement industry also uses some coal ash as a raw material, though the quantity is small.) About 7 MMT was embodied in coal for export.

This would leave roughly 72 MMT of ash in coal burned by electric power plants and industrial boilers. About 20 per cent of this is bottom ash. The other 80 per cent goes up the flue as smoke. It is standard practice for utilities to capture fly ash by means of electrostatic precipitators. The effectiveness of this system is now in the neighborhood of 99.8 per cent for the most modern units. But many industrial boilers and even some utilities are not so well equipped.

The EPA has estimated total suspended particulates emitted from stationary sources in the US to be 5.5 MMT in 1992 (IEA 1995). This was up slightly from 1991, but the general trend was declining (for example, from 7.684 MMT in 1980 and 6.433 MMT in 1985), so the 1993 number (missing) was probably about the same. The major sources of suspended particulates from stationary sources included quarries, cement plants, steel mills, incinerators, electric utilities, industrial boilers and domestic heating plants that burn fuel oil. The latter – being numerous and small – have few controls, and account for a disproportionate share of the total particulate emissions. However it is probable that fly ash from coal still accounts for 1 MMT or more of this total. Thus ash (dry weight) recovered and disposed of by electric utilities in 1993 must have been close to 71 MMT.

Coal ash contains significant quantities of heavy metals, as shown in Table 4.5. For instance, 2750 MT of arsenic would have been embodied in the ash (0.0093 per cent). Admittedly, the figures in Table 4.5 are only one estimate for one type of coal ash, and may be seriously in error, especially for the minor metals. It must be noted that the uncertainties could go either way. While most coal ash is captured, the waste ash must be disposed of somehow. Moreover, significant fractions of the more volatile trace metals – especially mercury and arsenic – still escape as vapor and re-condense downwind of the stack.[16]

Finally, the carbon in coal (along with the carbon in other fuels) is converted by combustion into carbon dioxide. The sum total in mass terms of all fossil fuels consumed in the US in 1993 was 1892 MMT, up from 1521 MMT in 1988 (Table 4.1). The carbon content is 75 per cent for methane (the major component of natural gas), and about 86 per cent for petroleum products (assuming ash and sulfur are removed at the refinery). In the case of raw coal, we must first subtract 10 per cent for ash and 8 per cent for sulfur, nitrogen, water and oxygen. Some of the sulfur and ash are removed by washing, as noted above. The combustible remainder of the coal is close to 90 per cent carbon, but overall the carbon content of clean coal *per se* is closer to 75 per cent.

The Carbon Dioxide Information Analysis Center at Oak Ridge National Laboratory has estimated that the average carbon content of fossil fuels used in the US is 84.7 per cent, whence carbon content in 1993 was about 1600 MMT. We can assume that nearly all of the fuel carbon is ultimately converted to CO_2 (5880 MMT). This includes the CO_2 from carbothermic reduction processes using coke, but not from calcination processes (lime and cement manufacturing, which are counted separately). However, it is important to bear in mind that significant quantities of fuels are diverted to 'non-fuel' use, ranging from carbothermic reduction to asphalt paving material to plastics and synthetic fibers. Some of this oxidation occurs rapidly, but some occurs very slowly over many years.

Emissions of CO_2 in the US from energy uses of fossil fuels *per se* in 1993 were 5.197 MMT (IEA 1995, p. 39). Emissions from agriculture, biomass

Table 4.5   Estimated US discharge of trace elements from coal combustion flows (kMT/year)

	1950 analysis	Discharged slag and fly ash Estimated 1980 (1.6*1950)	% of total discharge
Silicon	7 276	11 641	43.5
Iron	3 429	5 487	20.5
Aluminum	3 302	5 283	19.7
Calcium	1 370	2 192	8.19
Potassium	486	778	2.91
Magnesium	381	610	2.28
Sodium	220	353	1.32
Titanium	160	255	0.95
Zinc	24.3	38.9	0.145
Barium	20.6	32.9	0.123
Manganese	10.6	17.0	0.063
Vanadium	9.0	14.4	0.054
Strontium	7.3	11.6	0.043
Chromium	5.6	9.0	0.034
Nickel	5.1	8.1	0.030
Rubidium	4.8	7.7	0.029
Molybdenum	2.8	4.5	0.017
Copper	2.6	4.2	0.016
Arsenic	1.6	2.5	0.0093
Lead	1.5	2.5	0.0092
Cobalt	0.91	1.5	0.0054
Scandium	0.70	1.1	0.0042
Uranium	0.69	1.1	0.0041
Thorium	0.66	1.1	0.0040
Selenium	0.60	0.96	0.0036
Cesium	0.34	0.55	0.0021
Antimony	0.15	0.25	0.00092
Cadmium	0.15	0.23	0.00087
Bromine	0.09	0.15	0.00054
Mercury	0.005	0.01	0.00003
Total	16 724	26 759	

burning, waste incineration and other industrial processes, including carbothermic reduction, calcination and uses of fuels as feedstocks (for example, in ammonia and methanol production) are not included in this total, however. Also, this may not have included CO_2 from atmospheric oxidation of CO and VOC emissions, which were 83.96 MMT and 20.287 MMT respectively in 1993 (IEA 1995, Tables pp. 33, 35). We can estimate the CO_2 emissions from coal-burning electric power generation only, on the basis of 750 MMT of coal inputs at 75 per cent C times the ratio of atomic weights 44/12, or about 2065 MMT.

All NO_x emissions are combustion-related. Normally unreactive nitrogen in the air (or, as it happens, fuel-bound nitrogen in coal), combines with oxygen at high temperatures to form NO with some admixture of NO_2. EPA estimates total NO_x emissions for 1993 to have been 21.240 MMT, of which 9.639 MMT was produced by mobile sources (automobiles, motorcycles, trucks, aircraft, tractors and construction equipment). The rest (11.5 MMT) was produced by stationary sources, of which by far the greatest part came from electric power plants (below) (IEA 1995, Table p. 24).

Combustion processes also result in some releases of methane to the atmosphere, although agriculture, coal mining and gas processing and distribution account for most of it. The official EPA estimate for 1993 was 29 MMT (IEA 1995, Table p. 43). However, as we have noted, many of the components of this number are quite uncertain. An earlier but recent estimate

Table 4.6   Fuel inputs to the electric power sector 1993

Fuel type	%C	MMT
Bituminous coal	75	438.833
Sub-bituminous coal	75	260.864
Lignite	75	75.26
Diesel oil	87	1.765
Heavy fuel oil	87	22.415
Petroleum coke	99	1.105
Natural gas	75[a]	52.1
Coke oven gas	42[b]	6.5
Blast furnace gas	18[c]	84.4
Waste biomass/incineration	44[d]	1.800

Notes:
[a]   18.02 MMT/PJ.
[b]   43.8 MMT/PJ.
[c]   390.6 MMT/PJ.
[d]   PJ (= 32.4 MMT nat. gas equiv. = 100 MMT cellulose equivalent).

allocates 11.86 MMT of methane releases to all of industrial activities together, for the US in 1988 (Subak *et al.* 1992). We think the EPA estimate is more reliable, however.

It is of some interest to calculate losses from electric power production *per se*, since this sector is so important in its own right. Fuel inputs to the electric power sector, including combined heat and power (CHP) in 1993 are shown in Table 4.6.

We have already accounted for the carbon dioxide, sulfur and ash wastes. However, NO_x emissions depend on combustion conditions. At high temperatures, in the presence of excess air (as in electric power plants), this is a significant pollutant. Total emissions of NO_x by the electric power sector in US have been estimated by EPA to be 7.072 MMT for 1993 (IEA 1995, Table p. 24).

Endnotes

1. Basic statistical data in this section were derived mainly from two sources, the International Energy Agency of the OECD *Energy Statistics of the OECD Countries, 1992–1993* (IEA 1995) and World Resources Institute *Resource Flows: the material basis of industrial economics* (Adriaanse *et al.* 1997). We have converted all data for natural gas from the usual energy units (gigajoules, GJ, or terajoules, TJ) at the rate of 0.025 kg/TJ.

2. These numbers were cited in Adriaanse *et al.* (1997) but the original source was not cited.

3. As an indication of the range of uncertainty, we note a recent paper that suggests a global average overburden to coal multiplier of 5:1 (Douglas and Lawson, mimeo, undated c. 1996).

4. The mass balance constructed by the International Energy Agency allocates 0.493 MMT of oil to the drilling process itself (see below); it would seem reasonable to assume that this was used for drilling mud. If this was 3 per cent of the total, drilling muds must have weighed at least 15 MMT. On the other hand, if the drilling mud actually weighed nearly 30 MMT (as appears to be the case) then either more oil was used than is shown in the OECD statistics, or the 3 per cent figure is much too high.

5. They may have used Dutch data. Methane constitutes 72.7 per cent of crude Dutch gas, while non-hydrocarbons (mainly CO_2) constitute over 20 per cent (van Liere 1995, p. 33). If the Dutch ratio held for the US, it would imply a total mass of crude gas of roughly 497 MMT, compared to net production of 362 MMT in 1993. However, the non-hydrocarbon content of natural gas pumped in the US averages only about 1.5 per cent (Barns and Edmonds 1990, Table C2.1).

6. Actually the methane content ranges from 90–99 per cent. Since the other components, mainly ethane, are slightly denser, this mass estimate is very slightly too low. To get an idea of the possible correction, if the gas were 5 per cent ethane (C_2H_6), which has a molecular weight of 30 (compared to 16 for methane), the correction factor for mass would be $0.95 + 0.05(30/16) = 1.023$, or about 2 per cent.

7. These data are reported by 'Petroleum Administration for Defense' or PAD district, of which there are four, in MY 'Sulfur' Table 4. The 1993 figures added up to 2.847 MMT, but, data for one PAD district included two months of sulfur recovered by the Frasch process from underground deposits. Frasch sulfur was, of course, under-reported by the same amount. This obfuscation was deliberate, 'to conform with proprietary data requirements'. However, comparing year to year by category, it would appear that the under/over reporting was roughly 0.4 MMT.

8. US production of helium in 1993 was about 95 million cubic meters (MY 'Helium', Tables 2, 3). Production and consumption were approximately in balance for that year.

The density of helium gas is 0.1785 kg/m^3, so the mass of helium produced was about 17 kMT.

9. Natural gas is normally measured in volumetric terms, such as million cubic feet (mcf) or cubic meters (in Europe). The US Department of Energy confuses matters further by using English energy measures, such as trillion or quadrillion BTU (quads), while the International Energy Agency prefers metric energy units, namely terajoules (TJ = 10^{12} joules) or petajoules (PJ = 10^{15} joules). We have converted their data to mass, based on the standard heat energy content (enthalpy) of methane, namely 890.8 kJ/mole, 55.53 kJ/gm, or 55.53 TJ/metric ton. This translates to 18 kMT/TJ, or 0.018 MMT/PJ. (Methane weighs about 0.714 kg/m^3 so a cubic meter has a theoretical heat value of 39.7 MJ/m^3 or 1065 BTU/cf in English units.) The usual heat value assumed for natural gas in the US is slightly lower, namely 1000 BTU/cf. If we assume this lower number for heat value the mass of natural gas consumed would be correspondingly greater than our number (that is, by 6.5 per cent). However the mass difference must consist of unreactive gases, such as carbon dioxide or nitrogen gas.

10. It is estimated that, worldwide, 34 per cent of natural gas is flared or vented (van Liere 1995, p. 33). This happens mainly in remote regions where gas processing and transmission facilities are impractical.

11. The basic data for this section come from the International Energy Agency publication *Energy Statistics of OECD Countries 1992–1993* (IEA 1995, pp. 251–3). The publication consists of detailed energy balances, by country. All figures for solid and liquid fuels are given in mass units, but natural gas is given in energy units. We have converted their gas data to mass, based on the weight and energy content of a cubic meter of methane, namely 18.01 metric tons/TJ, or 0.01801 MMT/PJ.

12. Benzene, ethylbenzene, toluene and xylenes constitute, respectively, 0.1, 0.51, 0.19 and 0.88 per cent of average crude oil by volume (Gaines and Wolsky 1981). They are, of course, a much higher percentage of the volatiles.

13. In this section we also use the OECD/IEA energy balance data previously cited (IEA 1995).

14. To be specific, there are seven major regions with different characteristics:

   Northern Appalachia: medium quality and high sulfur (mostly 1.5–3.5 per cent).
   Central Appalachia: high quality, low sulfur, suitable for coking and export (0.7–1.0 per cent).
   Illinois: mediocre quality, high ash, high sulfur (mostly 2–3.5 per cent).
   Rocky Mountain: subbituminous and bituminous, low sulfur (0.5–0.6 per cent).
   Powder River Basin: subbituminous, low sulfur (0.3–0.5 per cent).
   Also, coal is mined in the southern Appalachians and in Alaska.

15. Coal cleaning is now a sophisticated process with a fairly long history in northern Europe. By contrast, the technology was only adopted in the US after the energy crisis of the 1970s. Sulfur occurs in the coal in three forms, mineral sulfides (pyrites), mineral sulfates, and organic sulfur compounds bound into the coal matrix. The coal cleaning technologies currently employed can remove 10–50 per cent of the sulfur (WEC 1992, p. 11), although there are exceptions.

16. US coal is unusually low in ash, most of which is recovered. By contrast, most other countries bum coal that has a much higher ash content – 15–25 per cent or more – very little of which is recovered. Thus the problem of heavy metal pollution from coal burning will be far more serious in eastern Europe, the former Soviet Union, China and India.

5 Extractive materials: Minerals and metals[1]

5.1 Introduction to the chapter

This chapter, like Chapter 4, deals with industries that extract non-renewable resources and process them into finished materials other than fuels and chemicals. As before, the focus is on materials accounting, with an emphasis on emissions and wastes.

We have conceptually divided the processes of mining, concentration (or winning), reduction or smelting, and refining as shown schematically in Figure 5.1. There are four stages of separation. The first two, being physical in nature, are normally assigned to the mining sector (SIC 10) or the quarrying sector (SIC 14). The last two, being thermal or chemical in nature, are assigned to the stone and glass sector (SIC 32) or the primary metals sector (SIC 33). However, for analytical convenience we view the sequence as a whole. At each separation stage, wastes are left behind and a purified product is sent along to the next stage. In principle, the wastes can be determined approximately by subtracting outputs from inputs. For a more precise answer, exogenous inputs to the beneficiation process must also be taken into account.

Unfortunately, from the analytic point of view, published data are rarely available in appropriate forms. There are significant imports and exports of concentrates and crude metals (and even some crude ores). But trade data are often given in terms of metal content, rather than gross weight. Domestic data are also incomplete, due to the large number of data that are withheld for 'proprietary' reasons. Thus, in several cases, we have been forced to use indirect methods, based on process data, to estimate the input quantities of concentrates. There are two types of waste associated with extraction *per se*. These are (i) earth displaced in the process of searching for and removing ore (overburden) and (ii) unwanted contaminants (gangue) removed on-site or at the mill by physical methods, such as screening, washing, settling, flotation, centrifuging and so on. The material shipped to the next stage of processing is, typically, a concentrate that is fed into a downstream smelting or refining process.[2]

Downstream materials processing activities such as cement manufacturing and metal ore smelting and refining generate further separation wastes, such as slags, as well as air and water pollutants. These arise partly from the use of fossil fuels to drive these processes and partly from the need to discard unwanted contaminants (notably sulfur). However, for convenience, all combustion-related wastes were discussed together in Chapter 4.

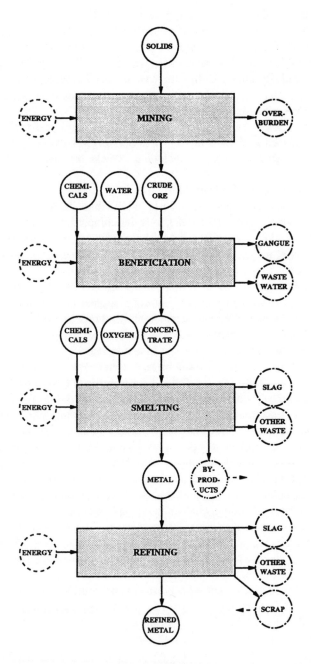

Figure 5.1   Metals processing relationships

5.2   Non-metallic minerals and industries (SIC 14, SIC 32)[3]

Non-metallic minerals are mined or quarried in very large tonnages, mostly domestically (see Table 5.1). Stone (including limestone) is the largest item (1118 MMT), followed by sand and gravel (895 MMT). Imports and exports are comparatively small. Unlike the case of metals, overburden and wastes are small in relation to production except for clay, where the waste amounts to 29.6 MMT, phosphates (76.8 MMT) and potassium salts (28.6 MMT).[4]

Portland cement (SIC 3241) is an important industry. Total tonnage of clinker produced in the US in 1993 was 66.96 MMT (MY 'Cement', Table 6), finished cement produced (including cement produced from imported clinker) was 70.27 MMT (ibid., Table 7), 71.1 MMT of all types of cement were shipped from US plants (ibid., Table 14) and total US production of hydraulic cement was reported as 75.11 MMT (ibid., Table 21), although this figure excludes some minor categories (aluminous, and natural cements) which might add as much as 1 MMT, but probably less. There is obviously some potential for confusion, especially since the US Bureau of Mines data are based on surveys with incomplete coverage (91 per cent for 1993). Most of the input materials were natural minerals, including limestone, 'cement rock', clay and shale, silica, and gypsum. Inputs to Portland Cement accounted for by the 'Cement' chapter of Minerals Yearbook added up to 117.165 MMT (see Table 5.2)

Unfortunately, different chapters in Minerals Yearbook are inconsistent with each other. Limestone is obviously by far the most important input. According to the 'Cement' chapter (Table 4) the input of limestone was 78.96 MMT, but according to the 'Stone' chapter (Table 14) it was 80.3 MMT. The 'Cement' chapter includes a category called cement rock, amounting to 19.186 MMT; the 'Stone' chapter has no such category, although Table 13 of that chapter allocates total stone inputs to cement of 84.318 MMT (obviously including limestone) while Table 14 mentions 0.801 MMT of dolomite, Table 18 notes 0.242 MMT of sandstone and quartzite and Table 19 adds 2.448 MMT of cinder and scoria. These are presumably included in cement rock. However, most of the latter is evidently hidden in the 'not elsewhere classified' category.

There are several other minor inconsistencies. The 'Cement' chapter notes inputs of 4.2 MMT for clay and 5.066 MMT for shale. The 'Clays' chapter allocates 7. 540 MMT of clay and shale (Table 8) plus 0.207 MMT of kaolin (Table 20) to the cement industry. The 'Cement' chapter mentions inputs of 3.696 MMT of gypsum, but the 'Gypsum' chapter allocates just 3.290 MMT to cement ('Gypsum' Table 4). Finally, the 'Cement' chapter acknowledges 0.038 MMT of blast furnace slag as an input, but the 'Slag' chapter implies that a significant fraction of 1.69 MMT (granulated) is so used ('Slag' p. 1055). It would be enormously helpful if the US Geological Survey could manage to sort out these internal inconsistencies.

It is well known that the cement manufacturing process releases large amounts of CO_2 from limestone calcination. The carbon dioxide emissions from clinker manufacturing (excluding fuel consumption) should amount to 44 per cent of the original mass of calcium carbonate (and other carbonates). Limestone used in the Portland cement manufacturing industry is about 85 per cent $CaCO_3$ and cement rock averages about 40 per cent $CaCO_3$ (van Ost 1997) so at least 32.5 MMT of CO_2 would have been emitted during calcination.[5] There should be a mass difference between inputs to the Portland cement manufacturing process, and outputs of the process, at least this great. In fact, the difference seems to be 117.165 − 66.96 = 50.20 MMT. This leaves about 17.7 MMT of input mass unaccounted for, which is a surprisingly large gap. Even if some of the inputs listed in Table 5.2 were, in fact, used for other types of cement, the discrepancy is much too large.

Fuel inputs for clinker production include 10.03 MMT coal, 0.452 MMT natural gas, 70 kMT scrap tires, 90 kMT other waste solid fuels, 0.67 MMT liquid waste fuels, which we take to be used engine and machine oils, and 1.03 billion kwh of electricity (MY 'Cement', Tables 6, 7). We do not have fuel figures for other types of cement. Combustion wastes from these fuels was mostly carbon dioxide, plus water vapor. Sulfurous fractions in the fuels react with the lime in the cement and remain in the cement, resulting in a small component of calcium sulfate.

Lime (CaO) is another commercial product made by calcining limestone. In 1993 US production of lime was 16.7 MMT, of which 2.35 MMT was hydrated lime or 'slaked lime' ($Mg(OH)_2$), plus 3.0 MMT of dolomitic lime and 'deadburned dolomite' (MgO) (MY 'Lime', Table 1). Calcination of limestone and dolomite releases CO_2 in a ratio of 0.785 tons per ton of CaO 1.1 tons per ton of MgO. Hence this industry consumed 28.6 MMT of raw crushed limestone plus 0.67 MMT or dolomite and released 13.0 MMT of CO_2 to the atmosphere. Industrial uses are extremely diverse, but the steel industry used about 30 per cent of the total (5.11 MMT, of which 3.56 MMT was used in basic oxygen steel-making and 1.14 MMT was used in electric arc furnaces), paper and pulp consumed 1.03 MMT, sugar refining consumed 0.7 MMT (MY 'Lime', Table 7, revised) and non-ferrous (copper) ore concentration by froth flotation took around 0.33 MMT according to our calculations (below) and acid neutralization for the ore leaching (SX–EW) process probably consumed 0.29 MMT. Use for environmental purposes in 1993 amounted to 4.2 MMT, of which flue gas desulfurization accounted for 1.8 MMT (ibid.). Uncalcined limestone in the amount of 2.361 MMT was also used for this purpose.

Phosphate rock mining and processing is another extremely important activity, since phosphate fertilizers are absolutely essential for modern agriculture. Unfortunately the ore is not of very high grade, and is rather

Table 5.1   Production and waste allocation for US industrial mineral production from domestic and foreign ores, 1993 (kMT)

Mineral	A. Total material handled USBM 1993 p. 47	B. Ore treated or sold USBM 1993 p. 58	C. Domestic production USBM 1993 p. 4	D. Exports USBM 1993 pp. 31–33	E. Imports USBM 1993 pp. 38–40	Apparent consumption calculated C – D + E	Over-burden loss calculated A – B	Concentration loss calculated B – C
Asbestos	70	45	13	28	31	17	25	32
Barite	1 147	773	315	18	834	1 131	374	458
Clays	70 657	41 074 p. 259	41 074	4 154	39 430	76 350	29 583	0
Diatomite	3 267[b]	662[e]	599	165	2	436	2 605	63
Feldspar	3 326[b]	776	770	18	7	759	2 550	6
Gypsum (crude)	22 564	15 932	15 812	344	7 587	23 055	6 632	120
Magnesium compounds	2 762[b]	1 627	698	117	495	1 076	1 135	929
Mica (scrap)	427[b]	388	88	6	22	104	39	300
Perlite	908[b]	604[e]	569	26	70	613	304	35
Phosphate rock	218 248[c]	112 302[c]	35 494	4 831	632	31 295	105 946	76 808
Potash	23 167[c]	34 233[c]	11 686[h]	925	7 204	17 965	13 953	22 547
Pumice	536	469	469	18	143	594	67	0
Salt	39 694 p. 961	39 694 p. 961	38 665	688	5 868	43 845	0	1 029
Sand and gravel total	912 818[d]	894 920	894 920	2 882	1 360	893 398	17 898	0
Sodium compounds, total	19 219[b]	9 319[f]	9 319[f]	2 887	252	6 684	9 900	0
Stone, crushed	1 175 632	1 118 824	1 116 000	4 824	8 400	1 119 576	56 808	2 824
Stone, dimension	1 858[b]	1 235 p. 1154	1 232	270	310	1 272	623	3
Talc & pyrophilite	996[d]	977[e]	818[i]	135	100	782	20	159
Vermiculite	190	190	187	7	30	210	0	3

Subtotal	2 497 486	2 274 043	2 168 727	22 344	72 778	2 219 161	248 462	105 316
Other[a]	3 966[d]	3 889[g]	3 889	1 242	3 014	5 660	78	0
Total	2 501 452	2 277 932	2 172 615	23 586	75 791	2 224 821	248 539	105 316

Notes:

[a] Boron, bromine, iodine, peat, sulfur, tripoli and zeolites.

[b] 'Materials handled (93)' estimated as 'ore treated or sold' (93) times the 1988 ratio of materials handled to ore treated or sold as given in USBM 1989; that is, $M(93) = O(93) * M(88)/O(88)$.

[c] *Source:* Adriaanse *et al.* (1997), p. 57.

[d] Overburden estimated at 2% of ore treated.

[e] 'Ore treated (93)' estimated as 'domestic production' (93) times the 1988 ratio of ore treated or sold to domestic production as given in USBM 1989; that is, $O(93) = P(93) * O(88)/P(88)$.

[f] Total not broken down to natural and synthetic in 1993. 1993 natural component calculated from 1992 ratio and added to soda ash.

[g] Ore treated or sold estimated as equal to domestic production.

[h] Total estimated assuming 14% K_2O content (Adriaansee *et al.* 1997, p. 57).

[i] 'Production (93)' estimated as 'underground production' (93) times the 1988 ratio of total production to underground production or sold as given in USBM 1989; that is, $p(93) = u(93)*p(88)/u(88)$.

Table 5.2   Mineral inputs to Portland cement, US 1993 (MMT)

Mineral	Source	Output side Quantity	Input side Cement (Table 4)
Limestone	Stone (Table 17)	80.3	78.958
Common clay	Clays (Table 8)	7.54	4.200
Cement rock (including marl)			19.186
Coral			0.754
Shale			5.066
Sand and calcium silicate			2.046
Sandstone, quartzite			0.571
Dolomite	Stone (Table 14)	0.8	
Other crushed stone (84.3 – 80.3 – 0.8)	Stone (Table 13)	3.2	
Kaolin	Clays (Table 20)	2.07	
Bauxite	Aluminum (Table 17)	0.43	
Gypsum	Gypsum (Table 4)	3.29	3.696
Granulated blast furnace slag	Slag, p. 1055[a]	1.69	0.038
Fly ash		?	0.888
Iron ore		?	1.097
Other n.e.c.			0.666
Total			117.166

Note: [a]   It is interesting to note that in Germany, 7.4 MMT of slag were sold in 1993, of which 39 per cent (2.88 MMT) went to the cement industry (MY 'Slag', p. 1057).

Source: MY 1993; detail tables and Cement Table 4.

contaminated, especially with cadmium, fluorine and uranium. (In fact, uranium was recovered from phosphate rock in the past.) In the US 451.8 MMT of raw materials were handled to produce 224.1 MMT of crude phosphate rock in 1988 (MY 1988 'Mining and Quarrying Trends', Table 2 'Materials Handled', p. 67). The difference of 227.7 MMT was overburden, which was mostly left in previously mined areas. The crude ore was then concentrated to 45.4 MMT of fertilizer grade phosphoric acid. In 1993, by contrast, the corresponding table (MY 'Mining and Quarrying Trends', Table 2, p. 47) provided only the data on concentrated ore (that is, fertilizer grade phosphoric acid), namely 35.531 MMT.[6] However, in the 'Phosphates' article (MY 'Phosphates', Table 1), production of crude ore was given as 106.79 MMT, while production of concentrates was given as 35.494 MMT, less than half of the 1988 value.

This is curious, since output of concentrates fell only 22 per cent from 1988 while output of crude ore fell by more than 52 per cent. The quality of the ore surely did not increase, so concentrate produced from ore mined in

1993 was probably about 22 MMT. Drawdowns of stockpiled ore must have accounted for the difference. At any rate, on a proportional basis, we think it safe to assume that overburden remained in the same proportion to crude ore in 1993 as in 1988. Thus, overburden from phosphate mining in 1993 was probably about 110 MMT. In other words, total materials handled in that year was probably about 217 MMT. Subtracting the fertilizer grade concentrate produced from this ore (22 MMT) yields a 'hidden flow' of 195 MMT.[7]

Other than the products mentioned above, it appears that the major waste emissions from the stone, clay and glass sector (exclusive of losses in quarrying and concentration) are primarily related to combustion of fossil fuels. The calcination of gypsum to plaster releases water vapor (21 per cent by weight). The glass and ceramics industries consume a great deal of energy for heat, but produce little waste of significance, except particulates. The ceramics sector generates some solid wastes in the form of broken bricks and tiles. An EPA contractor estimated dry wastes from the sector to be about 18 MMT in 1983 (SAI 1985). EPA's latest estimate of airborne emissions (particulates and CO, primarily) is about 1.0 MMT (USEPA 1991). We have no estimate of water use by the stone, clay and glass sector. However EPA estimated total (wet) wastes from the sector to be 560 MMT (USEPA 1986). This must refer mainly to water used for phosphate rock concentration, since most of the other processes in the sector are dry.

Incidentally, it is worth noting that phosphate rock concentrate, or 'fertilizer grade phosphoric acid' is produced by dissolving the crude phosphate rock in concentrated sulfuric acid – known as the 'wet process'. This refining operation is considered to be part of the inorganic chemical industry (SIC 28741) and will be mentioned again in the next chapter. (It is the largest consumer of sulfuric acid.) The product is reckoned to be about 50 per cent phosphoric acid (H_3PO_4). For 1993 this amounted to 10.3 MMT of phosphorus pentoxide (P_2O_5) which is the standard unit of measure in the industry.

Overall, we estimate overburden wastes for the non-metallic minerals for 1993 to have been 223 MMT. Further details are given in Table 5.1.

5.3   Metals mining and concentration (SIC 10)

The US Bureau of Mines estimates that mineral exploration and mine development activities in 1993 (not including energy fuels) generated more than 1450 MMT of waste material, mostly from overburden stripping, but also from test boring and other developmental operations (MY 'Mining and Quarrying Trends', Table 2). This is probably an underestimate, since much of this sort of activity was not reported. (We noted previously that both overburden and concentration waste from phosphate mining were omitted from this tabulation.) Bureau of Mines data, supplemented from other sources, yields a total of 1313.5 MMT of overburden for metal ores in 1993, of which non-ferrous metals contributed 1184.5 MMT and iron ore mining 129 MMT (Adriaanse et al. 1997). The totals are dominated by just two metals, copper and gold, with iron a distant third.

Domestic iron ores (SIC 101) are concentrated from low grade taconite ores by several means, including magnetic separation. Crude ore input from US mines was 180.906 MMT. The final product consists of pellets, of which 1993 production was 55.651 MMT. The crude iron ore processed in 1993 was 180.91 MMT (MY 'Iron Ore' p. 469). Iron ore concentration wastes therefore amounted to approximately 180.91 – 55.651 = 148.2 MMT.

It is convenient to discuss copper ores (SIC 102), lead/zinc ores (SIC 103) and molybdenum ores (SIC 1061) together.[8] The concentration process used for most minerals in this group is froth flotation. It is used, especially, to separate sulfide minerals of copper, lead, zinc, molybdenum and silver from gangue minerals such as silicates, aluminates, and carbonates. In the case of iron ore, it is mainly used to remove impurities (for example, sulfides). It is also used to concentrate phosphate rock and, to some extent, for coal cleaning.

The most recent US data available is for 1991 (Edelstein 1993).[9] In that year (excluding coal) 410 MMT of mineral ores were concentrated by froth flotation, yielding 62 MMT of concentrates and 348 MMT of (dry equivalent) mineral wastes (ibid., Table 2). Grinding mills required 7.6 billion kwh of electricity and 220 kMT of rods and balls. Water used in the process was 746 billion gallons, or 2820 MMT. Chemical reagents used for flotation amounted to 574 kMT, plus 22 kMT of effluent treatment chemicals. Of the grand total of 596 kMT, 312 kMT was lime, 66 kMT was fatty acids and soaps, 64 kMT was fuel oil, and 52.5 kMT was sulfuric acid, leaving only 100 kMT for all other chemicals (ibid., Table 4). These figures are probably underestimated by 15 per cent, or a little less (see endnote 8). Wastes from flotation are generally disposed of in ponds, mostly in dry areas. Typical unit consumption of these reagents in non-ferrous metal mills is shown in Table 5.3.

In 1991 copper and copper-molybdenum ores concentrated by flotation (reported to US Bureau of Mines) amounted to 243 MMT and yielded 4.39 MMT of copper concentrate (27 per cent Cu) and 61 kMT of molybdenum concentrate (53 per cent Mo); the process consumed about 302 kMT of lime and 25 kMT of other chemicals (Edelstein 1993, Tables 9, 10). Other sulfides, included lead–zinc ores (12.3 MMT), yielding 585 kMT of lead concentrate (74.1 per cent Pb), 560 kMT of zinc concentrate (55.9 per cent Zn) and 117 kMT of copper and lead–zinc concentrates (ibid., Table 11). These mills consumed about 14.5 kMT of chemicals, of which 2.3 kMT was lime. Zinc ores (2.87 MMT) yielded 193 kMT of concentrates (63.2 per cent Zn) and consumed very minor quantities of reagents (ibid., Table 12). Iron ore processed amounted to 29.3 MMT and yielded 26.2 MMT of concentrate (65.7 per cent Fe); flotation consumed 17 kMT of reagents (of which 4 kMT was lime) (ibid., Table 13). Phosphate rock concentration was a major activity: 96.7 MMT of ore was processed, yielding 21.88 MMT of concentrate (33.8 per cent P_2O_5) and consuming 210 kMT of reagents, including soap and fatty acids (66 kMT), fuel oil (64 kMT) and sulfuric acid (52.5 kMT) (ibid., Table 16).

In 1993 the amount of copper and copper molybdenum ore concentrated (excluding ores leached) was 262.00 MMT (MY 'Copper', Table 5). Unfortunately, this figure does not agree with another figure for crude copper ore, namely 469.186 MMT from the same reference (MY 'Mining and Quarrying Trends', Table 2). We suspect a confusion of terminology may be at fault. However, accepting the smaller number from the 'Copper' chapter, and extrapolating in proportion, 4.73 MMT of copper concentrate, containing 1.275 MMT of recoverable copper (plus 66 kMT of molybdenum concentrate containing 35 kMT of recoverable molybdenum) would presumably have been produced in 1993. This agrees quite well with reported 1993 data, namely 1.266 MMT of recoverable copper (MY 'Copper', Table 5) and 36.8 kMT recoverable molybdenum (MY 'Molybdenum', Table 1). Based on the same extrapolation, the 1993 consumption of flotation chemicals would have been 360 kMT, of which 330 kMT was lime. Concentration wastes from copper–molybdenum ore processing by froth flotation in 1993 would therefore have been 262.0 + 0.36 – 4.77 = 257.7 MMT.

One other extraction method is increasingly used for copper ore, namely solvent extraction–electro-winning (SX–EW), which accounted for 27 per cent of US primary copper production in 1993 (now 30 per cent). In 1993 28.71 MMT of copper ore was leached. The sequence starts with sulfuric acid leaching. The acid is a byproduct of smelting operations. According to the Bureau of Mines 2.1 MMT of byproduct acid was used for heap-leaching of copper ores in the US in 1993, while 0.18 MMT of acid was used for leaching other ores (MY 'Sulfur', Table 7). Concentration is by solvent extraction, not froth flotation. We have no data on other chemicals used for this purpose, although we suspect that 290 kMT of lime was used for acid neutralization. The copper sulfate leach solution can be reduced by scrap iron to yield a copper precipitate called 'cement copper', which is then smelted by conventional means. Or (more likely), it is electrolytically reduced to 'cathode copper', which is subsequently refined electrolytically to ultra-pure 'anode copper'. It is difficult to define a meaningful concentrate in this case. Copper recovered by means of this process was 0.491 MMT in 1993. Taking into account sulfuric acid and lime consumed, concentration losses from the SX–EW process would have been 28.71 + (2.1 + 0.29) – 0.49 = 30.6 MMT.

Copper–molybdenum concentration wastes for 1993 by froth flotation and acid leaching would therefore amount to 257.7 + 30.6 = 288.3 MMT. However, if the larger figure for 'crude copper ore' noted earlier (469.2 MMT) is

Table 5.3 Typical flotation reagent consumption in non-ferrous metal mills (grams/metric ton of ore)

	Pb–Zn sulfides Les Malines France	Pb–Zn oxide + sulfide Zellidja Morocco	Cu–Pb–Zn Brunswick Mining and Smelting Canada	Ni sulfide Falconbridge Canada	Cu sulfide Lornex Canada	Au cyanidation + CIF Homestake USA	Cu–Zn pyrite Pyhasalai Finland
Acids							
Sulfuric acid				500–600			5000[b]
Alkalis							
Lime	1000		2500	225–400	1100	1200	3150
Sodium carbonate		550	3300				
Sodium hydroxide		246					
Modifier							
Copper sulfate	200	120	815	35–60			330
Sodium cyanide	10	13					28
Zinc sulfate	60	91					
Sodium sulfide		2800				550	
Sodium silicate		2700					
Sulfur dioxide			700				
Starch			100				

correct (perhaps reflecting some physical means of concentration prior to froth flotation) it would follow that total copper concentration wastes would necessarily be increased by the same amount, namely $469.2 - (262 + 28.7) = 178.5$ MMT. This is frankly puzzling. We wish the Geological Survey would clarify.

Gold mining (SIC 1041) is a special case. Gold occurs in nature in pure metallic form, or alloyed with silver and copper, tellurium, bismuth or selenium, but generally not in compounds. However, large nuggets are extremely rare and gold ore consists of tiny grains of the pure metal interspersed with large volumes of other minerals from which it must be separated physically. Underground mines extract gold from lodes. Surface mines may be open pits or placer-type (using a water stream to dislodge sedimentary materials). US gold production in 1993 was 331 metric tons (MY 'Gold'). Ore processed, in toto was 500 MMT, but over half of this was primarily mined for other metals (copper, lead, zinc, silver, and so on). However gold ore as such amounted to 238.7 MMT which was also essentially the amount of concentration waste (MY 'Gold', Tables 4, 5). The overburden removed in the mining process is estimated to be 779 MMT for the US in 1993 (MY 'Mining and Quarrying Trends', Table 2), or 3.26 tons per ton of ore. (Incidentally, this table also sets a higher figure for ore output, namely 248.4 MMT.)

Quite a lot of gold (and silver) is recovered as a byproduct of copper and lead mining. The recovery process in this case is very complex. However, where gold is mined for its own sake, the first stage of separation is usually gravitic settling. A small amount of gold ore is treated by froth flotation (Edelstein 1993). By far the most common method of extraction is cyanidation, which is apparently used for all gold ore mined as such (MY 'Gold', Table 5). The technique, called 'heap leaching', is to pile up the ore (after grinding) and treat the ore pile with sodium cyanide (MY 'Gold', p. 417).[10] A pregnant solution is drawn off to a recovery plant. Cyanide consumption was not published by the Bureau of Mines for 1993, but total US consumption for this purpose in 1988 was about 82.5 kMT (MY 1989 'Mining and Quarrying Trends', p. 56).[11] This is equivalent to 410 tons of sodium cyanide consumed per ton of gold produced. Assuming the same technology was applicable in 1993, US cyanide consumption for gold recovery would have been 136 kMT. It is worth pointing out that the heap leaching process does not convert the cyanide to any other harmless chemical, *per se*. Only natural processes of degradation – by bacterial action and oxidation – decompose the cyanide. The mining operations merely try to contain the waste in ponds, although there are many reports of leakage into streams and ground waters. The final products of cyanide decomposition (by oxidation) would be CO_2 and NO_x.

Aluminum ore (bauxite) mining (SIC 1099) in the US is a very minor activity. Domestic output of bauxite is only about 30 kMT (used for non-metallurgical products). Almost all bauxite is imported. It is a relatively high grade ore (about 30 per cent Al). It is further concentrated to nearly pure Al_2O_3 by the Bayer process, which belongs to the inorganic chemical industry (SIC 2819). However, since this process is a part of the metallurgical reduction and refining sequence, we note that it consumed about 0.39 tons of lime or 0.075 tons of limestone and 0.35 tons of caustic soda or 0.075 tons of sodium carbonate (soda ash) per ton of alumina, based on a typical version of the Bayer process (for example, Hall *et al.* 1975).

Mining activities in 1988 altogether consumed 2.145 MMT of industrial explosives, of which 82.5 per cent was ammonium nitrate based (MY 1989 Mining and Quarrying Trends', Table 15). Unfortunately this data was not broken down by use, so we do not know how much was used in coal mines, how much in stone quarries and how much in copper or other metal ore mines. Even the aggregate data are not included in the 1993 Yearbook, but the trend was clearly rising and if the use of explosives is proportional to total material handled in mining and quarrying (except for sand and gravel and gold) – as seems plausible – then the 1993 total should have been similar or slightly higher. We therefore assume 2 MMT of ammonium nitrates was utilized by all of the mining (and quarrying) industries in 1993, plus 0.3 MMT of other explosives, also nitrogen based.

When nitrate explosives are used, they generate NO_x.[12] Unfortunately, very little has been published on this source. A colleague of ours has calculated using process simulation modelling software (Aspentech ©) that about 5 per cent of the mass of explosive was probably converted to N_2O, 14 per cent to NO and 5 per cent to N_2O (Axtell 1993). This implies N_2O emissions of 0.1 MMT and NO_x emissions of about 0.38 MMT from the use of ammonium nitrate explosives alone. We note that N_2O is one of the more potent greenhouse gases, and that its concentration in the atmosphere has been increasing in recent years without any clear explanation. We suspect that mining is part of the problem.

Metal ore concentration activities consumed approximately 0.8 MMT of lime in 1993 of which about 0.16 MMT was for aluminum (the Bayer process for alumina), 0.35 MMT was for copper ore (our estimate) and the remainder (0.29 MMT) was for other ore concentration processes (MY 'Lime', Table 5).[13] It appears that total concentration wastes for metals mined and concentrated domestically in 1993 were about 681.8 MMT (Table 5.4). The total is again dominated by gold, copper and iron.

5.4 Iron and steel (SIC 331)

By far the major product, in tonnage terms, is crude (or pig) iron.[14] US blast furnace output of pig iron in 1993 was 48.155 MMT (MY 'Iron and Steel', Table 1). This material has an iron content of 94 per cent and a carbon

Table 5.4 Production and waste allocation for US metals production from domestic and foreign ores, 1993 (MMT)

Domestic Mine Production 1993 (MMT)

	Material in (A+B)	Overburden (A)	Multiplier	Domestic ore out (B)	Source A & B
Bauxite	0.57	0.19	0.48	0.39	108
Copper–Molybdenum	860.16	563.55	1.90	296.61	337
Gold	816.74	596.00	2.70	220.74	[a]
Lead–Zinc	4.35	0.34	0.08	4.01	47
Zinc	6.30	0.36	0.06	5.94	47
Silver	6.92	4.53	1.90	2.39	[b]
Molybdenum	n.a.	n.a.		n.a.	
NF Total	*1695.03*	*1164.96*		*530.07*	
Iron	309.89	128.99	[c]	180.91	469
Total	*2004.92*	*1293.95*		*710.98*	

Domestic Concentrate Production 1993 (MMT)

	Crude ore input (B')	Source B	Concentration wastes B'–C	Concentrate (C)	Concentrate gross Source C
Bauxite/alumina	11.92	109	7.09[d]	5.29	109
Copper–Molybdenum	296.61	337	294.21[e]	5.20	[e]
Gold	220.74	[a]	220.88	0.00	407
Lead–Zinc	4.01	47	3.51	0.50	[g]
Zinc	5.94	47	5.54	0.40	[h]
Silver	2.39	[b]	2.39	0.00	1045
Molybdenum	n.a.		n.a.	0.03	p. 675
NF Total	*541.60*		*533.61*	*11.42*	

Iron   180.91   469   148.20[i]   66.11
Total   722.51   681.81   77.53

Domestic Refinery Output 1993 (MMT)

	Domestic concentrate (D)	Source	Net imports (E)	Source	Concentrate consumed (D+E)	Primary Output	Solid waste from smelting and refining
Alumina/aluminum	5.29	109	3.94	34	9.23	3.70	0.00
Copper	5.20	337	0.09	338	5.29	1.79	4.20
Lead	0.50	47	0.04	34	0.54	0.34	0.52
Zinc	0.40	47	0.05	34	0.45	0.24	est. 0.40
Other	0.20	j			0.20		
NF Total	*11.59*		*4.11*		*15.71*	*6.06*	*5.12*
Iron	66.11	469	9.04	i	75.14	48.16	19.00
Total	*77.70*		*13.15*		*90.85*	*54.22*	*24.12*

Notes:

a   Adriaanse *et al.* p. 57, gives overburden. Overburden multiplier = 2.7.

b   Silver from silver ore only, p. 1045. 1993 data on pure silver ore withheld. Ratio to metal assumed same as 1989. Overburden to ore ratio assumed same as copper.

c   Adriaanse *et al.* p. 57, implies multiplier of 0.71

d   Dry equivalent. Includes net imports of crude ore. Wastes include caustic soda and lime inputs to Bayer process.

e   P. 335 with average metal content of concentrate estimated at 1.75 per cent. Wastes include weight of rods, balls, flotation reagents and other chemicals.

f   Waste include cyanide.

g   Concentrate composition 60 per cent Pb.

h   Concentrate composition assumed 55 per cent Zn.

i   P. 471 less import share (pp. 474, 475). Wastes include lime and coal detritus.

j   Includes gold, silver, molybdenum, beryllium, magnesium, maganese, platinum group, titanium, uranium and all other withheld.

Source: Page number sources are from MY 1993. Overburden multipliers are from *et al.* p. 57

content of 4.5 per cent. It is entirely used for carbon steel production, mostly (> 90 per cent) via the basic oxygen process. (Electric minimills use scrap metal, almost exclusively.)

Blast furnace feed consumed in 1993 was 77.068 MMT (MY 'Iron and Steel', Table 2), of which 60.730 MMT was pellets (produced at mines, or imported) and 12.451 MMT was sinter produced at the integrated steel mills, which consumed about 6 MMT of upstream 'reverts' (dust, mill scale). The other blast furnace feed was 1.924 MMT of scrap. The US consumed 14.097 MMT of imported ores and agglomerates, mostly pellets, in 1993 (MY 'Iron Ore', Table 14) and exported 5.061 MMT (ibid., Table 12).

Blast furnace inputs (mainly pellets) averaged about 63 per cent iron, 5 per cent silica, 2 per cent moisture and 0.35 per cent other minerals (phosphorus, manganese, alumina). The iron content of the feed was 47.3 MMT; roughly 30 per cent (22.5 MMT) was oxygen combined with the iron. Slag consists of the silica and other non-ferrous minerals in the sinter and pellets, plus the fluxes. Total iron blast furnace slag production in the US in 1993 was 12.3 MMT, or 0.255 metric tons of slag per metric ton of pig iron. (About 20 per cent of this mass originates as mineral ash from the coking coal.)

In the blast furnace the oxygen in the iron-bearing concentrates reacts with carbon monoxide. The reduction process requires excess CO. The carbon monoxide is actually the reducing agent within the blast furnace. In 1993 just 21.537 MMT of coke were consumed (plus other fuels for heat) to produce pig iron. The coke includes 2.8 MMT of ash from the original coal (28 MMT, at 10 per cent ash), so its carbon content was about 18.7 MMT. Most of this combines with the oxygen in the feed, but pig iron also contains 4.5 per cent C, so 2.16 MMT of the carbon from the coke remains in the metal. Thus $18.70 - 2.16 = 16.54$ MMT of carbon from the coke combines with oxygen to produce a mixture of carbon monoxide (CO) and carbon dioxide (CO_2). The final product, 'blast furnace gas', has excess CO, hence energy value. It can be utilized as low quality fuel within the integrated steel mill or in an electric power plant.

Blast furnace gas averages 25–27 per cent CO and 13–15 per cent CO_2 plus 1–2 per cent H_2 the remainder being nitrogen from the air. (The hydrogen is produced by the reaction of water vapor (steam) and CO, at high temperatures, which yields hydrogen and carbon dioxide.) Based on trial assumptions of 26 per cent CO and 14 per cent CO_2 and knowing the amount of carbon available (16.54 MMT) we can deduce that the total quantity of blast furnace gas produced must have been approximately 232 MMT, embodying close to 58 MMT of oxygen.[15] Of this, 22.5 MMT of oxygen was combined with iron in the blast furnace feed and the remainder (35.5 MMT) came from blast air. Since air is 21.2 per cent oxygen and 78 per cent nitrogen by weight, we can deduce that 169 MMT of air was consumed, containing 132 MMT of nitrogen, or 57 per cent of the BFG. This is slightly inconsistent with our original assumptions and leaves the final product with too much hydrogen, but the balance is near enough for present purposes. A diagrammatic summary of the mass flows in the steel industry (1993) is shown in Figure 5.2.

Major purchased inputs at the reduction stage, other than concentrates, are fluxes. The most important of these is limestone (and dolomite). Data on usage of these materials as fluxing agents in smelting and steelmaking are not provided by the US Bureau of Mines. However, one clue is the fact that iron slag from US blast furnaces (12.3 MMT) averages 41 per cent CaO and slag from steel furnaces (6.7 MMT) averages 46 per cent CaO (McGannon 1971). The overall average is just over 44 per cent. This calcium oxide in the slag must have originated in the lime – or limestone – used in the blast furnaces or steel furnaces, or in the production of pellets at the iron mines. Iron and steel slag produced in 1993 amounted to 19.0 MMT (MY 'Slag', Table 1). This implies an input of 8.35 MMT of lime or 14.9 MMT of limestone. However, 5.14 MMT of quicklime was consumed by the iron and steel industry as such (MY 'Lime', Table 5). This leaves 3.21 MMT of CaO to be supplied from other sources, most likely embodied in pellets or sinter. This was probably introduced as limestone in the pelletizing process, since the lime appears to be accounted for.

Subsequent refining of pig iron and scrap iron to carbon steel is done in a further refining stage, normally the basic oxygen furnace. In this furnace pure oxygen (separated cryogenically from the nitrogen in air) is blown through molten pig iron to burn off the excess carbon. The process generates enough heat to keep the iron molten even as it becomes purer (and the melting point rises with purity). The final result is nearly pure iron, which can then be converted into carbon steel or alloy steel by the addition of ferromanganese and other ferroalloys in controlled quantities. Steel furnaces produced an additional 6.7 MMT of slag in 1993. However, iron and steel slags are no longer considered wastes, since virtually all slag produced is marketed for a variety of uses, including road surfacing and cement manufacturing

Other inputs to steel-making, as reported by the Bureau of Mines in 1993, included fluorspar (49.7 kMT as a fluxing agent (MY 'Fluorspar', Table 2) and 0.78 MMT of ferroalloys (MY 'Iron and Steel', Tables 16 and 17). The most important ferroalloys were manganese (336 kMT) and ferrochrome (194 kMT). One other input was sulfuric acid for steel pickling (28 kMT) (MY 'Sulfur', Table 7).

Coke ovens and steel rolling mills are significant sources of hazardous wastes, even though the coke oven gas is efficiently captured for use as fuel, and about 44 kMT (N-content) of byproduct ammonia, mainly as ammonium sulfate, is produced as a byproduct. This material is used as fertilizer. Coke is

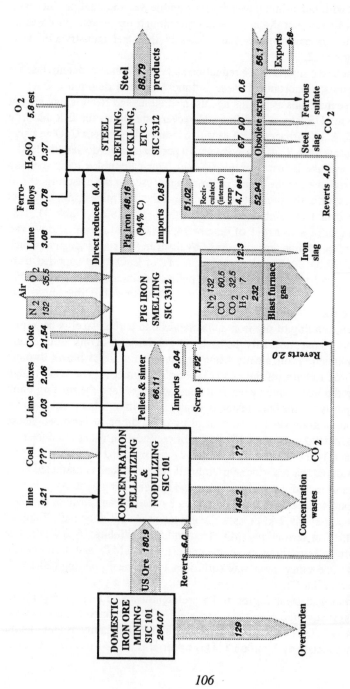

Note: Scrap consumption in iron and steel production is probably underestimated by up to 4 million tonnes. Recirculated scrap may be underestimated by a similar amount.

Figure 5.2   Mass flows in the US iron and steel sectors, 1993 (MMT)

cooled by rapid quenching with water, and some tars, cyanides and other contaminants are unavoidably produced. Unfortunately, materials balances cannot be used to estimate these wastes. However, they probably constitute a significant fraction of both water and airborne wastes from the primary iron and steel sector.

Also, in the rolling process steel is cleaned by an acid bath ('pickling'), resulting in a flow of dilute wastewater containing ferrous sulfate or ferrous chloride (depending on the acid used). The excess acid is usually neutralized by the addition of lime. In 1993 about 0.37 MMT of 100 per cent sulfuric acid (0.074 MMT S content) were used for this purpose, producing 0.57 MMT of ferrous sulfate. Ferrous sulfate can, in principle, be recovered for sale. However the market is insufficient to absorb the quantity potentially available (which is dilute and dirty in any case), whence most is waste.

5.5   Non-ferrous metals smelting, primary (SIC 333)

The major tonnage non-ferrous metals are aluminum, copper, lead and zinc. Gold, silver and uranium are special cases which we discuss separately below. Aluminum is the only important metal that is reduced exclusively by electrolysis, although copper from a copper-bearing solution is also reduced electrolytically in the SX–EW process to 'cathode copper'. Both cathode copper and blister copper from smelters are subsequently refined electrolytically.

Virtually all aluminum ore (bauxite) is imported. The first domestic step in the sequence is to produce pure aluminum oxide (alumina), via the so-called Bayer process (SIC 2819), which was mentioned previously. In 1993 11.92 MMT of (mostly) imported bauxite ore was concentrated to 5.29 MMT of alumina (mostly calcined) in the US and another 3.94 MMT was imported. This process also theoretically consumed 0.039 tons of lime (CaO) and 0.035 tons of caustic soda (NaOH) per ton of alumina (Hall *et al.* 1975). The Bureau of Mines reported consumption of 0.157 MMT of lime for this purpose (MY 'Lime', Table 5), which implies that about 0.15 MMT of caustic soda was also consumed. The concentration waste – an alkaline mixture of silica and iron oxides known as 'red mud' – was therefore 11.92 – 5.29 + 0.39 = 7.02 MMT.

The second step is electrolytic reduction. The alumina is dissolved in a molten bath of cryolite, a sodium–aluminum fluoride, which conducts electricity. The oxygen in the dissolved alumina reacts with a carbon anode, made from petroleum coke. The electrolytic reaction yields a mixture of carbon monoxide and carbon dioxide. If the anode were completely oxidized to CO_2 the theoretical reaction would require 0.333 tons of carbon per ton of metallic aluminum, while if only CO were generated, the carbon requirement would be twice as high, or 0.667 tons/ton. According to one source, a typical reaction consumes 0.51 tons of carbon anode per ton of primary aluminum produced (Hall *et al.* 1975; also Altenpohl 1982 p. 16). In this case the output gas would amount to 1.31 tons/ton and would contain equal amounts of carbon (but unequal amounts of oxygen) in each form, or roughly 39 per cent CO and 71 per cent CO_2 by weight. If the electrolysis is adjusted to utilize carbon anodes more efficiently, the output gas will contain a correspondingly smaller percentage of carbon monoxide. Apparently the output mix from the cell currently contains between 10 per cent and 20 per cent carbon monoxide (anon. US Bureau of Mines). The oxygen is derived entirely from the alumina, of course.

US production of aluminum metal in 1993 was 3.695 MMT, so we assume that carbon anode consumption was 1.88 MMT. Then, according to our 'theoretical' reaction, waste gas from the electrolytic reaction was 4.84 MMT, of which 1.84 MMT was CO. This gas (which also probably contains a small amount of hydrogen) would have had some fuel value and it could possibly have been used in the anode manufacturing process. Eventually, of course, the carbon monoxide would have been completely oxidized, whence the total CO_2 output from aluminum production in 1993 was probably about 6.92 MMT.

According to older process descriptions, primary aluminum plants con-sumed about 20 kg of fluorine per metric ton of aluminum, partly as hydrofluoric acid (HF) and partly as particulates. This is due to the gradual breakdown of cryolite at the anode. Losses are compensated by inputs of aluminum fluoride. However, fluorides are toxic and the aluminum industry now recycles about 90 per cent of the fluorides, reducing actual makeup F consumption to about 2 kg/metric ton (Altenpohl 1997). Total airborne emis-sions in 1993 from primary aluminum production in the US (3.695 MMT) were, therefore, 3.0 MMT of CO_2 (from the coke), 0.15 MMT of alumina particulates (Al_2O_3) and also about 7 kMT of fluorides (F equivalent).

In the case of heavy metals from sulfide ores (copper, lead, zinc, nickel, molybdenum, and so on), the sulfur is oxidized to SO_2. Roughly 1 metric ton of sulfur is associated with each metric ton of copper smelted, 0.43 metric tons of sulfur per metric ton of zinc, and 0.15 metric tons of sulfur per metric ton of lead. Most of this sulfur (90 per cent) is now captured and immediately converted to sulfuric acid. In 1993, byproduct sulfuric acid (100 per cent basis), was produced at US non-ferrous metal refineries, as follows: copper (3.643 MMT), zinc (0.398 MMT), lead (0.202 MMT), for a total of 4.242 MMT, or 1.40 MMT (S content) (MY 'Copper', Table 8). In the case of copper, most of this acid (2.28 MMT) was used by mines for leaching copper ores for the SX–EW process (MY 'Sulfur', Table 7).

As mentioned previously, leaching accounted for a significant proportion (27 per cent) of copper concentrates produced in the US in 1993. In fact, 262

MMT of crude copper and copper–molybdenum ore was mined and concentrated by flotation in 1993, yielding 1.266 MMT of copper, while 28.707 MMT of ore was mined and leached, yielding 0.491 MMT of copper. Other metal ores and precipitates from old tailings added another 65 kMT of recoverable copper (MY 'Copper', Table 5). Thus 1.801 MMT of recoverable copper in the form of concentrates was produced in 1993 along with 291.3 MMT of copper flotation and leaching wastes.

The next stage in the traditional sequence is smelting. Copper concentrates, together with limestone, silica and scrap copper, are roasted and smelted. In the case of copper smelting, typical concentrates fed to the smelter/convertor consist of 27 per cent Cu (Edelstein 1993, Table 9), 25–30 per cent S and 43–48 per cent other minerals, principally iron. The most important copper mineral is chalcopyrite ($CuFeS_2$). Sulfur dioxide is driven off and recovered as byproduct sulfuric acid, as already noted. The process typically involves two stages, although there are a number of variants. The first output of chalcopyrite ore smelting is typically a mixture of copper and iron sulfides ($CU_2S \cdot FeS$) known as 'matte'. This is subsequently 'converted' by oxidation of the copper, iron and sulfur. The latter is converted to SO_2. Silica (SiO_2) is added in the convertor where it combines with the iron oxide to form a molten slag ($FeO \cdot SiO_2$) that floats on top of the heavier molten copper. The oxidation reactions are all exothermic and no reductant is needed. However, in practice, some fuel (natural gas or coal) is consumed to achieve the high temperatures that are necessary.

Based on relatively old process descriptions it can be estimated that about 0.336 MMT of limestone was used in the smelting process, along with 1.07 MMT of silica (Gaines 1980). These combined with the iron and other minerals in the ore. According to the same source, 0.334 tons of 'waste gas and dust' are generated, along with 3.2 tons of slag per ton of refined copper (ibid.). Thus, the gaseous wastes and slag produced in the standard blister process in 1993 would have been roughly 0.42 MMT and 4.2 MMT respectively. Newer 'flash' technology (which has largely replaced the earlier roasting stage) has probably changed the numbers, somewhat, but we have no current data on wastes. We also have no information on wastes from the newer acid leach SX–EW process; however there is reason to believe that substantial quantities of lime may be needed for acid neutralization purposes (see endnote 13).

Blister copper production in 1993 from domestic ores (1.270 MMT) and electrowon (cathode) copper from the SX–EW process (0.491 MMT), are further refined electrolytically to yield very pure (> 99 per cent) anode copper. Copper refinery output in 1993 was 1.790 MMT (MY 'Copper', Table 6) which included 88.6 kMT from imported materials.

Based on the 1991 survey on froth flotation, 585 kMT of lead concentrate (74 per cent Pb), 560 kMT of zinc concentrate (56 per cent Zn), plus 95 kMT of lead–zinc concentrate (31 per cent Pb–Zn) was recovered from 12.33 MMT of domestic lead–zinc ores (Edelstein 1993, Table 11). The recoverable lead in these domestic concentrates was about 448 kMT. The main lead mineral is lead sulfide or galena (PbS). Concentration is accomplished by a series of flotation operations (which also separate recoverable copper and zinc fractions). Lead concentrates are about 74 per cent Pb (Edelstein 1993, Table 11), 11 per cent S and 15 per cent other. The concentration wastes for these lead–zinc ores in 1991 was therefore 12.33 − (0.585 + 0.095) = 11.68 MMT.

In addition, 193 kMT of zinc concentrate (63 per cent Zn) was produced from 2.87 MMT of domestic zinc ores (Edelstein 1993, Table 12), for an implied concentration waste of 2.87 − 0.19 = 2.68 MMT. The main zinc mineral is the sulfide, sphalerite (ZnS). Total recoverable zinc accounted for in 1991 was approximately 449 kMT, in 848 kMT of concentrates, of which 655 kMT was from lead–zinc ores and the rest from zinc ores.

In 1993, according to Minerals Yearbook 4.008 MMT of lead ore was mined, and overburden waste was specified as 533 kMT (MY 'Mining and Quarrying Trends', Table 2). Recoverable lead content of domestic ore in 1993 was 355 kMT (MY 'Lead', Table 1). This implies an ore grade of 8.9 per cent, which is implausibly high. Based on the figures for 1991 in the previous paragraphs the lead–zinc ore grade was actually 3.62 per cent (Pb). This implies that for 1993, when recoverable lead content was 0.355 MMT, the amount of lead–zinc ore mined in the US should have 9.8 MMT; concentration waste from that ore would have been 81 per cent of the 1991 number, or 9.25 MMT.

Again, using 1991 ratios, this implies zinc concentrates from lead–zinc ores of 455 kMT for 1993 (plus 72 kMT of lead–zinc concentrate) containing about 265 kMT of recoverable zinc. Total recoverable zinc mined from all domestic ores in 1993 was 488 kMT. Thus, 223 kMT (Zn), or 355 kMT of zinc concentrates, must have been from zinc ores (that is, not from lead–zinc ores), considerably more than the 121 kMT attributed to 2.87 MMT of such ores in 1991. Using this ratio, 1993 zinc ore output would have been a factor of 1.84 (223/121) more than the 1991 level, or 5.29 MMT. In fact, 5.942 MMT of crude zinc ore was mined in the US in 1993, plus overburden and other waste of 0.352 MMT (MY 'Mining and Quarrying Trends', Table 2). Based on the latter number, zinc ore concentrations wastes must have been 5.942 − 0.355 = 5.587 MMT in 1993. The zinc ore grade in 1993 was thus 223/5.942 = 3.75 per cent (Zn).

The smelting step for lead begins with sintering. The sinter process converts sulfides to oxides and drives off the sulfur dioxide, which is captured to produce sulfuric acid. Limestone and silica are added, as in the case of copper, to combine with the metallic impurities. The lead does not oxidize, despite the presence of oxygen, because the oxygen combines preferentially with carbon. Coke is not actually a reductant in this case either. In 1993 lead smelted and refined from domestic ores amounted to 310 kMT, plus another 25 kMT from imported lead concentrates (MY 'Lead', Table 4).

Based on published process descriptions we estimate that 0.58 MMT of limestone and 0.38 MMT of silica were consumed in the lead sinter process, along with 0.24 MMT of coke, and 0.4 MMT of slag, dust and 'reverts' (Burkle 1980). Dust and reverts are recycled. The final waste outputs would have been about 0.52 MMT of slag and 3 kMT of lead-bearing particulates, along with significant quantities of blast-furnace gas containing a mixture of CO, CO_2 and H_2 similar in composition to that from iron-smelting. Lacking details of the process, we assume for simplicity that this off-gas is generated in the same proportions to coke input as in iron smelting, whence it would have consisted of a mixture of carbon monoxide (about 0.67 MMT), carbon dioxide (about 0.36 MMT) plus nitrogen from the air (1.55 MMT) and a little hydrogen. When the blast furnace gas was burned, the final CO_2 generation would have been about 1.41 MMT.

Zinc concentrate is converted first to impure zinc oxide by roasting and calcining. Some is consumed directly in this form (by the tire industry). The remainder is reduced to metallic form (slab zinc). The electrolytic process involves dissolving the oxide in sulfuric acid, followed by electrodeposition on aluminum cathodes. The electrothermic process involves reducing the oxide by smelting in a furnace with coke. Primary zinc metal refined in the US in 1993 was 240 kMT, of which 26 kMT was from imported foreign concentrates (MY 'Zinc', Table 4). (Secondary sources added 141 kMT.)

We have insufficient process information to estimate slag and other waste output, except by analysis of the composition of the concentrate. In the case of zinc, a typical average concentrate would be about 60 per cent Zn and 30 per cent S, with other minerals (for example, iron) accounting for 10 per cent. Since the smelter feed is relatively pure zinc sulfide, slag production is small. An informal estimate by a commodity specialist at the US Bureau of Mines is 100 kg/metric ton. We have no information on fuel input or waste gas output.

Total slag production for the three main non-ferrous metals was therefore roughly 4.7 MMT in total. The production and smelting waste numbers for other non-ferrous metals (except gold) are insignificant. Silver is almost entirely produced as a byproduct of copper, zinc or lead. Uranium mining was important a few years ago, but uranium no longer appears to be produced to a significant extent in the US.[17] A diagrammatic summary of the mass flows for the US non-ferrous metals industries (1993) is shown in Figure 5.3.

In summary, the total solid materials handled associated with metals mining in the US in 1993 was about 2070 MMT, excluding water used for flotation. Of this 1313.5 MMT (dry weight), was overburden. Concentration

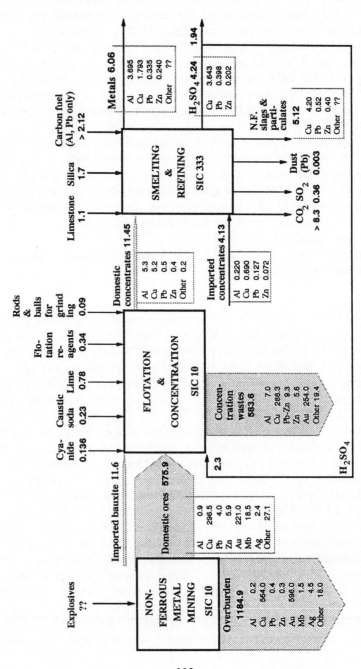

Figure 5.3   *Mass flows in the US non-ferrous metals sector, 1993 (MMT)*

112

wastes were an additional 727.1 MMT, leaving 77.7 MMT of concentrates produced domestically. (The ratio of concentration waste to concentrate is almost 9.5:1.) Smelting yielded 54.62 MMT of crude primary metals, mainly pig iron, from 90.85 MMT of concentrates (including imports and reverts). Altogether, based on mass-balance considerations (see Figures 5.2 and 5.3), we estimate solid smelting and refining wastes for primary metals, excluding CO_2, to have been 5.1 MMT in 1993, embodying calcium, silicon and other light oxides used in the non-ferrous smelters and refineries. In addition, about 19 MMT of iron/steel slag was produced, which was marketed commercially, mainly for road ballast.

As regards gaseous wastes, they consist of a mix of carbon monoxide and carbon dioxide, embodying the oxygen content of the original ores – mostly iron ore – which is released as CO and CO_2).[18] In the case of iron smelting and lead smelting the gas is 'blast furnace gas' with enough fuel value to be used as a heat source, for example, by electric generating plants. In these two cases, and also for aluminum, we have attempted a rough calculation. Gaseous wastes also included about 0.15 MMT of S (in SO_2), and some fluorides from aluminum smelters. We have not included the airborne or waterborne wastes from coal or petroleum coking. The major airborne emissions from smelting, other than CO_2, are CO, NO_x and particulates. In both cases, blast furnaces are the major sources. The coking quench waters and some spent acids used for pickling constitute the major waterborne wastes. However, these wastes cannot be estimated by mass-balance techniques.

We also note that explosives used in mining and quarrying probably generated around 0.4 MMT of NO_x and 0.1 MMT of N_2O in 1993, although much of this should be attributed to coal mining and stone quarrying. Finally, we note again the use of very toxic cyanide in gold mining, at the rate of 410 tons of potassium cyanide per ton of gold taken from the ground.

Water used in the flotation processes for metal and phosphate ore and concentration in 1985 was 3580 MMT, as noted above, but much of this – perhaps half or more – was for phosphates. The 1983 Census of Manufactures reported water intake by the entire mining sector (including coal, oil and gas) to be 4500 MMT (3280 mgd), while reported discharges were only 3900 MMT (2840 mgd), implying an evaporative loss of 600 MMT. Since the flotation processes alone account for much more than this, it is hard to reconcile the figures. Either some of the flotation water is actually discharged (or seeps) into rivers, or the coal mining, oil and gas sectors produce much more water than they consume. The latter seems likely. Actually, EPA reported that the oil and gas sector alone produced somewhere in the neighborhood of 1800 to 2400 MMT of excess water, which would help to explain the apparent discrepancy. In any case, the Census data seem to be incomplete, since 12 per cent of the water withdrawals was designated as for

'cooling' (mainly in the gas fractionation sector) and 44 per cent was designated as 'process', while the remaining 44 per cent was unallocated. Clearly,
a much more detailed study of water use and waste production in the mining
sector seems called for.

An EPA contractor, Science Applications Inc. (SAI), estimated the 1983
solid wastes from iron and steel production at 6.0 MMT and from non-
ferrous metals at 6.5 MMT (SAI 1985). These estimates were not specifically
designated as 'dry' so some water content can be presumed. EPA estimates
airborne emissions from the primary metals sector as a whole to be 2.8 MMT,
including particulates and CO, but not including CO_2 (USEPA 1991). Both
sets of estimates are roughly consistent with the above.

Endnotes

1. We want to express our particular appreciation for assistance by Marilyn Biviano, Chief,
   and several of the commodity specialists at the Mineral and Materials Analysis Section,
   US Geological Survey (formerly US Bureau of Mines), who kindly reviewed a draft of
   this chapter and corrected numerous errors and misunderstandings. Particular thanks are
   due to Dan Edelstein and Hendrik van Ost. They are not responsible for any remaining
   errors.
2. In the case of iron, concentrates for blast furnaces (pellets and sinter) are treated differently. Pellets are produced at the mine, while sinter is included in the smelting sector
   rather than in the mining sector. For consistency, we adopt this convention. In the case of
   aluminum, the 'concentration' stage is taken to be the chemical conversion of bauxite ore
   into pure aluminum oxide (alumina). This process is conventionally included in the
   inorganic chemical industry (SIC 2819). Phosphate rock concentration (yielding fertilizer
   grade 'superphosphate' is included in the fertilizer industry (SIC 2873). Phosphorus metal
   and phosphoric acid from phosphorus are both also included with inorganic chemicals in
   SIC 2819.
3. Data on materials handled is from MY (1993 edition), pp. 45–9. The rest of the data on
   metals and minerals came from individual chapters. We also utilize a recent publication of
   the World Resources Institute, entitled *Resource Flows: the Material Basis of Industrial
   Economies* (Adriaanse *et al.* 1997).
4. We have calculated concentration wastes in Table 5.1 as the difference between gross ores
   and product. This does not distinguish between concentration wastes occurring outside
   the US from exported raw ore and domestic concentration wastes, but with the exception
   of potash, very little non-concentrated ore is exported. This table also neglects mass
   inputs (such as lime) to the concentration process.
5. Calcination splits the carbonate $CaCO_3 \rightarrow CaO + CO_2$. The atomic weights of calcium,
   carbon and oxygen are 40, 12 and 16 respectively, adding up to 100. The molecular
   weight of CO_2 is 44.
6. But this same number was mislabelled in the table and appeared both under the headings
   'crude ore' and 'total'.
7. By comparison, WRI calculated a 'hidden flow' of 183 MMT, which was probably arrived
   at by subtracting the whole 35.5 MMT of current production from a very similar estimate
   of total materials handled (Adriaanse et al., 1997). At any rate, we take this as confirmation
   of our estimate of overburden.
8. The published information on molybdenum is rather confused. In an earlier US Bureau of
   Mines report it was stated that 170 million short tons of materials were handled at
   molybdenum mines in the US in 1988, of which 140 million short tons were attributed to
   'crude ore' at surface mines (MY 1989 'Mining and Quarrying Trends', Table 2). However these numbers appear to be inconsistent with information on molybdenum ore grade,

which ranges between 0.2–0.5 per cent molybdenite (MbS_2) in molybdenum deposits, and from 0.02–0.08 per cent molybdenite in copper ores (MY 'Molybdenum', p. 671). These disparate figures are mutually consistent if (and only if) the 'materials handled' data from the 1989 'Minerals Yearbook' include copper ore processed for molybdenum recovery. But, in that case, one cannot arrive at a total 'materials handled' by adding molybdenum together with copper. No doubt the same problem arises with respect to silver, lead and other metals that are extracted partly as byproducts.

9. Data given in the survey report applies only to respondents. Only 133 plants provided details, out of 260 possible. Of the respondents, 85 were metal or mineral producers and 48 were coal producers. Of the 130 non-respondents, 100 were coal cleaning plants (probably small operators) and 30 were metal or mineral producers. Coverage of metallic sulfide concentration plants was estimated to be 90 per cent of production; coverage of iron ore producers was estimated to be 85 per cent of output; coverage of mineral preparation plants was estimated to be 85 per cent for phosphates and glass sand, 75 per cent for potash, and 58 per cent for feldspar; no attempt was made to estimate the fractional coverage in the case of coal.

10. In the past (and even today in small-scale or illegal mining operations) gold in very fine grains was aggregated and recovered by amalgamation with mercury. The combined mercury–gold amalgam was then heated to drive off the mercury (which boils at a low temperature), leaving the gold. This process is causing significant mercury pollution in several parts of the world, such as in the Amazon region of Brazil and parts of West Africa.

11. The figure actually given was only for the state of Nevada, but it was also stated that Nevada accounted for 55 per cent of US consumption of cyanide for gold ore processing. We made the appropriate adjustment.

12. Ammonium nitrate is $NH_4.NO_3$. An explosive, by definition, is unstable. In the presence of a little heat to ignite the reaction, the atoms recombine preferentially into water vapor ($2H_2O$) and N_2O. In the presence of oxygen there will also be other products, such as NO and NO_2.

13. The estimates for aluminum and bauxite were based on data in MY 'Lime', Table 5. Tonnage data for copper and 'other' were suppressed and only dollar value data were included in that table. We assumed that the average price for lime used by the copper and 'other' ore concentration activities was the same as the average price paid for lime used in the aluminum industry, where tonnages were given. As it happens, this calculation agrees almost exactly with the estimate extrapolated from 1991 data on froth flotation, as discussed in the text (Edelstein 1993). We cannot account for 'other', but the most plausible use is the SX–EW process for copper extraction, which consumes large amounts of sulfuric acid and might reasonably be expected to require significant quantities of lime for acid neutralization.

14. This material is usually called 'pig' iron for historical reasons. It was formerly solidified in ingots called 'pigs'. Nowadays most crude iron moves on to the steel furnace as a liquid, to conserve energy.

15. The equations are $C = [(12/28)(CO/BFG) + (12/44)(CO_2/BFG)]BFG$ and $O_x = [(16/28)(CO/BFG) + (32/44)(CO_2/BFG)]BFG$ where BFG is the quantity of blast furnace gas produced, O is the quantity of oxygen consumed, CO and CO_2 are the quantities of monoxide and dioxide generated respectively and C is the quantity of carbon available from the coke (16.54). We have four unknowns. A third and fourth equation result from assuming $CO = 0.26$ BFG and $CO_2 = 0.14$ BFG. Substituting, we get $16.54 = 0.0438$ BFG $+ 0.0273$ BFG $= 0.0711$ BFG and $O = 0.148$ BFG $+ 0.102$ BFG $= 0.250$ BFG. Solving, we obtain BFG $= 16.54/0.0711 = 232$ MMT and $O = 58$ MMT.

16. Uranium mining in the US produced about 15 MMT of ore in 1980. This was reduced (mostly by flotation) to 19.5 kMT of U_3O_8 concentrate ('yellow cake'), which yielded 4.74 kMT of refined uranium oxide (nuclear fuel). Thus 3600 tons of ore were needed to produce one ton of concentrated UO_2 pellets (LeBel 1982, Table 6.1). Uranium production in the US has been declining sharply; production in 1991 was 0.58 MMT of ore, and 1.15 kMT of 'yellow cake', down 96 per cent from 1980. Uranium mining added 15

6 Chemical industry material flows and wastes: Inorganic chemicals

6.1 Introduction

This chapter and Chapter 7 together comprise a systematic materials flow analysis and derivation of aggregate production wastes for the US chemicals industries (SIC 28), taken as a whole. Most of the inputs to and some of the outputs of the chemical industry can be estimated, with reasonable accuracy, from well-established, albeit scattered, government and industry production statistics. However, as in the earlier chapters, there are serious gaps. Unlike most other sectors of the economy, however, some knowledge of the chemical transformation processes themselves is also needed. Combining both production and process information, it is possible to account for most chemical uses and large volume wastes by means of the materials balance methodology.

All material inputs to the chemical industry, as any industry, must ultimately become outputs, either as products or as wastes, as shown in Figure 6.1. It is not necessary to know much about the details of chemical processes to assert that any inputs not embodied in products must end up in some waste stream. The basic scheme of this chapter and the next requires us to account for both inputs and outputs. The difference, according to the mass balance principle, must be wastes and losses. However, the situation is greatly complicated by the fact that some chemicals are used within the 'boundary walls' of the industry to make other chemicals. As a consequence the total mass of chemicals manufactured within the 'fence' is considerably greater than the mass of feedstock inputs or the mass of outputs 'over the fence'.

In working with the published statistics further complications arise. First, a great many statistics are literally missing, due to laws that forbid the government to publish data that might 'reveal the operations' of an individual firm. The net result is to protect the activities of monopolies or near-monopolies from scrutiny. Due to continuous industry consolidation, with fewer and fewer producers of each chemical, the availability of data to the public has become progressively worse in recent years, as will be seen later.

An additional complication arises from the distinction between 'production' and 'sales'. Sales (or shipments) are always less than (or equal to) production; the difference reflects use *within* an establishment or firm. In general, it is production that is of interest. However, it is useful to have both figures. In fact, when the two figures are identical it can be concluded that the

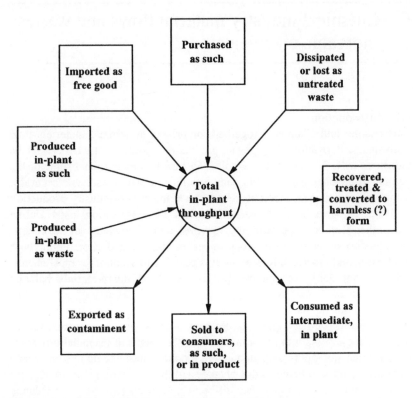

Figure 6.1 Materials balance for a chemical species

product is 'final', that is used as such and not subsequently converted into another chemical product. Conversely, when production of a chemical is much larger than sales, it can be concluded that the product is an intermediate, since most of it is used within the same firm that produced it.

Where appropriate we compare the results of our approach with other published estimates of waste residuals. In several instances, significant discrepancies are identified. One major virtue of our approach is to clearly distinguish between dry and wet wastes. Another virtue is that it enables us to estimate waste streams from dissipative and/or consumptive uses, especially of heavy metals and halogens. The conventional measurement based approach is relatively unsatisfactory in dealing with non-point sources.

Clearly, many chemical products are used dissipatively. This applies to pesticides, solvents, fuel additives, cleaning agents, catalysts, plasticizers, and a number of other categories. We note that certain products such as solvents and cleaning agents, are doubly hard to track if they are widely distributed and ultimately consumed by small businesses, farms or private households that are not covered by the EPA's Toxic Release Inventòry (TRI). These points are not in dispute. However, they raise serious doubts about the value of TRI as an indicator of overall toxic hazard. It is doubts of this sort that have led us to attempt a materials balance analysis of the chemical industry as a whole.

The complexity of the chemical industry, and the large number of its products make this task difficult. However, some simplification is possible by focussing attention very strictly on inputs to, and 'final' products of the industry, disregarding intermediate conversions for the most part (except with regard to production losses). Because many chemical products are used largely, or entirely, to make other chemical products, final output tonnage is considerably smaller than total production. For example, European production of elemental chlorine in 1992 was 8.61 MMT, while only 1.367 MMT was shipped outside the industry. The remainder, 7.322 MMT was either consumed or lost within the industry (Ayres and Ayres 1997).

For our purposes it is convenient to classify chemicals by key element(s) rather than by four digit SIC's, although there is obviously some correspondence.[1] The major categories are: nitrogen-based, sulfur-based, phosphorus-based, halogen-based, sodium-based, other metal-based, and carbon-based (organic). The organic group can be further subdivided into chemicals built from methanol and light olefins, chemicals based on aromatics (benzene, toluene, xylene) and chemicals based on fatty acids and other organics. The organic chemicals are discussed in Chapter 7.

6.2 Nitrogen-based chemicals[2]

Ammonia, most ammonia compounds, nitric acid and urea all belong to the fertilizer group SIC 2873. Fixed nitrogen (in the form of ammonia and its derivatives) is an interesting case, since the nitrogen is from the atmosphere, combined with hydrogen from natural gas and steam. The theoretical synthesis reaction (which occurs only at high temperatures and pressures) is $3CH_4 + 6H_2O + 4N_2 \rightarrow 8NH_3 + 3CO_2$ which implies that 1 ton of ammonia requires 0.353 tons of methane and 0.795 tons of water (steam) as feedstocks and generates 0.97 tons of carbon dioxide, not including the carbon dioxide produced by combustion for heat.

In reality, synthesis reactions are not quite so efficient, but the CO_2 output (which takes up all of the carbon) is necessarily proportional to the methane input, in the ratio of atomic weights (44/16 = 2.74). In one commercial process 0.479 tons of natural gas are consumed as 'feed' per ton of ammonia, in addition to 0.0971 tons/ton as fuel (SRI 1989). Based on this process gross 1993 US ammonia production of 15.65 MMT (12.87 MMT, N) would have required very nearly 9 MMT of methane, mainly (83 per cent or 7.48 MMT) for feedstock. The methane feed embodied 5.61 MMT of carbon and 1.87 MMT of hydrogen, whence 0.92 MMT of hydrogen must have been derived from steam. This implies a water input (as feed) of 8.28 MMT. The ammonia synthesis process would have generated 20.55 MMT of CO_2 from the methane used as feedstock, not including the contribution from fuel combustion. The oxygen balance works out as 14.94 MMT in the carbon dioxide, of which $8.28 - 0.92 = 7.36$ MMT was derived from feedwater and the rest (7.58 MMT) from the air.

In addition to US production, an additional 2.28 MMT (N) was imported (net) for consumption, for a total ammonia supply of 15.145 MMT (N). In addition, there were significant imports and exports of other N-chemicals. The major (net) import item was urea (1.363 MMT, N) and the total of imports was 1.856 MMT (N) and a total mass of 5.087 MMT. Major US export items were ammonium phosphates (1.424 MMT, N), urea (0.303 MMT, N) and ammonium sulfate (0.159 MMT, N). The total of these exports was 2.036 MMT (N), with a total mass of 10.565 MMT.

Fertilizers consumed in the US in 1993 accounted for 68 per cent of the total ammonia supply, or 10.314 MMT (N) (MY 'Nitrogen', Table 6). The biggest single use of ammonia was to manufacture urea (23.3 per cent), followed by direct fertilizer use of anhydrous ammonia (21.7 per cent), ammonium phosphates (16.2 per cent), nitric acid (10.9 per cent), and ammonium nitrate (8.6 per cent). Ammonium sulfate is also an important fertilizer but most of it is a byproduct of other chemical processes or coke ovens; it accounts for very little of the ammonia (0.7 per cent). All other uses of ammonia accounted for 18.5 per cent of supply (see Figure 6.2).

The most important first level uses of ammonia other than those already mentioned are hydrogen cyanide (HCN), acrylonitrile (ACN) and caprolactam. HCN is a starting point for several chains, including methyl methacrylate (MMA), although the latter actually contains no nitrogen. Acrylonitrile is a major ingredient of synthetic rubber and acrylic fibers. Caprolactam is the monomer of nylon 6. Aniline, an important dye and epoxy intermediate, is derived from nitric acid via nitrobenzene. Adipic acid, a nylon-66 monomer, is manufactured from phenol or cyclohexanol by a process that also uses nitric acid, but adipic acid itself contains no nitrogen. Melamine, another important plastic monomer, is made from urea.

Overall output of these N-based materials in 1993 was much larger than their nitrogen content, as might be expected. Production of ACN was 1.129 MMT (27.5 per cent N); caprolactam output was 0.65 MMT (13.1 per cent N); aniline production was 0.449 MMT (15 per cent N); MMA output was 0.521 MMT (0 per cent N), while melamine output was 0.122 MMT (66.7 per cent N) (CEN 1995). Production of HCN in 1988 was 282 kMT (N), or 544 kMT total. We do not have data on HCN for 1993.

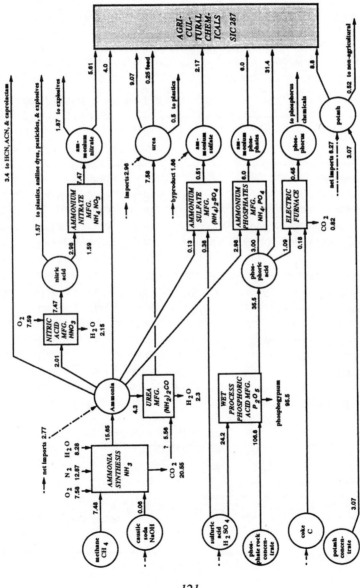

Figure 6.2 Materials flows in the production of agricultural chemicals in the US, 1993 (MMT)

A more detailed account of nitrogen flows for the US economy for 1988 has been given elsewhere (Ayres and Ayres 1996). In that year ammonia supply was 14.746 MMT (N), nearly the same as in 1993. The main results are summarized in Figure 6.2 which accounted for 96 per cent of the total supply (production plus imports) in that year. The two major categorical uses of nitrogen chemicals, other than for fertilizers and animal feed, for plastics, synthetic fibers and rubber (for example, melamine, nylon, nitriles) and explosives, which took 4.5 per cent and 5.25 per cent respectively of the N. Table 6.1 shows US production of major N-based chemicals in both 1988 and 1993.

One process–product chain that is of special interest is the cyanide family. It begins with ammonia, which is partially oxidized to an intermediate, hydro-

Table 6.1   US production of major N-based chemicals, 1988 and 1993

		1988		1993	
	N%	kMT	kMT(N)	kMT	kMT(N)
Total counted		31629	12888	31587	13285
Urea[a]	46.6	7826	3650	8308	3875
Ammonia, 100%	82.2	7630	6275	7647	6289
Ammonium nitrate, 100%	35.0	3404	1191	3744	1310
Nitric acid, 100%	22.2	3625	806	3744	832
Terephthalic acid + DMT	3.3	4642	155	3223	108
Acrylonitrile-butadiene-styrene[b]	6.5	1097	71	1326	86
Acrylonitrile	26.4	1112	294	1129	298
Ammonium sulfate, 100%	21.2	1058	224	1100	233
Aniline	15.0	467	70	450	68
Polyamide, nylon type[c]	12.1	257	31	348	42
Ethanolamines[d]	15.2	276	42	320	49
Melamine	66.6	94	63	122	82
Nitrile rubber[e]	9.2	75	7	78	7
Styrene-acrylonitrile[f]	13.2	67	9	48	6
Nitrogen	*100.0*	*24176*	*24176*	*26654*	*26654*

Notes:
[a] Includes thermosetting resins.
[b] Includes other styrene polymers.
[c] Composition assumed similar to Nylon 66.
[d] Composition assumed average of mono-, di-, tri- ethanolamine.
[e] Composition assumed to be 35 per cent acrylonitrile and 65 per cent butadiene.
[f] Styrene polymer.

Source: CEN 1996.

cyanic (prussic) acid, HCN. About 25 per cent of the HCN output is a byproduct of acrylonitrile (ACN). One of the uses of HCN is to manufacture methyl methacrylate, MMA (better known as 'plexiglass') with ammonium bisulfate as a byproduct that contains the nitrogen. Another major use is to manufacture adiponitrile, an intermediate for hexamethylene diamine (HMD), which is another nylon (610) monomer. A third major use of HCN is to make sodium or potassium cyanide (by direct reaction of HCN with NaOH or KOH). These chemicals are extensively used in gold, silver and copper mining, and also to a minor extent for metal plating and lead–zinc or copper–zinc ore flotation. Some complex ferri-cyanides are also still used as pigments, such as Paris blue and Prussian blue. All uses of metallic cyanides accounted for about 85 kMT (N) in 1988, and significantly more in 1993, due to expansion of gold mining activity. We note that, despite the extreme toxicity of these chemicals, they are being dispersed into the environment in large quantities, but almost totally unknown to the public due to lack of published data.

We have not attempted a complete rebalance of the N-chemical subsector for 1993. Overall, the allocation of N-based chemicals in 1993 was not much different from the 1988 allocation. Since it is impossible to be precise, we assume hereafter that 15 per cent of fixed nitrogen (that is, 2.7 MMT of ammonia) is consumed downstream in the production of synthetic organic chemicals such as plastics, synthetic fibers, synthetic rubber, organic dyes and drugs.

Process losses of nitrogenous chemicals within the sector are probably at least 2 per cent, bearing in mind the large number of small volume products not specifically listed. In terms of pollution of the environment, the 2 per cent loss rate suggested above is insignificant in comparison with dissipative uses of nitrogenous chemicals, of course. As mentioned in the last chapter, explosive decomposition of ammonium nitrate generates some N_2O. Adipic acid production also apparently generates N_2O, at least as it was carried out a few years ago (Thiemens and Trogler 1991). The adipic acid process may have been modified since then, however, either to capture the nitrous oxide or to reduce it catalytically. Based on estimated nitric acid inputs, the loss by this route alone for 1988 would have been 60 kMT (N) or about 95 kMT (N_2O).

6.3 Sulfur-based chemicals[3]

The major sulfur-containing natural raw materials are – or were – gypsum (hydrated calcium sulfate), 'alum' (hydrated aluminum sulfate), sodium sulfate, pyrites, sulfide minerals (ores of copper, lead and zinc), natural gas, petroleum, coal and elemental sulfur. Gypsum is used to make plaster-of-Paris and other building materials, but not chemicals, so we ignore it hereafter. Sulfur in coal is not economically recoverable at present, except as synthetic gypsum. We discussed this possibility briefly in Chapter 5. Most sulfur resources for the chemical industry are converted first either to elemental sulfur (S) or sulfuric acid (H_2). The exception is sodium sulfate (0.651 MMT), about half of which (0.322 MMT) was obtained from natural sources in 1993, mainly brines. Of course, synthetic sodium sulfate is a byproduct (or co-product) of other uses of sulfuric acid involving the neutralization of sodium hydroxide.

Elemental sulfur produced in the US in 1993 was 2.753 MMT (MY 'Sulfur', Table 1). In the past the primary source was natural deposits recovered by the so-called Frasch process. Elemental sulfur is now mostly recovered from natural gas processors and petroleum refineries. What is recovered in petroleum refineries was mostly also used there (0.959 MMT S-content), although some acid is also regenerated. Sulfuric acid production in the US was 35.40 MMT 100 per cent acid (11.886 MMT (S) in 1993) and the grand total of sulfur produced in elemental form or as acid was 14.639 MMT (S) (MY 'Sulfur', Table 7).

The acid is derived from elemental sulfur by controlled catalytic oxidation. It is mostly a product of the inorganic chemical industry, subsector SIC 28193, although it is also (as previously noted) a byproduct of copper, lead and zinc smelting. As noted in Chapter 5, smelters produced 1.387 MMT (S) but again, much of that (0.746 MMT S-content) was used in non-ferrous metal mining operations, mainly copper mining, by the acid leach process (MY 'Sulfur', Table 7). In the case of copper mines, copper precipitate (mainly sulfate) is recovered from the leach piles, and this is refined, but much of the leaching acid remains in the ore heaps where it presumably reacts with other minerals and remains as insoluble sulfates. It is the starting point for most sulfur based chemicals. See Figure 6.3.

There are a very few processes that utilize elemental sulfur but not sulfuric acid. In all, 2.753 MMT of elemental sulfur was used in 1993, of which more than 1 MMT was 'unidentified' (ibid.). The use of elemental sulfur in agriculture is classified as SIC 2879 (pesticides and agricultural chemicals not elsewhere classified). This use accounted for a surprising 0.914 MMT of sulfur in 1993. It is used in the sulfite pulping process (for paper), which was described briefly in Chapter 3. It consumed 27 kMT of elemental sulfur in 1992 and probably a similar or slightly larger amount in 1993 (MY 'Sulfur', Table 7). It is also used in beet sugar processing, where it is burned to make SO_2 as a bleach for the sugar syrup. The resulting sulfurous acid is neutralized by lime to form calcium sulfite, a waste (or soil conditioner). Elemental sulfur was consumed in significant quantities (571 kMT) in petroleum refining (SIC 29), possibly to make sulfur dioxide for bleaching purposes.

Only 260 kMT of elemental sulfur was specifically known to be used within the chemical industry (SIC 28) of which 74 kMT of that was for pigments, many of them metallic sulfides (MY 'Sulfur', Table 7). Other

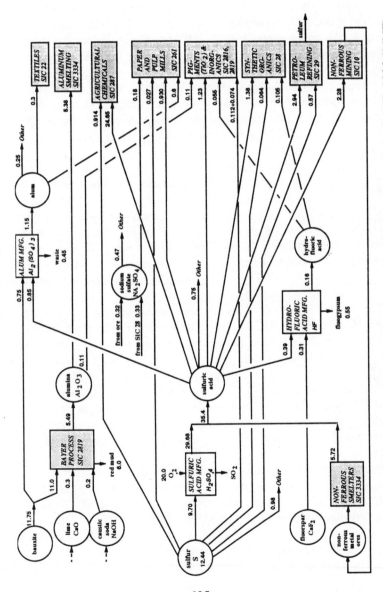

Figure 6.3 Materials flows in the production of major sulfur-based chemicals in the US, 1993 (MMT)

inorganic chemical uses of elemental sulfur (122 kMT S) include production of carbon disulfide (CS_2), sodium tetrasulfide, and phosphorus pentasulfide. Carbon disulfide is a former starting point for rayon, carbon tetrachloride and CFCs. We estimate, below, that phosphorus pentasulfide (a starting point for some downstream phosphorus chemicals) accounted for 30–35 kMT of elemental sulfur; it could be as much as 50 kMT).

Virtually all of the 64 kMT elemental sulfur reportedly consumed in SIC 2822 (synthetic rubber) must have been used for vulcanizing purposes, mainly for tires. The sulfur remains in the rubber and accounts for the stink when tires are burned. Tires contain around 1.5 per cent sulfur in relation to total weight, but closer to 6 per cent in relation to synthetic rubber content (Guelorget *et al.* 1993). Since US production of synthetic rubber was 1.993 MMT in 1993 (MY 'Nonrenewable Organics', Table 13), it would appear that tires and other rubber products should have embodied around 120 kMT (S). Thus about 56 kMT is unaccounted for. However, we have no further information on this point.

The biggest single use of sulfuric acid, already mentioned, is in phosphate rock processing. As noted in Chapter 5, crude phosphate ore produced in 1993 (after beneficiation by flotation) was 106.790 MMT to which 24.2 MMT of sulfuric acid was added during treatment. This accounted for 7.906 MMT (S) in 1993, or 54 per cent of the total supply. The sulfur used in this process is embodied directly in the concentration waste stream (as phospho-gypsum). The quantity of fertilizer grade phosphoric acid was 35.494 MMT The difference (95.5 MMI) was concentration waste, none of which is currently utilized for any purpose.

The second biggest use of sulfuric acid outside the chemical industry was in petroleum refining (SIC 29, 291). The acid is typically made on site from sulfur recovered from gas or petroleum, and is used basically for purposes of bleaching. Altogether this use accounted for 0.959 MMT (S) in 1993 (MY 'Sulfur', Table 7). Another important use of sulfuric acid outside the chemical industry is in the sulfate (Kraft) pulping process, which accounted for 0.934 MMT or 0.304 MMT (S), also discussed previously in Chapter 3. The 'pickling' process for cleaning rolled steel prior to galvanizing or tin-plating used 28 kMT (S) as acid. Automotive batteries accounted for a further 28 kMT (S).

Inorganic chemicals, including fertilizers, consume significant quantities of sulfuric acid. Ammonium sulfate – actually classified as a nitrate fertilizer (SIC 2873) – is the biggest: 2.07 MMT of which 0.526 MMT (S) in 1993 (MY 'Nitrogen', Table 5). But less than a quarter of the ammonium sulfate (23.4 per cent) or 123 kMT (S) was produced directly for fertilizer use as such (MY 'Sulfur', Table 7). The remainder was recycled as a byproduct of other N-chemical processes, mainly hydrogen cyanide (HCN) and caprolactam (one of the monomers for nylon 6,6), as indicated schematically in Figure 6.2.

Aluminum sulfate or 'alum' was once mined (for use as a fixative for dyes). It is now essentially all synthetic, produced from bauxite and sulfuric acid. Total production of aluminum sulfate $(Al_2(SO_4)_3)$ in 1993 was 1.15 MMT (17 per cent Al_2O_3) with a sulfur content of 278 kMT (S) (MY 'Aluminum' Table 18). Based on the chemistry, the process probably required 0.75 MMT of bauxite and 0.85 MMT of sulfuric acid (100 per cent) and generated about 0.45 MMT of waste similar to 'red mud'.

Another big inorganic carrier, but not consumer, of sulfur was synthetic sodium sulfate. The total output of sodium sulfate in the US in 1993 was 651 kMT, of which half – about 325 kMT – was from natural sources (brines) and the rest was probably from byproducts of other chemical processes (MY 'Sodium Sulfate', p. 1094). For instance, cellulosic fibers such as rayon (SIC 2823), consumed 51 kMT (S), or 157 kMT of sulfuric acid in 1993 (MY 'Sulfur', Table 7). Evidently 157 kMT of sulfuric acid inputs, neutralized by 129 kMT of sodium hydroxide, would necessarily yield 228 kMT of sodium sulfate. This process alone would account for most of the synthetic sodium sulfate output.

In 1993 317 kMT (S) as sulfuric acid was used in the 'paint and pigment' sectors (SIC 2816, 285, 286) and 'other' inorganic chemicals sectors (2819) (MY 'Sulfur', Table 7). Most of this presumably was used in the sulfate process for producing titanium dioxide from ilmenite slag, generating impure calcium sulfate as a waste product. (See the discussion of titanium dioxide production, later in this chapter.) Elemental sulfur was used for manufacturing some sulfide pigments.

The 'other inorganic chemicals' category (SIC 2819) consumed 233 kMT (S) as sulfuric acid in 1993 (MY 'Sulfur', Table 7). Inorganic chemicals that actually embody sulfur include aluminum sulfate and sodium sulfate (mentioned above), magnesium sulfate (42.7 kMT, 9.45 kMT S) mainly for animal feeds and fertilizer, copper sulfate (46.4 kMT, 9.27 kMT S), mainly for wood preservatives, and zinc sulfate (20 kMT, 3.96 kMT S). Other processes use the acid but leave the sulfur in a waste. One example is hydrofluoric acid production from fluorspar, by the reaction $CaF_2 + H_2SO_4 \rightarrow 2HF + CaSO_4$. US consumption of acid-grade fluorspar in 1993 was 320.7 kMT (MY 'Fluorspar', Table 2), which yielded 159 kMT of HF and presumably consumed 390 kMT (121.7 kMT S) of sulfuric acid. This process generated 320.7 + 390 – 159 = 552 kMT of 'fluo-gypsum'. None of this waste material is utilized for beneficial purposes, at least in the US, although it could have been used as a substitute for natural gypsum.

Setting aside the aluminum sulfate, and assuming sodium sulfate to be a byproduct, we can account for 144.3 kMT (S) in the 'other inorganic chemicals' category, leaving about 88 kMT (S), or 0.27 MMT of sulfuric acid unaccounted for. Unfortunately, this is not nearly enough to allow for the production of aluminum sulfate ('alum') from bauxite, noted above, which itself must have consumed at least 285 kMT (S) or 0.85 MMT of (100 per cent) sulfuric acid. We can only assume that this use of sulfuric acid – probably by the aluminum producers – was, for some reason, included in the 'unidentified' category, which amounted to 1.832 (S) in 1993, or 12.5 per cent of total consumption (MY 'Sulfur', Table 7). The other possibility is that alum is produced on site by major users, such as integrated pulp and paper companies, which are large sulfuric acid consumers. (These companies are also large sodium sulfate producers, from internally recycled 'black liquor'; the latter production is not fully reported.)

Very few organic chemicals for final use embody sulfur. Most of them are sulfonates, used in detergents. According to the US International Trade Commission's annual report on synthetic organic chemicals, production of sulfonic acids and salts (for detergents) was 0.932 MMT in 1990. Sales of surface active agents of all kinds amounted to 2.013 MMT in 1992 (USITC 1992). (The 1993 edition does not organize the data in a comparable way.) According to the US Bureau of Mines, 45 kMT (S) was embodied in sulfonated fats and oils and related surface-active agents for detergents (mainly SIC 2843) in 1993 (MY 'Sulfur', Table 7). It is reasonable to assume that soap and detergent production has not changed much from 1990 to 1993. This implies that about half of the total mass of surface-active agents consists of sulfonated fatty acids with an average sulfur content of about 4.5 per cent.

Sulfuric acid use in all of the other organic chemicals sectors (including plastics and synthetic rubber (SIC 2822), cellulosics (SIC 2823), drugs (SIC 283), surfactants (SIC 284), industrial organic chemicals (SIC 286), and pesticides (SIC 2879) amounted to 523 kMT (S) (MY 'Sulfur', Table 7). As we have seen, some of this – perhaps 40 kMT (S) – may have been recovered as marketable sodium sulfate from cellulosics, while 45 kMT was embodied in surface active agents (detergents) for final consumption. A much smaller amount, not more than 22 kMT, was embodied in drugs and pesticides. The remainder (we estimate 425 kMT (S) plus or minus 20 kMT (S)) was lost in processing within the organic chemical industry sectors.

In 1989, 0.72 MMT (S) of 'spent' sulfuric acid was recycled as sulfuric acid (MY 1989 'Sulfur', p. 1033). Most of this recycling was within the petroleum refining industry. There are no recent data on spent acid recovery.

6.4 Phosphorus-based chemicals[4]

Phosphate rock is the only source of phosphorus chemicals, including fertilizers. Phosphoric acid (P_2O_5) is the end product of phosphate rock processing. As noted at the beginning of this chapter, 106.79 MMT of phosphate concentrates were treated in 1993 by the so-called 'wet process'. This process consumed 24.6 MMT of 100 per cent sulfuric acid or 7.906 MMT of embodied sulfur (see Section 6.3), yielding 35.5 MMT of so-called 'superphosphate' (P_2O_5) and 95.9 MMT of 'phospho-gypsum' waste consisting mainly of (impure) calcium sulfate. Evidently this single process accounts for most of the solid waste (in mass terms) from the whole US chemical industry.[5]

Fertilizers (SIC 2873) now account for close to 90 per cent of all phosphorus produced in the US; 82 per cent was consumed domestically and 8 per cent was exported in 1993. The remainder was used for other chemicals. Of the 1993 production (11.940 MMT, P_2O_5 equivalent), exports – mostly as ammonium phosphates – accounted for 1.018 MMT, leaving 10.922 MMT for domestic consumption (MY 'Phosphates', Table 4). Most of this, 9.724 MMT (88.4 per cent) was 'wet process' phosphoric acid (H_3PO_4) (ibid.). Elemental phosphorus production in the US in 1993 was 1.092 MMT (P_2O_5 equivalent), or 445 kMT (P), and only about 6 per cent of this (27 kMT) was reconverted to P_2O_5, for 'triple superphosphate' production. The rest was used to manufacture phosphorus chemicals. A schematic diagram of the relationships among fertilizer chemicals is shown in Figure 6.2.

Actually there is a whole range of sodium phosphates and polyphosphates that are used for soaps, detergents and water softeners. They range from the strongly alkaline ($Na_3P_2O_4$) to the strongly acid (NaH_2PO_4).[6] US production of sodium tripolyphosphate, or STPP ($Na_5P_3O_{10}$), a major water-softening component of synthetic detergents was 0.497 MMT in 1988 (US Department of Commerce 1988), with a phosphorus content of 0.125 MMT. According to the US Bureau of Mines, about 50 per cent of elemental phosphorus in 1989 (which was 225 kMT) was used to manufacture STPP (MY 1989 'Phosphates', p. 772). This corresponds to a P-content of about 110–20 kMT, or slightly less than the 1988 figure. Another detergent-builder of growing importance was tetrasodium pyrophosphate or TSPP ($Na_4P_2O_7$).

Later published statistics on STPP and other alkali-phosphates are unavailable. However, elemental phosphorus production in 1993 (445 kMT) was significantly higher than in 1989. Thus 1993 production of phosphorus chemicals was proportionally larger than 1989 production. In the late 1980s the detergent industry was reducing phosphate consumption and was shifting to an alternative, tetrasodium pyrophosphate, which contains less phosphorus. However, this shift appears to have stalled or even reversed. In fact, based on data on consumption of soda ash (in a later section) we estimate that around 345 kMT of phosphorus was embodied in STPP, TSPP and other inorganic chemicals used for soaps, detergents and water softeners in 1993. This would correspond to roughly 1 MMT of products.

This leaves about 100 kMT (P) for other phosphorus chemicals that are still unaccounted for. Most of them start from elemental phosphorus, by way of phosphorus pentasulfide (P_4S_5) or phosphorus trichloride (PCl_3). The former is made by direct reaction of phosphorus metal and elemental sulfur, while the latter is made by direct chlorination. One use of phosphorus pentasulfide is in the manufacture of zinc dithiophosphate, a lubricating oil additive. This use accounted for 15 kMT of phosphorus metal in 1974 (Lowenheim and Moran 1975); this use is almost certainly somewhat greater today. Phosphorus trisulfide (P_4S_3) is also used for match manufacturing and pyrotechnics. We estimate that phosphorus sulfides took 25–30 kMT of phosphorus and 30–35 kMT of sulfur in 1993, though it could be somewhat more.

The starting point for organic phosphate synthesis is phosphorus trichloride (PCl_3). Production figures are not published, but on the basis of absorbing 1 per cent of chlorine output (see chlorine below), we can conclude that about 30 kMT of phosphorus metal would have been required, plus or minus 10 kMT. The trichloride is later converted to phosphorus oxychloride ($POCl_3$) by direct reaction with chlorine and phosphorus pentoxide P_2O_5. The oxychloride, in turn, is the basis of organic phosphate esters that now have many uses. The most important of them is the plasticizer tricresyl phosphate (TCPP). Phosphate esters, such as aryl phosphate, are also used as flame retardants and fire resistant hydraulic fluids. Such phosphate esters totalled 43 kMT (P_2O_5) in 1990 (USITC 1991); a different source puts the phosphate share of the US flame retarder market at 20 per cent or 80 kMT for 1991 (Roskill 1992, Table 8 and text). Detailed data for each chemical are not published, but the phosphorus content is rather small (8.5 per cent in the case of TCPP). TCPP is also used as a gasoline additive. About 30 kMT or so of phosphorus remains unaccounted for, but that is hardly surprising.

6.5 Halogen-based chemicals

Halogen-based chemicals are mostly produced from elemental chlorine. They are the major product (with sodium hydroxide, or 'caustic soda') of the chlor–alkali industry, SIC 2812. The exceptions are sodium chloride (salt or halite) used as such for a variety of purposes including snow removal, for cattle feeding and food processing, calcium chloride from brine and used for snow removal, potassium chloride (sylvite), used as potash fertilizer. One other chemical, sodium chlorate (for bleaching paper pulp) is manufactured from sodium chloride.

Elemental chlorine together with sodium hydroxide (NaOH) (caustic soda) are co-produced by electrolysis of sodium chloride (salt), mainly in the form of brine. In 1993 US salt production was 29.913 MMT, imports were 5.440 MMT and 18.361 MMT was consumed by chlor–alkali producers (MY 'Salt' Table 2). US chlorine output in 1993 was 10.871 MMT, 10.913 MMT or 10.853 MMT, while sodium hydroxide output was 11.451 MMT, 11.661 MMT or 11.312 MMT, depending on the source of the data.[7] Net imports for

1993 were 255 kMT, so the supply was slightly larger than domestic production. The wastes from this process (mostly 'spent' brines) amount to about 8 per cent of the weight of the products, or about 1.4 MMT. The mass balance is made up from water on the input side, and a small amount of hydrogen released at the anode of the electrolytic cell. This hydrogen is usually recovered and burned on-site for its heat energy value (Figure 6.4). A small amount of chlorine is produced by the electrolysis of potassium and magnesium chlorides, the latter being primarily a byproduct of the production of magnesium metal.

For a detailed account of chlorine uses we have to rely on a special study by the Chemical Manufacturers Association for 1993 (Swift 1995), which also used the figure 10.9 MMT for domestic production. Major uses of chlorine in the US in 1993 outside the organic chemicals sector included inorganic chemicals manufacturing (1.674 MMT or 15 per cent), of which hydrochloric acid produced by direct reaction of hydrogen and chlorine accounted for 349 kMT and titanium dioxide purification took 458 kMT (Swift 1995).[8] Sodium hypochlorite (bleach) took most of the rest, about 630 kMT, as calculated subsequently.[9]

Pulp and paper bleaching consumed 1.211 MMT (10.9 per cent) in 1993, according to this source;[10] water and sewage treatment consumed 568 kMT (5.1 per cent) and 'miscellaneous uses' took 1.112 MMT (10 per cent) (ibid.). The remainder (6.75 MMT, or 60 per cent) was consumed in the production of organic chemicals. It should be noted that chlorine use for pulp bleaching is declining, due to the discovery of dioxin traces in bleached paper products. As a consequence – whether justified or not – this bleaching process has been almost completely phased out in Europe and is currently being phased out, albeit more slowly, in North America. The likely near-term future alternative is 'oxygen bleaching', using chlorine dioxide (from sodium chlorate), hydrogen peroxide or ozone. The widely used Rapson R8 process generates chlorine dioxide on site from sodium chlorate, sulfuric acid and methanol, producing sodium sulfate as a byproduct (MY 'Sodium Sulfate', p. 1096).

Evidently, much of the chlorine embodied in the identified chemicals, especially hydrochloric acid, is subsequently consumed in the production of other chemicals. Reported *shipments* of HCl in 1993 in the US were 3.168 MMT (CEN 1996). This evidently neglects HCl produced and consumed within the same establishment. By far the major single use of hydrochloric acid in the chemical industry is in the production of ethylene dichloride by oxychlorination (EDC), which is normally paired with vinyl chloride monomer (VCM) production where HCl is a byproduct. The result is that slightly over half of the chlorine embodied in EDC is derived from HCl. Based on US production of EDC in 1993, this would account for at least 3 MMT of HCl that was produced and used within the same establishment. There are also some other linked

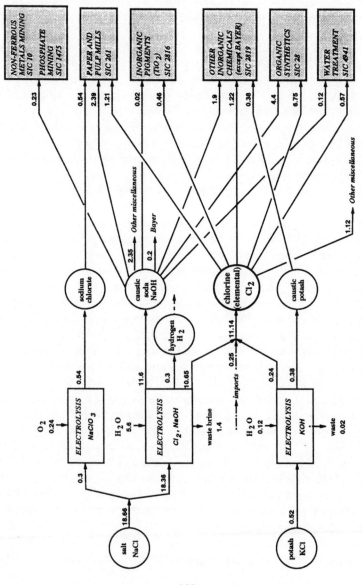

Figure 6.4 Materials flows in the production of major chlorine-based chemicals in the US, 1993 (MMT)

process complexes that both produce and use HCl, which probably account for an additional 1 MMT or so. We return to this point below.

Apart from elemental chlorine for water treatment and pulp bleaching, and HCl for water treatment, metal cleaning, and various minor uses, the products that moved 'over the fence' to other sectors or final consumption were mainly inorganic bleaches, chlorinated solvents (including CFCs) and plastics. By far the most important of the plastics that actually contain chlorine is polyvinyl chloride (PVC) – the end of the EDC–VCM sequence – which accounted for about 24 per cent of US chlorine consumption in 1993 (Swift 1995). Reported US 1988 and 1993 production of major Cl-based chemicals is shown in Table 6.2.

By far the biggest single intermediate other than HQ is EDC, the intermediate leading to PVC. However PVC only accounted for 24 per cent of

Table 6.2   US production of major Cl-based chemicals, 1988 and 1993

		1988		1993	
	Cl%	kMT	kMT(Cl)	kMT	kMT(Cl)
Total counted		19532	13350	25054	17105
Ethylene dichloride	71.7	5909	4234	8139	5831
Vinyl chloride monomer	56.7	4109	2331	6234	3536
PVC and copolymers	56.7	3787	2148	4652	2639
Hydrochloric acid 100%[a]	97.2	2928	2847	3168	3080
Phosgene	80.9	272	220	998	808
Sodium chlorate 100%	33.3	242	81	489	163
Methyl chloride	70.2	271	190	385	270
Chloroform	89.1	238	212	216	192
Methyl chloroform	73.1	328	240	205	150
Methylene chloride	83.5	229	191	161	134
Perchloroethylene	85.5	226	193	123	105
Carbon tetrachloride	92.2	239	318	88	81
Polychloroprene (neoprene rubber)	40.0	82	33	70	28
Trichloroethylene	80.9	272	74	66	53
Ethyl chloride	55.0	400	38	62	34
Chlorine	*100.0*	*10212*	*10212*	*10911*	*10911*

Note: [a] Refers to shipments (plus imports minus exports), not production, which is considerably larger due to in-house consumption.

Sources: 1993 data from Swift 1995. 1988 data from CEN 1996 and USITC 1991.

produced elemental chlorine in Europe; part of the chlorine contained in EDC is reclaimed again as HCl. EDC also has other end products, such as trichloro-ethylene and perchloro-ethylene. Some is also exported. Another important intermediate is epichlorohydrin, an intermediate to epoxy resins; phosgene ($COCl_2$) is an intermediate to isocyanate pesticides and urethane resins. Chlorinated benzenes are also intermediates to a variety of products.

A detailed analysis of chlorine flows in Europe for 1992, based on a very detailed survey of the European chlorine industry sponsored by the European association of chlorine producers (Euro Chlor) yields some interesting results (Ayres and Ayres 1997). The flow diagrams are not reproduced here, but one key result (for Europe) is worth mentioning: if elemental chlorine output was reckoned at 100 units, then shipments of elemental chlorine and hydrochloric acid 'over the fence' to other sectors, for example, for water treatment, pulp bleaching and other minor uses amounted to 15.7 units. Chemical products embodying chlorine (mainly PVC) accounted for about 51 units. Losses of chlorine within the sector were, therefore, 33.3 units. Of course there was recycling within the sector, almost entirely in the form of byproduct HCl. This reflux amounted to 53 units, making a *total* chlorine input flux of 153 units. On this basis, products crossing the fence carried 41.6 per cent of the input flux, 33.7 per cent was recycled and 24.7 per cent was lost as wastes. Although there are minor differences between European and US practice, many of the above macro-relationships would be quite similar.

A point of some interest is that European chlorine production in 1992 was 8.610 MMT, while HCl output (96 per cent byproduct) was 5.774 MMT. Thus the ratio of elemental chlorine output to HCl output in Europe was about 1.5:1. On this basis, we would expect US HCl production to be in the neighborhood of 7.3 MMT, plus or minus 20 per cent or so, since the product mix and the technologies in use are quite similar in Europe and the US. (The main differences are that more chlorine is used for pulp bleaching in the US than was the case in Europe, while somewhat less is used to produce PVC.) However, it seems safe to assume that actual HCl production in the US was much larger than the reported shipments (3.168 MMI), and that the true figure is at least 6 MMT and possibly as much as 7 MMT. Most of the byproduct HCl is produced in the organic chemicals sector, especially from chlorination of organic feedstocks such as methane, ethylene, propylene and benzene, where a chlorine atom replaces a hydrogen atom, and the hydrogen then recombines with another chlorine. Except for oxychlorination of EDC, however, most of the uses are elsewhere.

We have no US data on the uses of HCl. However, if the European pattern is applicable, we would expect that about 18 per cent went back to the inorganic sector, 4 per cent each went to pulp and paper and water treatment, respectively, while 15 per cent went to 'other' uses, such as metal treating (steel pickling), brine treating, oil well acidizing, food processing, and mining (SRI 1991). In the US several of these uses are much more important than in Europe, whence the 'other fraction' may have been greater than 15 per cent. Among the inorganic chemical uses, the largest was actually for recycling back to elemental chlorine by the so-called Kel-chlor process. Acid neutralization was also important. A third use of HCl in Europe was to produce calcium chloride ($CaCl_2$) from lime.

The chlorine-containing wastes are mostly dissolved salts, for example, NaCl, MgCl and $CaCl_2$. These result from neutralization of HCl by sodium or calcium hydroxides (caustic soda and slaked lime), respectively. To illustrate with a typical example, the production of household bleaches such as sodium hypochlorite (Na(ClO)) involves chlorination of sodium hydroxide. In the old process half of the chlorine input and half of the caustic soda input ended as NaCl and became an instant waste. Based on this process, to produce 650 kMT of sodium hypochlorite bleach (47.5 per cent Cl) would require not 315 kMT but about 630 kMT of chlorine. Similarly, the caustic soda requirement would not be just 335 kMT but double that amount. However the modern process uses the inputs more efficiently, by the reaction $NaOH + Cl_2 \rightarrow NaClO + HCl$, producing HCl as a salable byproduct. So, to produce 650 kMT of sodium hypochlorite still requires 650 kMT of chlorine, but only half the caustic soda formerly required, as well as yielding nearly 350 kMT of HCl.

Virtually all uses of chlorine are dissipative, with the major exception of PVC, which is used for structural purposes (for example, water and sewer pipes, siding, window frames, calendered products and bottles). PVC from vinyl chloride monomer accounts for 24 per cent of US elemental chlorine output.

Most of the uses (for example, of solvents) are not in the chemical industry itself. However, chlorination processes are relatively inefficient. Hence, recycling of waste streams is commonplace and a fairly large proportion of the input chlorine eventually becomes a production waste in manufacturing other downstream chemicals. For instance, in the production of VCM from ethylene dichloride, the loss rate is around 3 per cent (Manzone 1993). About 60 per cent of this waste stream consists of non-volatiles (heavy ends), is 'recycled' into chlorinated solvents and 40 per cent is volatiles that are destroyed by incineration, with some recovery of hydrogen chloride. In general, a 3 per cent loss rate for chlorination processes seems realistic.

The other halogens are bromine, fluorine and iodine. The latter is not used in significant quantities. Bromine consumption in the US in 1993 was 177 kMT (MY 'Bromine', Table 1). The production process involves substituting elemental chlorine for bromine in dissolved bromine salts (for example, from brine or seawater). About 0.45 kg chlorine plus some lime and sulfuric acid, is used per kg of bromine recovered (MY 'Bromine'). Thus 80 kMT of chlorine was consumed. Bromine salts (dissolved in brine) must have weighed about 230 kMT. All of the bromine was used ultimately in organic chemicals. Exact figures are unavailable, but the US Bureau of Mines estimated that in 1993 about 10 per cent was used in drilling fluids (mostly as calcium and zinc bromides), and 15 per cent was used in water treatment as a biocide for slime control.

Fire retardants – tetrabromobisphenol-A (TBBP-A) and decabromodiphenyl oxide (DBDPO), known as 'halons' – accounted for about 27 per cent of total bromine usage, or 48 kMT (B). About 16 per cent was used in agriculture as a soil fumigant (methyl bromide) while 12 per cent (21 kMT) was consumed as ethylene dibromide (EDB) added to leaded gasoline as a scavenger to prevent lead deposition on valves.[11] Dyes and photographic chemicals consumed 10 per cent (for example, in a red pigment known as pigment 168 for metalized paint for automobiles) and pharmaceuticals took 6 per cent. Evidently around 60 per cent was used in organic chemicals, half olefin-based and half aromatic (for example, phenol) based. There are no published data on production of specific bromine chemicals, even though many of them are highly toxic and some halons are known to contribute to the stratospheric ozone depletion problem.

Fluorspar (>97 per cent CaF_2) consumption in the US was 447 kMT in 1993, but this included non-chemical uses, such as fluxes for the steel industry (50 kMT) and 'other', including production of synthetic cryolite and aluminum fluoride for the aluminum industry directly from spar (77 kMT). Most chemical uses begin with hydrofluoric acid (HF), produced by the action of sulfuric acid on mineral fluorspar (discussed previously). US production of the acid in 1993 was 159 kMT, as mentioned previously. Some HF was used in petroleum refining (as an alkylation catalyst) and a small amount was probably used in uranium refining (uranium hexafluoride, UF_6). Some was used in the production of synthetic cryolite and aluminum fluoride, which is required by the Hall–Heroult electrolytic smelting process for aluminum. This use is declining as the aluminum industry now obtains most of its fluorine directly from spar or from fluosilicic acid (a byproduct of phosphate rock processing). Also, the aluminum industry is recycling its fluorine more and more efficiently (to reduce emissions). In 1993 63 per cent of the HF (95 kMT F) was consumed in the manufacture of CFCs and HCFCs (MY 'Fluorine' p. 364). Although CFC production was declining, thanks to the ban (which took effect in 1995) the three major CFCs still accounted for about 128.4 kMT (F), or about 135 kMT of HF.[12] In addition, other CFCs and the fluorocarbon polymers (for example, 'Teflon') presumably accounted for most of the rest.

A minor source of fluorine chemicals was phosphate rock processing. In 1988 this industry produced 46.6 kMT of fluosilicic acid (H_2SiF_6), with a fluorine content equivalent to 90 kMT of fluorspar (Ayres and Ayres 1996, Chapter 7). This substance is largely consumed for toothpaste and municipal water treatment, but it is also used to produce aluminum fluoride We have no data for 1993, but since output of phosphate rock declined, it is reasonable to suppose that output of fluosilicic acid did so also.

6.6 Alkali-metal-based chemicals

The major alkali metals are sodium, potassium, calcium and magnesium. These enter the economic system as salt (NaCl), soda ash (Na_2CO_3), potash (KCl), limestone ($CaCO_3$) and dolomite ($MgCO_3$), respectively. The first three occur both as natural minerals, and as brines. The chlorides of sodium and potassium have few chemical uses as such. In both cases, the first step is electrolysis of the brine to produce elemental chlorine and sodium or potassium hydroxide, respectively.

Sodium carbonate, or soda ash, is normally utilized as such. The calcium and magnesium carbonates are solid minerals that are first calcined (by heating) to drive off CO_2 before chemical usage. The traditional names for the calcined products are 'quicklime' – or simply lime – (CaO) and 'dead-burned dolomite' (MgO). On reacting with water they become hydroxides. It will be seen that very few final products of the chemical industry that are shipped 'over the fence' actually embody any of these four alkali metals. The exceptions are mainly sodium phosphates and silicates. Almost all of the mass of the alkali metals utilized for chemical purposes is for neutralizing sulfuric or hydrochloric acids, producing metallic sulfates and chlorides that are of little or no value in themselves.

The major source of sodium chemicals is common salt (sodium chloride). As mentioned in connection with chlorine in the last section, in 1993 US salt production was 29.913 MMT, imports were 5.440 MMT and 18.361 MMT was consumed by chlor-alkali producers (MY 'Salt', Table 2). The latter produced, in turn, somewhere between 11.312 MMT and 11.661 MMT of sodium hydroxide as a byproduct of chlorine production (see endnote 10). It is by far the most important sodium chemical.

One other important industrial inorganic chemical, sodium chlorate ($NaClO_3$) – used for pulp bleaching in the pulp sector – is made directly from sodium chloride by electrolysis. Sodium chlorate output in 1993 was 0.536 MMT. This was mostly used as a source of chlorine dioxide for bleaching woodpulp. The chlorine in this process is ultimately neutralized by caustic soda and ends up as sodium chloride in the wastewater from the pulp sector. However, except for sodium sulfate (which is partly of natural origin and partly produced synthetically for its own sake), most other sodium chemicals are either recovered as byproducts or they start from sodium carbonate (soda ash), not from caustic soda.[13]

The next most important sodium chemical is soda ash. Its historical import-ance arises from its ancient use in glass-making, which still accounts for nearly half of all usage.[14] In the nineteenth century LeBlanc, and later Solvay developed synthetic soda ash processes. Some plants using the Solvay ammo-nia-soda process are still operating in Europe. The US supply is obtained entirely from natural brines or underground deposits of so-called trona ore, which is comprised of sodium carbonate, sodium bicarbonate and water of crystallization.[15] US output in 1993 was 8.959 MMT (MY 'Soda Ash', Table 1). Apparent domestic consumption in 1993 was 6.348 MMT, the remainder being exported (ibid.). The largest single use was in glass manufacturing. Chemical industry usage in 1993 was 1.476 MMT, presumably for inorganic chemicals (SIC 2819), plus 0.806 MMT for soaps and detergents (SIC 284) (MY 'Soda Ash', Table 3). Other significant uses included pulp and paper (139 kMT), water treatment (116 kMT) and flue gas desulfurization (183 kMT) (ibid.).

It is worth reiterating that both soaps and detergents and water treatment chemicals depend on sodium phosphates, as pointed out earlier. The starting points for most of these chemicals appear to be monosodium phosphate (NaH_2PO_4) and disodium phosphate (Na_2HPO_4). Monosodium phosphate is probably produced by a neutralization reaction between caustic soda (NaOH) and phosphoric acid; disodium phosphate is made by reacting soda ash (Na_2CO_3) with phosphoric acid (H_3PO_4) releasing CO_2 (Shreve 1956, pp. 359–60). Sodium tripolyphosphate or STPP ($Na_5P_3O_{10}$) is made by heating a mixture consisting of one mole of the mono- and two moles of the di-sodium phosphates together and allowing it to cool and crystallize with appropriate temperature control. The tetra-sodium pyrophosphate, or TSPP ($Na_4P_2O_7$), is made by calcining disodium phosphate at high temperatures to drive off excess water molecules. Trisodium phosphate, TSP (Na_3PO_4) is made from disodium phosphate by reaction with sodium hydroxide. Evidently the so-dium content of STPIP was two-thirds from soda ash and one-third from caustic soda. The same ratio holds for TSP. The sodium in TSPP is entirely derived from soda ash. Lacking any other firm data, we assume that, overall, soda ash is the source of roughly 80 per cent of the sodium in this group of chemicals. Caustic soda is the source of the remainder.

Soda ash consumed for soaps, detergents and water treatment chemicals in 1993 amounted to 0.922 MMT, with a sodium content of almost exactly 400 kMT, of which about 32 kMT went to synthetic organic detergents (sulfonated fatty acids).[16] Thus 368 kMT went into sodium phosphates. To this, we add a notional 92 kMT of sodium from sodium hydroxide (recalling that 20 per cent of the total sodium is assumed to be from that source), for an estimated total of 460 kMT (Na). US production of STPP in 1988 was 497 kMT, with a phosphorus content of 125 kMT and a sodium content of 154 kMT (US

Department of Commerce 1988). Later statistics on STPP are unavailable, but STPP production is probably about the same.

There are no published data on the other alkali-phosphates, but given the known importance of TSPP (which contains less phosphorus) the overall phosphorus/sodium ratio is probably slightly lower than that of STPP; we guess 100:75. (This line of argument suggests that the total phosphorus content of these sodium-phosphorus chemicals in 1993 was $(3/4)*(460) = 344$ kMT, which is roughly consistent with what we have already deduced about phosphorus chemicals.) The total mass of sodium phosphates can be estimated roughly as a little less than three times the mass of STPP, or approximately 1.4 MMT. We note that the phosphates are inorganic chemicals and thus *not* included in the mass of synthetic organic surface-active materials (about 2 MMT) produced by the synthetic organic chemical industry.

There are several other major uses of soda ash in the inorganic chemical industry. One of them is the production of sodium silicate (Na_2SiO_3) from silica. The basic reaction is $Na_2CO_3 + SiO_2 \rightarrow Na_2SiO_3 + CO_2$, under reducing conditions. (Actually, the chemistry is much more complicated and there are several sodium silicates, with the general formula $N_2O(SiO_2)_n$ where n is a variable.) The silica used in this process is the mineral quartzite (white sand). It is either dissolved in hot caustic soda under pressure or fused with soda in a furnace. Production of sodium silicate in 1993 was 0.91 MMT (CEN 1995). The minimum quantity of soda ash required as input for this reaction was 0.79 MMT, or slightly more than half of the total consumption of soda ash for all inorganic chemicals other than phosphates for detergents (1.476 MMT). The indicated quantity of silica required was 0.45 MMT. Another, smaller use of soda ash is in the manufacture of sodium dichromate. The indicated requirement for that purpose in 1993 was about 0.1 MMT. (See the discussion of chromium chemicals, later.)

It is worth noting that sodium carbonate is essentially $Na_2O.CO_3$ and most, if not all, chemical uses of sodium carbonate involve a substitution of some other radical for, and release of, carbon dioxide. On an atomic weight basis, the 1.476 MMT of soda ash that was consumed by the inorganic chemical sector implies a release of 0.605 MMT of CO_2 to the atmosphere.

Major uses of sodium hydroxide in Europe for 1987 were: inorganic chemicals (23 per cent of which the preparation of alumina by the Bayer process accounted for 6 per cent and sodium hypochlorite (bleach) accounted for 3 per cent); organic chemicals (17 per cent); pulp and paper (14 per cent); cellulosics (4 per cent); soap and detergents (4 per cent); unspecified acid neutralization (12 per cent), petroleum refining (2 per cent), dyeing of textiles (4 per cent), water treatment (1 per cent), and miscellaneous purposes (19 per cent) including exports and synthetic cryolite for aluminum manufacturing (SRI 1989). Counting cellulosics, soap and detergents and most of the unspecified acid neutralization as part of the 'organics' sector, broadly defined, increases the total share of the latter to 37 per cent. However, in recent years data of this sort have become increasingly scarce, and we have been unable to find any reliable source of data on recent uses of caustic soda in the US, except for the single figure on usage in the pulp and paper sector cited in Chapter 3 (Table 3.1), which was 2.39 MMT or 20.6 per cent of 1993 US consumption (MEB 1995). This was larger than the corresponding European figure. Otherwise we rely partly on European data and partly on mass balances for key individual processes.

Sodium hypochlorite bleach is made by reacting chlorine with caustic soda. As noted in the last section in connection with chlorine, for each molecule of sodium and of chlorine in the product, a molecule of caustic soda is consumed. Thus, production of 650 kMT of the bleach in 1993 would have consumed about 350 kMT of caustic soda.

Soap and fatty acid production are major consumers of caustic soda. (Soap is a sodium salt of a fatty acid.) The fatty acids, in turn, are generally produced by sulfuric acid treatment of animal or vegetable fats and oils. In 1993 1.2 MMT of fats and oils were converted into fatty acids, of which 0.35 MMT were saponified to soap (AS Table 188). The saponification process is essentially the neutralization of a fatty acid to produce a soluble sodium salt, such as sodium stearate or sodium palmitate. An average for soap is difficult to obtain, but for sodium palmitate $(NaO(C_{15}H_{31})CO)$ the sodium content is 8.3 per cent. If this fraction applies approximately for all soap, the sodium content in 1993 would have been 29 kMT and NaOH consumption for purposes of saponification would have been 50 kMT. Sodium salts of coconut oil acids (274.8 kMT), and tallow acids (459.8 kMT) are major components of liquid detergents. Production in 1988 was 275 kW and 460 kMT, respectively (USITC 1989). Figures for 1993 would be slightly larger, between 750 and 800 kMT. Accordingly we cannot readily estimate the average sodium content of this material. But for one common detergent ingredient, alkyl aryl sulfonate $((C_{12}H_{25})C_6H_4SO_3Na)$ the sodium content is 6.32 per cent and the sulfur content is 8.88 per cent. If these fractions apply to all detergents, the total sodium and sulfur embodied in the products would have been 54 kMT (94 kMT NaOH) and 75 kMT, respectively. In these two cases – soap and liquid detergents – the sodium is embodied in the final product.

European consumption patterns for 1989 cited previously – which are admittedly not necessarily applicable to the US – suggested that inorganic chemicals consumed 23 per cent and organic chemicals (broadly defined) about 37 per cent of total production, or 60 per cent altogether. However, paper and pulp consumed a larger share in the US (20.6 per cent versus 14 per cent), whence other uses were presumably reduced in proportion. On this basis, and lacking better data, it seems reasonable to assign 56 per cent of total output, or 6.5 MMT to SIC 28. Since the end-product of caustic soda is almost always a sodium salt of some acid, it is reasonable to assume that the caustic soda is used where the acids are used. Except in the case of soaps and detergents, (which are salts of fatty acids, as noted above) sodium hydroxide is not embodied in organic products. Thus, to anticipate a later discussion, we estimate that dissipative losses (that is, acid neutralization) of caustic soda within the organic chemical industry as a whole in 1993 accounted for about 4.4 MMT.

To cite a few examples, rayon production (mentioned above) consumes 0.68 kg per kg of product; the manufacture of ammonia requires about 4 kg per metric ton of product; the extraction of benzene from light oils (in the petroleum refining sector) requires 14.5–28.5 kg per metric ton; glycerine requires 100 kg per metric ton; caprolactam, the monomer for nylon 6, requires 125 kg of NaOH per metric ton of product; 63 kg of NaOH is required per metric ton of adipic acid from cyclohexane. In none of these cases is the sodium embodied in the product. In virtually all cases, NaOH is used as a process intermediate, or simply to regulate the acidity or alkalinity (pH) of the reaction. At the end, it neutralizes, or is neutralized by some acid.

Allowing for sodium embodied in soaps and detergents and subtracting from the imputed total of 6.5 MMT for all chemical uses implies that 2 MMT of caustic soda was used in miscellaneous inorganic chemical processes. Again, most of this was probably for acid neutralization. We can only account specifically for a few chemical products containing sodium – other than byproducts – that are derived directly from sodium hydroxide, such as sodium hypochlorite and synthetic cryolite. However, by our calculation, sodium hypochlorite production by itself consumed 0.685 MMT of caustic soda, while the Bayer process for producing alumina from bauxite also consume about 0.2 MMT of caustic soda. Still, this is less than half of the total to be accounted for.

'Potash' consists of a number of potassium chemicals, but the major one by far is potassium chloride (KCl). US production was 3.067 MMT in 1993, but most of the domestic supply (9.3 MMT) was imported from Canada (MY 'Potash', Table 1). While most potash goes directly to fertilizer and animal feeds, non-agricultural uses in 1993 amounted to 521 kMT (ibid. Table 6). We have no specific information on the nature of those uses, but it seems likely that they are mostly in the inorganic chemical sector. The starting point for most potassium chemicals would be potassium hydroxide (KOH), produced by electrolysis of potassium chloride. Chemically pure potassium salts would then be produced by reacting KOH with an acid. Based on this assumption, potash could have accounted for a little over 2 per cent of US chlorine output (0.24 MMT) and KOH production in 1993 could have been 0.38 MMT (see Figure 6.4). In reality, these are probably overestimates.

Magnesium chemicals consist mainly of caustic-calcined magnesia (MgO), of which 131 kMT was produced in 1993, magnesium hydroxide $(Mg(OH)_2)$ of which 252.5 kMT was produced, and magnesium sulfate $MgSO_4$, of which production was 42.7 kMT (MY 'Magnesium', Table 13). The calcined magnesia is used for animal feeds and fertilizers, and for special cements, insulating wallboard and pharmaceuticals. It is also used for water treatment, sulfur removal from flue gas and acid neutralization for process wastes (for example, ore concentration). The hydroxide is mainly used in the pulp and paper industry. The sulfate is used for animal feeds and fertilizers. These chemicals are closely analogous to the corresponding sodium and calcium chemicals, and have similar uses.

6.7   Alumina, silicon, pigments and other metal-based chemicals

All aluminum-based chemicals are produced from aluminum oxide, or alumina (Al_2O_3), or aluminum hydroxide $(Al_2(OH)_3)$, which is also known as aluminum hydroxide trihydrate. Alumina is manufactured from bauxite, mostly imported, by the so-called Bayer process. In 1993 US bauxite consumption for alumina production was 11.002 MMT, yielding 5.49 MMT gross weight, and 5.29 MMT calcined equivalent (MY 'Aluminum', Table 15). The apparent weight loss (dry) was 5.51 MMT, consisting mostly of 'red mud' and particulates. For each ton of alumina produced, 37 kg of limestone $(CaCO_3)$ and 37.5 kg of caustic soda (NaOH) are required, or about 196 kMT of limestone and 200 kMT of caustic soda. These also become part of the Bayer process waste stream, which amounted to roughly 6 MMT (dry weight) in total.

Alumina is the primary feedstock for the electrolytic reduction of aluminum metal. According to the Bureau of Mines, 91 per cent of US alumina output (4.8 MMT) went to refineries. Alumina imports (net) were 2.7 MMT. In 1993 US primary aluminum production was 3.695 MMT, which would have required 7.25 MMT of alumina feedstock, based on a calculated 1.96 kg of alumina per kg of primary aluminum, including 0.03 kg of alumina per ton (110 kMT) converted to aluminum fluoride and/or synthetic cryolite. This would correspond to roughly 150 kMT of cryolite $((3NaF)AlF_3)$ and 110 kMT of aluminum fluoride (AlF_3) produced and consumed by the aluminum industry (see 'fluorine' above). The production of synthetic cryolite also required on the order of 120 kMT of caustic soda.

Chemical uses of alumina are mainly for water treatment, in water softeners or in detergents (as a substitute for phosphates). The Bureau of Mines reported in 1993 US aluminum sulfate production of 1.144 MMT (containing 17 per cent Al_2O_3) – see the discussion in the section on sulfur chemicals above – plus 770 kMT aluminum hydroxide trihydrate $(Al(OH)_3)$, and 114 kMT of aluminates (MY 'Aluminum', Table 18). Aluminum trihydrate is the leading wood preservative chemical; it accounts for about half of a total market for wood preservatives that was estimated at 400 kMT in 1991 (Roskill 1993). Except for minor uses in detergents, no aluminum chemicals are used in the production of synthetic organic chemicals.

Silicon chemicals of importance include sodium silicates (mentioned above in connection with sodium), silanes and silicones. Sodium silicates are made from silica (sand) and soda ash. The others are made from silicon metal as a starting point. As already noted, 1993 production of sodium silicates was 0.91 MMT. They are used for a variety of purposes. In 1974 the breakdown of uses was as follows: silica gel and catalysts (35 per cent); additives to soaps and detergents (18 per cent); pigments (14 per cent); boxboard adhesive (8 per cent); water treatment, pulp and paper and ore flotation (6 per cent); roofing granules (3 per cent) and 'other' (16 per cent) (Lowenheim and Moran 1975). Most of these markets are relatively stable although the use for adhesives may be declining.

Other silicon chemicals are derived from silicon metal. The data is extremely difficult to unearth. The US Bureau of Mines published annual data on silicon metal usage during the early 1980s, through 1986, followed by a two-year gap, followed by a single year (1989). In that year production of silicon metal in the US was reported to be 139.5 kMT, excluding semiconductor grades, while consumption was 180.5 kMT *not* excluding semiconductor grades (MY 1989 'Silicon', Tables 1 and 3). There were net imports for consumption of 38.06 kMT of silicon metal (MY 1989 'Silicon', Tables 4 and 5), leaving a discrepancy of 3 kMT, which was probably ultrapure silicon. At any rate, in 1989 the USBM reported that 1.6 kMT went to steel alloys and 49.9 kMT went to aluminum alloys. The USBM assigned 129.1 kMT to 'miscellaneous and unspecified uses', including silicones, silanes and fumed silica.[17] No mention at all was made of silica for optical fiber production.

The question remains how to allocate the 'unspecified' output among silicones, semiconductors and fumed silica. A serious effort to untangle this mess was made by the metals data consulting firm Roskill Ltd (UK), based on a reconstructed historical time series allowing for low demand for aluminum alloys in the early 1980s, that shows remarkable growth for the 'unspecified' (that is, silicone) uses. The Roskill estimate was 94.7 kMT (Si) for silicones, up from 55 kMT just three years earlier, with total imputed 1989 silicone output of 264 kMT (Roskill 1991, Table 104). We see no reason to challenge the USBM's assignment to aluminum or steel alloys in 1989, so this would leave 34.4 kMT for other chemical uses, including silanes for ultrapure silicon for semiconductors, silicon for photovoltaic (PV) cells, silicon for optical fibers and fumed silica production in 1989. All of these markets are growing very rapidly and all are based on silanes.

The US Department of Commerce reported tetrachlorosilane production of 49.1 kMT for 1990 and 54.8 kMT for 1991, a growth rate of 18.5 per cent per annum (USDOC 1992). Assuming this growth rate continued, US silicone production for 1993 would have been in the range of 400 kMT, although the breast cancer scare associated with silicone breast implants undoubtedly depressed demand for some products.

Silanes are chlorinated compounds of silicon, notably silicon trichloride $SiHCl_3$ and silicon tetrachloride ($SiCl_{14}$). Silanes are produced by direct chlorination of silicon metal. Silanes are used both in the production of silicone resins and ultrapure polycrystalline or amorphous silicon for semiconductors and optical fibers. However, silanes are also byproducts of the current (Siemens) silicon purification process, which means they could easily be recycled – at least in principle – having no other use in themselves than to carry silicon from one point or condition to another.

The mass of silicon embodied in semiconductor devices is extremely small. It was probably about 750 metric tons in 1989 and probably did not exceed 1 kMT for the whole world in 1993, despite the extraordinary growth of semiconductor markets, because of parallel progress in micro-miniaturization. Of this global total, not more than 0.4 kMT was manufactured in the US. But the small size of the market for electronic grade silicon (EGS) is misleading because the purification process was extraordinarily inefficient. To produce 0.4 kMT of 'chips' at least 1.2 kMT of wafers would have had to be produced from 3.5–4 kMT of polysilicon. That, in turn, would have required roughly 18 kMT of silicon metal as a starting point.[18]

The optical fiber market is much larger in gross tonnage, and growing even faster, since miniaturization is less relevant. Optical fibers are made from specialty glass (or 'fused silica'), which is first purified chemically from silicon metal. The US market for fiber optics in 1993 was about $300 million, and was projected to grow at 20 per cent per year. We do not have data on the physical quantity of silica involved.

We have noted the inefficiency of the silicon purification process. What happened to all this silicon metal? Of the 3.5 or 4 kMT of polysilicon that was produced for electronic purposes in 1989, some was contaminated (especially in the latter stages) and lost to waste, but half or more was used to manufacture silicon PV cells and/or optical fibers. The remainder, in the order of 14 kMT (Si) was converted to silanes, in various mixtures.

It is unlikely that mixed silanes from silicon purification would or could have been used by the silicone industry. It is far easier to start from scratch and produce exactly the compound that is needed. (We suspect that the reported silicon tetrachloride figures do, in fact, refer to 'virgin' production for silicones.) However, it is relatively easy to convert mixed silanes to fumed silica by hydrolysis, that is, by simply 'burning' them to SiO_2 in an oxygen–

hydrogen flame. The chlorine can then be recovered and recycled as HCl. Thus, if all steps in the EGS process were carried out in the US, the US production of fumed silica in 1993 might have been about 14 kMT (Si) or 28.5 kMT gross weight, with a recovery of 48 to 62 kMT of HCl. If these silanes were *not* recovered, of course, one would have to assume a rather horrendous wastage, amounting to over 50 kMT of mixed chlorinated silanes. We doubt that this is occurring. But it would be nice to have some confirming data.

Titanium dioxide has already been mentioned. It is the most important metallic pigment – being used for most exterior paints, as well as in paper. Unfortunately we lack information on the weight of rutile and ilmenite ores, most of which are imported as concentrates. US production of the pigment in 1993 was 1.162 MMT, with a TiO_2 content of 1.090 MMT. There are two major processes. The major process for titanium dioxide production starts from the mineral ilmenite, which is first concentrated in an electric furnace. Worldwide, 87 per cent of titanium is obtained from ilmenite ores. So-called ilmenite slag (85 per cent Ti), is the form in which it is normally imported. The slag is then ground and treated by sulfuric acid. According to one source, the process consumes 2.9 tons of sulfuric acid and 2.03 tons of lime, as well as 0.075 tons of caustic soda per ton of product (SRI 1989). The solid waste from the process (roughly 5 tons of solid waste per ton of titanium dioxide) consists mostly of calcium sulfate mixed with a small amount of sodium sulfate.

However, the Bureau of Mines allocated only 1.2 MMT sulfuric acid (0.39 MMT S) to all inorganic pigments, and industrial inorganic chemicals except fertilizers and chemicals included in SIC 281 (MY 'Sulfur', Table 7). It is possible that most of this acid was used in titanium dioxide production, but not all (chromium, lead and zinc pigments also consumed small amounts). Evidently the sulfate process could not have accounted for more than about 30–35 per cent of the titanium dioxide output (say 0.35 MMT), and therefore generated about 1.75 MMT of wastes (dry).

The chlorine process starts from a concentrate of the mineral rutile, which is 95 per cent pure TiO_2. It is first chlorinated to titanium tetrachloride ($TiCl_4$, in a reducing atmosphere at high temperature. The tetrachloride is then oxidized either by pure oxygen or by steam. In the former case the chlorine is mostly recycled, but in the latter (older) process it is released as HCl and neutralized by lime. This process utilized 0.46 MMT of chlorine in 1993 (Swift 1995) and presumably generated 0.73 MMT of calcium chloride waste (based on the ratio of atomic weights). According to one source, for each ton of TiO_2 produced by the HCl neutralization route, roughly 1.2 tons of waste $CaCl_2$ is generated. Thus 0.73 MMT of waste $CaCl_2$ implies that 0.6 MMT of titanium dioxide (55 per cent) was produced by this route, leaving 20 per cent of output for the pure oxygen route. These estimates are obviously very approximate. Overall, we estimate that solid wastes from titanium dioxide pigment production in the US to be in the neighborhood of 2.5 MMT (dry).

Compounds of iron, chromium, copper, lead, titanium and zinc also have important chemical uses, especially for pigments. Iron oxide is a red pigment, largely from natural sources. Ferricyanides are important blue pigments (Paris blue and Prussian blue). There are no published data on iron-based chemicals. However, it is known that ferrous chloride and ferrous sulfate are byproducts of steel pickling with hydrochloric and sulfuric acids, respectively. Ferrous chloride is used to some extent as a soil conditioner. Ferrous sulfate (in low grade forms) is available in tonnages (2–4 MMT/y) far greater than usage. It is used to some extent to make iron oxide, to manufacture ferrites, as a catalyst, in sewage treatment, and so on. However, much of it must be disposed of as a waste.

About 25 per cent of zinc is consumed in chemical form. Zinc chemicals produced in 1993 were as follows: zinc oxide (directly from ore), 160 kMT; zinc sulfate 20 kMT; zinc chloride 4.34 kMT (MY 'Zinc', Table 11). Zinc oxide is used mainly in tire manufacturing (63 per cent). Only 3 per cent is used as a pigment for paints. Zinc chloride is mainly used as an electrolyte in dry cells. Minor quantities of zinc were used in pesticides (for example, zineb) and to manufacture catalysts.

The main chemical form of copper is copper sulfate ($CuSO_4$). US production in 1993 was 11.7 kMT (Cu content) or 29.2 kMT in gross weight (MY 'Copper', Table 7). Copper sulfate is the basis of most copper chemicals (fungicides, algicides, pesticides, catalysts, flotation reagents, and so on). Uses were for agriculture (59 per cent, mainly for fungus control), 31 per cent for industry (for example, as catalysts, flotation reagents and wood preservatives) and 10 per cent for water treatment.

Chrome chemicals are mostly derived from sodium dichromate ($Na_2Cr_2O_7$) manufactured from 'chemical grade' chromite ore ($FeCr_2O_4$) of which the US consumed 139 kMT in 1993 (MY 'Chromium', Table 12). The production process involves treatment of chromite ore (50 per cent Cr_2O_3) with sulfuric acid, limestone and soda ash (Lowenheim and Moran 1975). The recipe for 1 metric ton of sodium dichromate is 1.1 tons of ore, 1.5 tons of limestone, 0.8 tons of soda ash and 0.5 tons of sulfuric acid. The reaction occurs in two stages, $4FeCr_2O_4 + 8Na_2CO_3 + 7O_2 \rightarrow 8Na_2CrO_4 + 2Fe_2O_3 + 8CO_2$ and $2Na_2CrO_4 + H_2SO_4 \rightarrow Na_2Cr_2O_7 + H_2O + Na_2SO_4$. The sodium sulfate is recoverable. The limestone does not really participate in the reaction, but becomes part of the waste. On this basis the output of dichromate would have been 126 kMT, with 69.5 kMT of byproduct sodium sulfate, 38.5 kMT of Fe_2O_3 plus 190 kMT of limestone waste and 21 kMT of CO_2.

The sodium dichromate was allocated (c. 1990) as follows: chromic acid (55 per cent), followed by chromium oxide (10 per cent), chromium sulfate for leather tanning 8 per cent, green and yellow pigments (7 per cent), direct use in wood preservatives (2 per cent), drilling mud additives (2 per cent) other domestic uses (3 per cent) and exports (13 per cent) (ibid. p. 220). The largest use of chromic acid (70 per cent), and the largest use of chromium chemicals altogether, was for wood preservatives (in combination with arsenic and copper). This use evidently accounted for 41 per cent of chromium chemical usage, or 55.5 kMT of sodium dichromate equivalent. Chromic acid is also used for electro-plating and metal treatment (15 per cent of 1993 demand) and as the base for producing other chromium chemicals. Leather tanning (8 per cent of US dichromate demand in 1993) uses chromium (III) sulfate to protect the organic material from attack by micro-organisms. All chemical uses of chromium except for electroplating are essentially dissipative, although the chromium used wood preservatives and in 'chrome' tanning is tightly bound to the organic material and leaches or wears away only very slowly.

Lead chemicals are mostly sulfates and oxides are primarily pigments, but also the basis for other lead chemicals such as tetraethyl lead (TEL). The latter was once a major product, but no US production was reported in 1993. However, lead consumption in TEL is essentially proportional to bromine consumption in ethyl bromide (EDB), in the ratio of 2 units of lead for each unit of bromine, and EDB consumption in 1993 was definitely not zero. On this basis, 1993 lead consumption for TEL would have been about 40 kMT.[19] Total US production of 'other oxides' (SIC 28) was 63.6 kMT in 1993, but most of this was apparently for 'leaded' glass and ceramics (SIC 32) or lead-based paints (SIC 285) (MY 'Lead', Table 6). The subcategory 'other pigments and chemicals' (SIC 28) only reported consumption of 9.874 kMT. Lead pigments are no longer used for white paints. Red lead is still used for exterior metal protection (for example, on bridges) although this use also appears to be declining.

Nickel and tin chemicals are produced and used in minor amounts. US production was 1.8 kMT (Ni content), exports were 1.4 kMT (Ni content), and imports were 4 kMT (MY 'Nickel', Tables 3 and 4). These were mostly additives and catalysts. In the case of tin, 6.5 kMT (Sn content) of chemicals was produced in 1993 (MY 'Tin', Table 3). These chemicals are mostly used for fire retardants, stabilizers for plastics, fungicides and for protection of ship's hulls against barnacles.

All final uses are dissipative. Dissipative losses of toxic metals clearly outweigh losses from industrial processes, probably by a large margin. However, we do not discuss chemical uses of metals further in this chapter.

6.8 Summary

There is some potential confusion in classifying inorganic chemicals. For our purposes we class fertilizers and produced animal feeds (for example, urea) as inorganic. We do not include mineral products from natural sources that are consumed *as such* as chemical products. Examples include limestone, sulfur, salt, potash (KCl), soda ash and sodium sulfate from natural sources. We also exclude lime and calcined dolomite, which are not classified as chemicals. We also note that some byproducts of the organic chemical sector (Chapter 7) are clearly inorganic chemicals, but for consistency we do not include these in the totals calculated below. Examples in this category include byproduct sodium sulfate, ammonium sulfate, hydrocyanic acid and hydrochloric acid.

In 1993 the primary purchased inputs for the inorganic chemicals production sectors, in mass terms, were phosphate rock concentrate (106.8 MMT), salt (18.66 MMT), sulfur (13.4 MMT), bauxite (11.75 MMT), methane for ammonia synthesis (7.5 MMT), byproduct sulfuric acid from the non-ferrous metal sector (5.7 MMT), soda ash (1.5 MMT), and titanium mineral concentrates, rutile and ilmenite (1.3 MMT), plus HCl from the organic sector which we assume to be 1.3 MMT. In addition, there were minor inputs of silica (0.5 MMT), potash (0.5 MMT), fluorspar (0.31 MMT), bromine salts (0.23), chromite ore (0.14), and coke (0.18 MMT). We neglect limestone (lime) and dolomite, although lime is used in quite a few processes, because it is almost invariably used for acid neutralization and ends up in solid waste. However this requires some adjustment in the waste estimates, as will be seen later. Magnesia, copper, zinc and lead ores, and a few other minerals like borates are also neglected, both on input and output sides, although this results in a slightly greater underestimate of inputs than outputs.

Disregarding the minor minerals, as above, the total mass of purchased inputs was therefore approximately 169.8 MMT, *not* counting 5.6 MMT of CO_2 consumed in the production of urea, which might theoretically have been recycled from ammonia plants. If not, this must have been produced by burning a pure form of carbon (such as petroleum coke) in pure oxygen, which would add 5.6 MMT to the mass of purchased inputs. Neglected inputs of limestone and lime would also add slightly to this total. The only significant chemical products involving calcium are calcium chloride and calcium phosphates (for animal feed). Quantities are not large, but unfortunately we have no data.

To these must be added a number of non-purchased inputs, mainly oxygen (35.4 MMT) and nitrogen from the air (12.9 MMT), as well as process water (14 MMT) for the ammonia synthesis and chlorine electrolysis processes. These add up to 62.3 MMT. Thus total inputs amounted to 232.1 MMT.

The major primary products of the US inorganic chemical industry in 1993 were ammonia (15.65 MMT), sulfuric acid (33.34 MMT), chlorine (10.9

MMT), sodium hydroxide (caustic soda) (11.6 MMT), alumina (5.49 MMT), phosphoric acid (35.5 MMT), plus miscellaneous other acids, salts, and metallic pigments. These add up to 112.48 MMT. However, it is important to bear in mind that much of this is actually consumed within the sector.

Significant fractions of all of these primary products are also consumed within the organic sector. Ammonia is a fairly straightforward case. Counting fertilizers, animal feeds and cleaning agents as inorganic chemicals (broadly defined), we estimate that about 15 per cent (2.7 MMT) was consumed by the organic sector. Essentially all the rest was embodied in agricultural chemicals (SIC 287) (see Figure 6.2). Although ammonia is alkaline, it is too valuable to be used for acid neutralization with a very few exceptions (where the byproduct is usually recovered). Phosphoric acid, too, is almost entirely used for agriculture. Other inorganic phosphate chemicals (sodium phosphates) are used primarily for water treatment (we estimated a total of 1.4 MMT). Only minor amounts, on the order of 0.1 MMT (P) are consumed in organic synthesis.

Sulfur flows are more complex (Figure 6.3.). Most elemental sulfur is used to produce inorganic chemicals – mainly sulfuric acid – but 0.914 MMT was used directly for agricultural purposes (SIC 287) and 1.06 MMT was shipped to unspecified 'other' sectors. As regards sulfuric acid, again, the largest share was consumed in processing phosphate rock for fertilizer. Altogether, agricultural chemicals (SIC 287) absorbed 24.65 MMT (70 per cent) of 1993 output. However, 1.4 MMT went to organic synthesis and 6.9 MMT was consumed by other sectors, especially copper mining (SIC 10) and petroleum refining (SIC 29).

In the case of chlorine, we previously estimated that 16 per cent (1.77 MMT) is consumed to produce sodium hypochlorite, titanium dioxide and other inorganic chemicals, including bromine. Hydrochloric acid is a special problem. It is an inorganic chemical, and some is produced directly by chlorine hydrogenation, but almost all of it is produced as a byproduct of processes in the organic sector. Total byproduct output in the US is certainly much greater than the amount that was shipped (Table 6.2). On the basis of an earlier discussion we estimated that between 6 MMT and 7 MMT of the acid was produced in the US in 1993, of which virtually all (96 per cent) was byproduct. A median estimate would be 6.5 MMT. About 1.3 MMT would probably have been used within the inorganic sector, while about 1.7 MMT was probably exported to other sectors (paper and pulp, water treatment, metal treatment, and miscellaneous). The remainder (3.5 MMT) was probably re-used in the organic chemicals sector, mainly within the EDC–VCM–PVC chain. Needless to say, all of these estimates are uncertain by at least 10 per cent or 15 per cent each way.

In addition, 7.2 MMT of elemental chlorine went to organic chemicals synthesis and 1.9 MMT to other sectors (pulp bleaching, water treatment and ('miscellaneous uses'). In the case of caustic soda we have estimated that 2 MMT (17 per cent) is consumed in various inorganic processes, although we can only account specifically for a fraction of this. Organic chemicals probably consumed 4.4 MMT (Chapter 7), while pulp and paper accounted for another 2.39 MMT. Altogether 9.5 MMT of caustic soda was apparently consumed outside of the inorganic chemicals sector (see Figure 6.4).

It is difficult to estimate the total mass of sales of inorganic chemicals 'beyond the fence', because of imports, exports, byproducts (such as HCl, ammonium sulfate and sodium sulfate) and missing data. Products we can definitely account for, however, include 58.25 MMT of N- and P-based agricultural chemicals, mainly fertilizers, produced from primary materials (excluding potash and elemental sulfur, which are not products of the sector) as shown in Figure 6.2, plus 0.9 MMT of elemental sulfur (Figure 6.3). We can also account for roughly 15.8 MMT of basic inorganic chemicals that subsequently become inputs for organic chemical synthesis, namely ammonia (2.7 MMT), sulfuric acid (1.38 MMT), chlorine (6.75 MMT), caustic soda (4.4 MMT) and miscellaneous chemicals in relatively small quantities (0.6 MMT, consisting of P, S, F, Br, and so on). Here we exclude byproduct HCl produced and consumed within the organic chemicals sector. About 1.7 MMT of HCl was probably sold to other sectors, but most of this must be attributed to the organic sector (Chapter 7).

On the other hand, we must count 1.3 MMT of recovered HCl as an input *from* the organic chemicals sector *to* the inorganic chemicals sector. Furthermore, we have accounted for 13.4 MMT of the four basic chemicals sold to other sectors (mining, paper and pulp, petroleum refining, water treatment, and 'miscellaneous').

Finally, we must include a number of other chemical products – mostly metal-based – whose inputs have been counted specifically. The most important is alumina, almost all of which (5.4 MMT), was shipped out of the inorganic chemicals sector to aluminum smelters. Others include nitrogenous inorganics (ammonium nitrate explosives, cyanides, rocket propellants, and so on adding up to about 2 MMT, sodium phosphates and other inorganic phosphorus compounds (1.2 MMT), mainly for water treatment and detergents, aluminum sulfate (1.15 MMT) for paper and textile processing, titanium dioxide (1.09 MMT), sodium silicate (0.91 MMT), sodium hypochlorite (0.65 MMT) and sodium dichromate (0.17). Minor examples include hydrofluoric acid sold direct to the organic sector or 'embodied' in aluminum fluorides and synthetic cryolite for the aluminum industry (0.16 MMT F). All of the above add up to 98.5 MMT, which must be considered the approximate lower limit of output.

We can also account directly for some of the major wastes from the sector. The solid waste category includes phospho-gypsum (95.5 MMT), 'red mud'

(6 MMT), plus solid wastes from alum and titanium dioxide processes, hydrofluoric acid and sodium dichromate production adding up to about 4.15 MMT. But since we neglected lime as an input, we must also subtract the calcium component of these wastes, insofar – as in the case of the Bayer process the chloride process for titanium dioxide, and the sodium dichromate process – it was originally derived from lime or limestone. This subtraction reduces the total by at least 0.6 MMT. Waste water vapor generated as outputs by three key processes (nitric acid, urea and chlor-alkali) amounted to at least 5.9 MMT. (This does not include much larger process wastewater streams from washing and dilution).

In addition, we can account for at least 22.1 MMT of CO_2, mostly from ammonia synthesis and processes using sodium carbonate. As mentioned above, it would be logical to assume that some of this carbon dioxide (from ammonia) might have been captured and used for urea manufacturing. On the basis of the latter (rather optimistic) assumption, we can now account for *at least* 132 MMT of process wastes to set alongside the 232.1 MMT (plus some contribution from other minerals) of known inputs, both purchased – including byproduct HCl – and free. If the CO_2 used in urea production is not recycled, both inputs and wastes rise by 5.5 MMT (or more). Either way, the *maximum* mass of inorganic chemical products sold to other sectors or exported would seem to have been approximately 100 MMT plus the neglected inputs from limestone, dolomite, other metal ores and other minor minerals that contribute little or no mass to outputs. It would be surprising, in any case, if these neglected inputs added up to 1 MMT.

Thus we have reached an estimate of marketable output of inorganic chemicals from both above and below, arriving at a total of approximately 99 MMT. Since the figures calculated both ways agree closely, we suspect they are accurate within 2 per cent or so either way. There were many assumptions in the calculations, so even though the apparent lower limit was a little higher than the apparent upper limit, they are as close as can reasonably be expected. We suspect that a more careful analysis of the mass flows within the sector could reduce the uncertainty further, but without better data the effort would not be worthwhile. A similar analysis is attempted for the organic chemicals sectors in Chapter 7.

Endnotes

1. Many chemicals include two (or even more) key elements. In case one of them is a hydrocarbon base, we include it with the other element (for example, methyl chloride). Hydrocarbon-based chemicals apart, there are relatively few chemicals of importance that appear in more than one of these categories (for example, ammonium sulfate, ammonium chloride, phosphorus trichloride, diammonium phosphate, sodium chlorate).
2. Data in this section are taken largely from the article of 'Nitrogen' in US Bureau of Mines *Mineral Yearbook 1993*. As before, when the 1993 volume is referenced, we omit the year for convenience, that is, MY. In the case of nitrogen, all figures are given in terms of

contained nitrogen, not total mass. Nitrogen accounts for 82.2 per cent of the mass of ammonia.

3. The main sources of data for this chapter are US Bureau of Mines *Minerals Yearbook, 1993* (chapters on 'Sodium Sulfate' and 'Sulfur') and *Chemical and Engineering News* (CEN). The latter data base is available on the Internet. We refer to these sources respectively as (MY ...) and (CEN ...) for convenience.

4. We thank Tom Llewellyn of the US Bureau of Mines for his assistance. He is not responsible for any remaining errors.

5. It is important to emphasize this fact; to associate an undifferentiated 'waste coefficient' with the 'fertilizer sector' as a whole, or the 'inorganic chemicals' sector, in a country without a phosphate rock processing industry, would be grossly misleading. By the same token, it must be recognized that most countries in Europe that have significant phosphate rock processing sectors do not bother to control fluoride emissions, still less recover the fluorine for beneficial use. In countries like Algeria and Morocco this industry is extremely hazardous to workers and nearby residents.

6. The various sodium–phosphate molecules contain from 1 to 3 sodium atoms for each phosphorus atom, depending on alkalinity. Each time a hydrogen atom is substituted for a sodium atom, the molecule becomes more acid, and vice versa.

7. The first two figures for 1993 were from The Chlorine Institute and the Bureau of the Census, respectively, as cited in MY 'Salt', Table 9. The third figure for 1993 was from the magazine *Chemical and Engineering News* (CEN), June 24 1996 (and their on-line web page). The electrolytic process for chlorine production from brine yields 1.1 units of sodium hydroxide per unit of chlorine, with inputs of 1.75 units of sodium chloride. However, some chlorine is produced from magnesium chloride and some is regenerated from hydrochloric acid, so the ratios are not exact.

8. Most HCl (about 91 per cent) is recovered as a byproduct of one of the chlorination processes, especially the chlorohydrin process for propylene oxide production. The latter process consumed 502 kMT (4.6 per cent of supply) in 1993 but this chlorine is entirely recycled internally as HCl. The other major source of HCl is the process that converts EDC to vinyl chloride monomer (VCM); but HCl is also consumed by a parallel process that produces EDC by hydrochlorination of ethylene. These two processes are deliberately combined.

9. Swift did not give a specific number for use in manufacturing sodium hypochlorite. However the US Department of Commerce published data for production and shipments of chlorinated bleaches, which were mainly (85 per cent) sodium hypochlorite. Production and shipments were approximately equal and amounted to 635 kMT in 1991. We estimate 650 kMT for 1993. Unfortunately the quantity data are given as '100 per cent chlorine equivalent' with no explanation of what that means. We assume it means weight of active material, which would be NaClO. (The hypochlorite is always shipped as a solution, usually less than 7 per cent.)

10. The CMA disagrees with the association of paper and pulp manufacturers, which estimated chlorine consumption by the industry for 1993 to be 0.95 MMT (MEB c. 1995).

11. This use is being phased out as the anti-knock additive tetraethyl lead or TEL is phased out. But 1991 consumption of EDB was 24 kMT, and 1993 consumption (21 kMT) was not much lower. This implies that TEL consumption was also still significant.

12. The breakdown for 1993 was as follows: CCl_3F or CFC-11 (65 kMT at 10 per cent F); CCl_2F_2 or CFC-12 (168 kMT at 24 per cent F), and $CHClF_2$ or HCFC-22 (264 kMT at 34 per cent F) (USITC 1994).

13. As noted earlier, sodium sulfate is also a byproduct of rayon manufacturing.

14. The name comes from the historical fact that in Europe it was obtained by burning seaweeds: 13 tons of ash yielded 1 ton of soda ash. Potash was also derived from wood ash.

15. About 1.8 tons of brine are needed to produce 1 ton of soda ash (MY 'Soda Ash', p. 1070). Since production was nearly 9 MMT, there must have been about 7.2 MMT of spent brines or other wastes, mainly waterborne.

16. In addition, the same group of chemicals absorbed about 3 per cent of US caustic soda

(NaOH) output, or about 375 kMT (216 kMT Na content), although most of this probably went into soap manufacture. The sodium content of the sulfonated fatty acids – another type of synthetic detergent – must be proportional to the sulfur content (4.5 per cent) in a ratio of 23/32 (the ratio of atomic weights). This implies a sodium requirement for sulfonated fatty acids of 3.2 per cent or about 32 kMT for an assumed total production of 1 MMT.

17. Data for silicon metal production were given again in 1991 (176 kMT) but except for one of the smallest uses (in cast iron) all uses were 'unspecified' (MY 1991 'Silicon', Table 3). In the 1993 *Minerals Yearbook* silicon metal is not even distinguished from ferrosilicon, although US consumption in that year was 'estimated' at 220 kMT (USBM 1994, *Mineral Commodity Summaries*, 'Silicon'). This reticence is undoubtedly due to the small number of producers of all of the key products. For example, there are only three US producers of silicones and only one major producer of optical fibers (Corning Glass Co.).

18. For a detailed account see Ayres and Ayres 1996, Chapter 11 'Electronic Grade Silicon' and references therein.

19. The link arises from the fact that ethyl bromide is used as a scavenger for lead in gasoline. The ratio can be verified by checking historical statistics on bromine and lead consumption (for example, USBM 1985, chapters on 'Bromine' and 'Lead').

7 Chemical industry material flows and wastes: Organic chemicals

7.1 Organic (carbon-based) chemicals[1]

Organic feedstocks consist mainly of hydrocarbons, carbohydrates and fats. The first category is by far the most important. Most organic industrial chemicals are based on petrochemical (hydrocarbon) feedstocks derived from natural gas or petroleum refineries, with a smaller contribution from coal tar. There are three basic categories: (1) *paraffins (alkanes)*, which are saturated aliphatic (straight or branched-chain) hydrocarbons, the most important of which are methane, ethane, propane, isobutane, and n-butane; (2) *olefins (alkenes)*, unsaturated aliphatics with one or more double bonds, for example, ethylene, propylene, butylene, butadiene; (3) *cyclics and aromatics*, for example, benzene, toluene, xylenes, cyclopentane, cyclohexane and naphthalene. There is a fourth, *miscellaneous*, group of non-hydrocarbons including oxygenated compounds of organic origin, methanol, alcohols, cellulose, fatty acids and related chemicals.[2]

The statistics are both inadequate and confusing. As discussed in Chapter 4, the annual energy balances compiled by the International Energy Agency (IEA) of the OECD provided some explicit statistics on aggregate 'feedstocks' consumed by the petrochemical industry for each country. We used those numbers in preparing Figure 4.2 for 1993. The figure shows explicit flows of 44.22 MMT from gas processing and refineries to petrochemicals (although explicit *inputs* to petrochemicals add up to only 42.98 MMT). However, very large amounts of fuels and feedstocks are not specified as to destination or usage by the IEA. It is possible – indeed reasonable – to suppose that some of this unaccounted for material is also consumed as feedstocks by the petrochemical sector.

According to the US International Trade Commission (USITC), primary products from petroleum and natural gas for chemical conversion, including methane, C_2–C_4 olefins, C_5 and 'other' aliphatics (including methane), and aromatics, amounted to approximately 50 MMT in 1988, 54.1 MMT in 1991 and 54.72 in 1993 (USITC 1988, 1991, 1993). A detailed breakdown by category was published for 1988 and 1991, but data for 1993 was much less complete. Of the 1991 total, about 41.6 MMT consisted of aliphatic hydrocarbons (of which C_2–C_4 olefins accounted for 36 MMT) and 12.5 MMT consisted of aromatics and naphthenes. For 1993, unfortunately, the inputs were no longer broken down by source or compiled in a convenient form by the USITC. However, we suspect that since the totals for the two years are virtually identical, the subtotals are probably very nearly so. The USITC data for 1991 and 1993 is shown in Table 7.1. It is important to emphasize that these numbers refer only to chemical feedstocks produced domestically from petroleum and natural gas.

The US Bureau of Mines introduced a chapter on 'Nonrenewable Organic Materials' in its 1993 yearbook, reflecting the increasing importance of plas-

Table 7.1   US primary feedstock production (MMT)

		1991	1993
Aliphatics and olefins			
C_2	Acetylene	0.137	0.123
	Ethylene	18.123	18.149
		18.260	*18.272*
C_3	Propylene	9.774	9.739
C_4	Butadiene and butylene fractions	1.047	n.a.
	1,3-Butadiene for rubber	1.385	1.414
	1-Butene	0.425	0.239
	Isobutane	0.499	0.875
	Isobutylene	0.441	n.a.
	Other C_4	n.a.	n.a.
		6.340	*n.a.*
C_5	Isoprene	0.214	0.277
	Pentenes, mixed	0.189	n.a.
	Other C_5	1.294	n.a.
		1.697	*n.a.*
All other aliphatics (including methane)		5.558	n.a.
Aromatics and naphthenes			
Benzene, all grades		5.209	5.548
Toluene, all grades		2.857	2.277
Xylenes, mixed		2.866	0.377 o-xylene
			2.627 p-xylene
All other aromatics and naphthenes		1.537	n.a.
		12.469	*n.a.*
Grand total		54.098	54.720

Source: Data from USITC 1991, 1993.

tics, synthetic fibers, synthetic rubber, asphalt, lubricants and so forth in our industrial economy. Based on data from the US Department of Energy (USDOE) it provided an estimate for apparent domestic consumption of petrochemical feedstocks of 74.54 MMT, of which 66 MMT was domestic in origin and net imports were 9.47 MMT.[3] We also take note, incidentally, that the corresponding USBM figures for 1991 were 64.03 MMT for domestic feedstocks plus net imports of 8.23 MMT (ibid.). Thus total feedstock consumption according to USDOE accounting grew by over 3 MMT, from 1991 to 1993, but total consumption according to the USITC grew by only 0.6 MMT. This seems anomalous.

The explanation for this apparent disagreement between USITC and USDOE is probably that the USDOE defined feedstocks differently from the USITC. Whereas the USITC considered olefins (for example, ethylene and propylene) to be feedstocks, the USDOE defined feedstocks to be natural gas, natural gas liquids, naphtha and refinery off-gas. Indeed, C_2–C_4 olefins are derived to a large extent from so-called 'light ends' produced in petroleum refineries.[4] A typical US refinery might yield 1.3 per cent light ends (including refinery off-gas) by volume, from the initial distillation (Gaines and Wolsky 1981). However, subsequent refining processes such as catalytic cracking, catalytic reforming and delayed coking, also yield large – and variable – quantities of light ends. Separate data are not readily collected for light ends, natural gasoline or reformate, due to the prevalence of mixed streams generated and converted internally within the refineries.

Most of these volatile byproducts are used internally within the refinery complex. The mixed C_1 and C_2 gases (methane, ethane and ethylene) are partially used as fuel for steam generation to provide heat energy for the refinery itself. They are not counted as feedstocks by the USITC. The C_3 gases (propane, propylene) are collected and liquefied under pressure and partly consumed as domestic fuels (LPG). The C_4 gases (butylene, isobutane and n-butane) are mostly alkylated or blended directly into gasoline. Nevertheless, light ends also constitute a source of aliphatic petrochemical feedstocks. In brief, light alkane feedstocks like ethane (C_2H_6), propane (C_3H_8), and butanes (C_4H_8) – along with some naphtha and heavy gas oil (HGO) – are dehydrogenated in a pyrolysis furnace (within the refinery complex) to ethylene (C_2H_4), propylene (C_3H_6), butadiene (C_4H_6), butene, butylene (C_4H_8) and other C_4 olefins. Large amounts of hydrogen-rich off-gases are produced at this stage, but these are mostly used for hydro-treatment of naphtha or for hydro-forming within the refinery. Some C_4 and C_5 gases were used as octane-boosters in gasoline, or as solvents, and some were converted to hydrogen (mostly used in the refining process) or to carbon black.[5] Similarly, catalytic reformate (derived from naphtha), is the major source of aromatic feedstocks, known as BTX (benzene-toluene-xylene), although most of this material is subsequently blended into gasoline to increase the octane number. However most downstream synthetic organic chemicals are also derived from the above starting points or from the inorganic intermediates discussed previously.

In addition to the above, natural gas is both a feedstock and a fuel. It is difficult to determine objectively how much of the gas consumed is for one purpose rather than the other. Having said this, we can assume that both the USITC numbers and the USBM/USDOE numbers for 1993 are reasonably accurate, but that they refer to different stages of processing. In effect, the more narrowly defined USITC feedstocks are derived from the USDOE feedstocks. If so, we can safely adopt the USITC figures as a basis for further downstream analysis. However, we must bear in mind the fact that the USITC did not collect any data on imports, either of feedstocks or intermediates. Yet we know that, in some cases at least, imports are significant. For instance, 30 per cent of US methanol consumption in 1993 was imported (MY 1993 'Nonrenewable organic materials', p. 757).

In addition to hydrocarbons there are also some chemical products that originate from animal or vegetable materials. Cellulose (from wood pulp) is one of these. Output of 'cellulosics' in 1993, including rayon and cellulose acetate, was 229 kMT (fibers) and 37 kMT (resins) (MY 'Nonrenewable Organic Materials', Tables 6, 9). Since these products retain the cellulose molecular structure (Shreve 1956, p. 747), we assume that cellulose inputs were comparable in magnitude, or about 300 kMT, down from about 400 kMT in 1988. Animal and vegetable fats and oils (especially coconut and palm oils) are also starting points for industrial products such as surface-active agents. The USITC and IEA do not specify the quantity of raw materials for these products, but according to the US Department of Agriculture, animal and vegetable fats and oils for all industrial use, excluding animal feeds, amounted to 1.5 MMT (see Chapter 2 and Figure 2.3). Most of this was converted by the chemical sector into soaps, detergents and other surface active agents. We have already discussed sodium phosphates, which are important inorganic ingredients for detergents and water softeners. They are *not* included in the following.

To summarize, we have accounted for organic inputs (aliphatics, aromatics, fats and oils and cellulose) amounting to $54.7 + 0.3 + 1.5 = 56.5$ MMT in 1993. In addition, we must include 2.1 MMT of imported methanol (MY 'Nonrenewable Organic Materials', p. 757), 1.65 MMT of sulfuric acid (0.517 MMT S), 4.4 MMT of sodium hydroxide, 7.5 MMT of halogens (mainly chlorine), 2.7 MMT of ammonia and small amounts of phosphorus, silicon and various other metals (< 0.3 MMT). These further inputs add up to around 18.4 MMT. The grand total of purchased inputs therefore comes to roughly 75 MMT, not including imported intermediates (if any) or oxygen from the air. We return to the question of oxygen later.

7.2   Conversion

Most methyl and methylene (C_1) compounds (based on a CH_3 group) are methanol derivatives. The major examples include formaldehyde, methyl ether, methyl amines, methyl chloride, methyl-tert-butyl ether (MTBE), and so on. A schematic chart showing the relationships is shown in Figure 7.1. Ethyl or ethylene (C_2) compounds – based on a $CH_2=CH_2$ or $CH_2.CH_3$ grouping – now start from ethylene, although acetylene was an important feedstock earlier in this century. They include ethanol, ethyl ether, ethylene oxide, ethylene glycol, ethyl amines, ethyl chloride, ethylene dichloride, vinyl chloride, vinyl acetate, and so on. Methyl-ethyl combinations include acetic acid, acetone, acetic anhydride, acetaldehyde, etc. The ethylene derivatives are shown in Figure 7.2.

Higher order (C_3) compounds based on propylene (C_3H_6) include isopropyl alcohol (propanol), propylene oxide, propylene glycol, and acrylonitrile. Propylene derivatives are shown in Figure 7.3. Butene, C_4H_8 is usually converted to 1-3, butadiene (C_4H_6) or n-butyl alcohol (butanol). Butadiene is mainly used as a component of synthetic rubber. Methyl ethyl ketone (MEK) and glycerol are important downstream derivatives of n-butyl alcohol (butanol).

The aromatics, benzene, toluene, xylene(s) and naphthenes are all characterized by one or more rings of six carbon atoms, with some of the hydrogens replaced by other atoms (such as halogens) or groups, such as methyl, ethyl, hydroxyl (OH), carbonyl (CO) or amine (NH_2) radicals. Aromatic intermediates of importance include ethyl benzene, styrene, phenol, cumene, cyclohexane, maleic anhydride, phthalic anhydride, adipic acid, caprolactam, terephthalic acid (TPA), hexamethylene diamine (HMDA), nitrobenzene, chlorobenzene, toluene diisocyanate, and so on. (Some of these are combinations with olefins or alcohols.) Polymers from these building blocks include polyesters, polyethylene terephthalate (PET), polyurethanes, phenolics, alkyds and others. Synthetic fibers are among the most important categories of final products. Derivatives of benzene and toluene are shown schematically in Figure 7.4. Xylene derivatives are shown in Figure 7.5.

According to the International Trade Commission (USITC) total US production of synthetic organic chemicals in 1993 was 146.98 MMT (USITC 1993, Table 2), of which 82.565 MMT were sold. The remainder was consumed within the same establishment or transferred to another establishment of the same firm. However, even the sales figure included a great many chemicals used to make other chemicals and therefore consumed inside the sector. There is no public source of data on the exact mass of chemicals sold to end users outside the chemical sector. However, through careful application of the mass balance principle we can reduce the uncertainty by a large margin, as will be shown in the following paragraphs.

To calculate an upper limit of final outputs, we need to subtract the mass of all of the products that are definitely consumed *inside* the chemical sector.

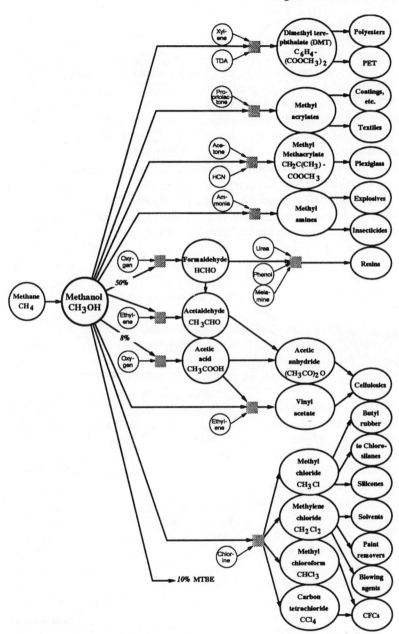

Note: *xx%* = % 1998 US production.
Source: Gains and Shen 1980.
Figure 7.1   Product flows from methanol, US 1978

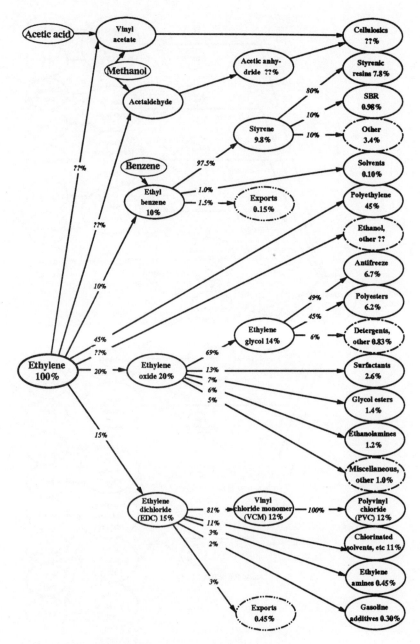

Notes: *yy*% = percentage of precursor. *xx*% = percentage of seedstock.
Source: Gains and Shen 1980.
Figure 7.2   Product flows from ethylene, US 1978

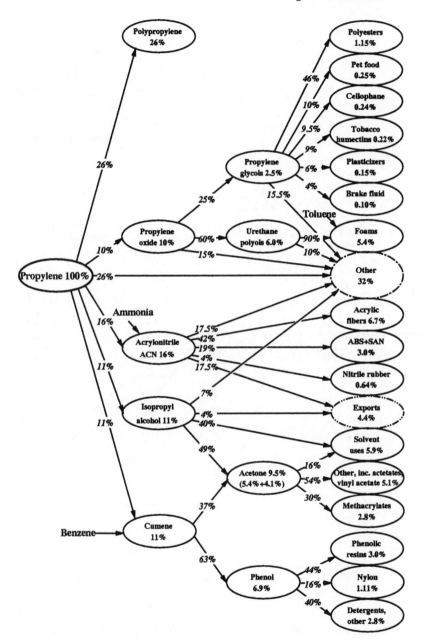

Notes: yy% = percentage of precursor. xx% = percentage of feedstock.
Source: Gains and Shen 1980.
Figure 7.3   Product flows from propylene, US 1978

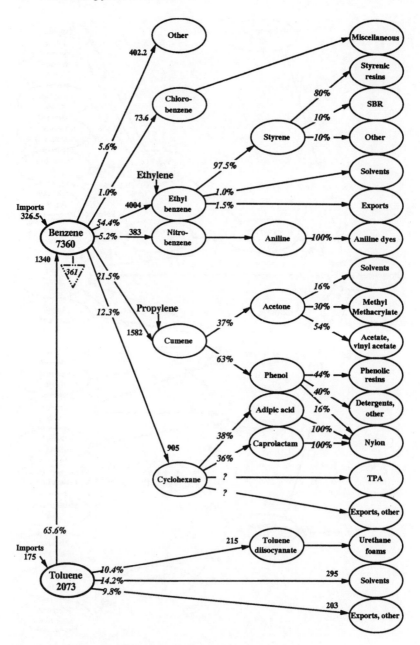

Notes: yy% = percentage of precursor. yy = US 1988 production (kMT).
Sources: IEI 1991; H.M. Mittelhauser Inc. 1979.
Figure 7.4   Product flows from toluene and benzene, US 1988 (kMT)

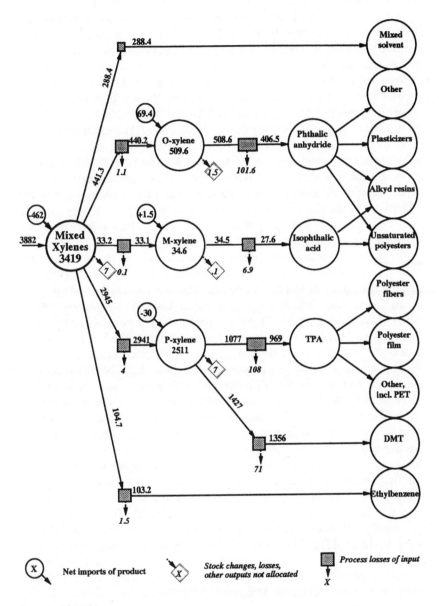

Source: IEI 1991.

Figure 7.5 Product flows from xylene, US 1988 (kMT)

For instance, to avoid double counting inputs as outputs we should subtract the domestically produced methanol, which was 4.765 MMT. Another category that can be subtracted, for the same reason, is the *cyclic intermediates*. This category (as defined by the USITC) includes the aromatic feedstocks (benzene, toluene and xylene, or BTX) as well as downstream cyclic chemicals such as ethylbenzene, cyclohexane, adipic acid, cumene, phenol, bisphenol A, styrene, and a number of others, although a few cyclic intermediates are omitted by the USITC for unknown reasons (see below). Total production of these chemicals in 1993, according to the USITC was 29.543 MMT, of which 10.981 MMT was sold and the rest was consumed by the same producer.

There are, of course, many non-cyclic intermediates that are almost never sold 'beyond the fence'. Formaldehyde, acetic acid, acetic anhydride, acetaldehyde, ethyl alcohol for chemical use, ethylene oxide, propylene oxide, isopropyl alcohol, methyl chloride, carbon tetrachloride, chloroform, phosgene, ethylene dichloride, vinyl chloride and vinyl acetate are all examples. However, adding them up individually is not only tedious, but essentially impossible due to lack of production data for many of the small volume chemicals.

The alternative is to identify end use chemicals as such. In these cases, it is sales 'across the fence' that we are interested in. The USITC identifies several explicit categories of end use chemicals. The first consisted of *plastics and resins* (polymers), including synthetic fibers. Total 1993 sales was 29.003 MMT (USITC 1993, Table 2). As it happens, this figure omits some things that properly belong in the plastics and resins category. The USITC allocated nylon and polyethylene terephthalate (PET) for fibres (1991 sales 1.604 MMT) and all water-soluble polymers (1991 sales 0.286 MMT) with 'miscellaneous end use chemicals', rather than with plastics and resins (USITC 1991, section 14). If these two were reallocated from miscellaneous to plastics and resins, and if 1993 sales was the same as 1991 sales (a plausible approximation), the extrapolated overall figures for 1993 sales of plastics and resins would be (roughly) 30.9 MMT. An industry magazine estimated 1993 sales of plastics and resins as 31.219 MMT, but this figure still omitted one plastic, ethylene vinyl acetate (EVA) for which no 1993 data were given, although reported sales in 1991 had been about 0.5 MMT (*Modern Plastics*, January 1994). For consistency, however, we use the USITC figures.

Another USITC end use category was plasticizers. Plasticizer sales in 1993 were 0.912 MMT (USITC 1993, Table 2). Synthetic *elastomers* (that is, rubber) was also in the end use category. Sales were 1.877 MMT (ibid.). The Bureau of Mines gives 1993 shipments of synthetic rubber of 1.993 MMT (MY 'Nonrenewable Organic Materials', Table 13). *Rubber processing chemicals* was also an identified category: sales in 1993 were 139 kMT (ibid.).

The USITC also explicitly identifies *medicinal chemicals* which correspond to SIC 2833 and 2834 (pharmaceuticals). Sales were 120 kMT (USITC

1993, Table 2). It breaks out *surface active agents*, which are part of SIC 2841 (soap and detergents) and SIC 2843 (other surface active agents); sales were 1.948 MMT (ibid.). It also broke out *flavor and perfume materials* (presumably of SIC 2844), which had sales of 72 kMT. Dyes and organic pigments were distinguished by the USITC, for some reason (probably tariff rates), although both belong to SIC 2865, which also includes cyclic intermediates. Taking them together, sales were 185 kMT (USITC 1993, Table 2). Finally, the USITC breaks out *pesticides and related products* (SIC 2879) with sales of 413 kMT (ibid.).

The sales of all of the categories listed in the last three paragraphs were to end users. Adding them up, we have sales 'across the boundary fence' of approximately 37.3 MMT, for these product categories.

Finally, the USITC identifies a set of miscellaneous end use chemicals that does not correlate with any particular SIC, or with the prior categories. Sales were 12.934 MMT in 1993 (USITC 1993, Table 2). This category includes chelating agents (for water treatment), enzymes, fuel additives (mainly MTBE), lubricating oil additives, polymers not included in the plastics and resins category – notably nylon and polyethylene terephthalate (PET), and urea for feed and fertilizer. We have already taken the liberty of shifting the polymers (estimated 1993 sales of 2.9 MMT) back into the plastics and resins category. According to the USITC, production of urea for feed and fertilizer was 8.047 MMT, but sales data for 1993 were suppressed (USITC 1993, Table 3.1, pp. 204–5). However, from the Bureau of Mines we had data on consumption of urea for fertilizers and animal feeds (3.029 MMT (N) or 6.49 MMT). We can probably equate consumption with sales. In any case, since this chemical has been accounted for already (under the heading of nitrogen chemicals), urea can be subtracted from miscellaneous end uses.

These two subtractions add up to 9.39 MMT. The unallocated 'leftovers' in the miscellaneous end use category is therefore $12.934 - 9.39 = 3.724$ MMT for sales. This is problematic, however, because production of one single product, the gasoline additive methyl-tert-butyl ether (MTBE) in 1993 was 6.748 MMT, and sales (to refineries) were 5.369 MMT (USITC 1993, pp.3–42). Another source gave production of MTBE as 5.852 MMT, as compared to 4.93 MMT the previous year (CEN 1995). Either way, there is clearly a problem with the USITC data, at least with regard to sales. Allowing for other products, we estimate that the USITC must have undercounted sales in the miscellaneous end use category by at least 3.3 MMT for 1993. Actual sales to end uses must have been about 7 MMT.

The justification for this statement is as follows. In 1991 total sales in this miscellaneous end use category were 10.712 MMT of which polymers accounted for 1.604 MMT, urea for fertilizer and animal feed accounted for 5.053 MMT and MTBE accounted for 2.498 MMT, leaving 1.557 MMT for everything else. If everything else added up to 1.6 MMT in 1993 (which is plausible, but cannot be verified directly because of the change in USITC's chemical classification system) then total sales, *including* MTBE and urea and polymers would have been 16.4 MMT, while sales to end uses *excluding* urea and polymers must have been close to 7 MMT, rather than 3.7 MMT. Unfortunately we cannot explain this anomaly.

One final large but less clearly identifiable category used by the USITC consists of *miscellaneous cyclic and acyclic chemicals.* According to the USITC, production in this category was 57.409 MMT, while sales were 23.981 MMT Miscellaneous cyclics in the USITC classification (as of 1991) included caprolactam and maleic anhydride, both of which are intermediates derived from benzene.[6] The 'acyclic' subcategory includes acetates (vinyl), aldehydes (formaldehyde, acetaldehyde, butyraldehyde, and so on), alcohols (methanol, ethanol, propanol, butanol, glycols, MTBE, and so on), amines, fatty acids (lauric acid, palmitic acid, stearic acid, and so on) ketones (acetone, methyl ethyl ketone, and so on), nitriles (including acrylonitrile and acetonitrile), chlorocarbons such as EDC and VCM, fluorocarbons and silicone fluids.

Evidently, the miscellaneous cyclic and acyclic category consists mostly of intermediates. However, there are exceptions. Several examples can be identified. One is ethylene glycol ('antifreeze'). Production in 1993 was 2.359 MMT and sales were 2.250 MMT (USITC 1993, pp. 3–32).

There are other known end uses for organic chemicals that fit mostly into this miscellaneous category, notably as solvents. In fact, the solvents market in 1992 was estimated at 5.16 MMT, altogether (MY 'Nonrenewable Organic Materials', p. 759). The largest category of solvents (38 per cent, or 1.96 MMT) consisted of hydrocarbons, such as toluene and xylene. The next largest group was alcohols, esters and ethers (33 per cent), followed by chlorinated hydrocarbons (11 per cent),[7] ketones (9 per cent) and glycols (6 per cent) (ibid.). Of the total demand, 54 per cent (2.8 MMT) was consumed *within* the chemical industry by the paints, coatings, printing inks and adhesives subsectors (SIC 2851, 2891, 2893) (ibid.). The remainder (2.4 MMT) was sold to other industries or final consumers 'beyond the fence'.

We have no specific data on brominated chemicals, but their major uses (as flame retardants) depends on the fact that bromine is heavier than chlorine. We know that 177 kMT of bromine was used in 1993 (MY 'Bromine', Table 1) and that 60 per cent (106 kMT) went to the chemical sector. It seems safe to assume that bromine constitutes half of the weight of these chemicals. We guess that brominated organic chemicals amounted to 200 kMT in 1993. We also extrapolated (above) that silicones amounted to 400 kMT in 1993.

In its new (1993) classification system, the USITC identifies several end use categories not identified in the earlier system (USITC 1993, pp. 3–279 *et seq.*). One of them is rosin ester gums (129 kMT for both production and sales); another was dye carriers and finishing agents used in the textile industry (34.8 kMT for production and 32.3 kMT for sales, (ibid. pp. 3–280, 281). A bigger category was additives to lubricants and gasoline other than MTBE. The totals for production and sales in 1993 were 521 kMT and 510 kMT (ibid. pp. 282–3).

Finally, and most mysterious, there is a catch-all category consisting of all the chemical products not elsewhere counted and involving 5.098 MMT of production and 2.567 MMT of sales. Of the sales, two-thirds (1.715 MMT) consists of unspecified hydrocarbon mixtures for unspecified purposes, although solvent uses are probably included among them. The other third consists of a number of chemicals, of which about 125 kMT are alcohol mixtures and the rest are unspecified. Two uses specifically mentioned are 'prepared binders for foundry molds' and 'carbon black feedstocks'. Since carbon black is consumed in large quantities by the tire industry, and for printing inks, it seems likely that this use accounts for a significant fraction of the unspecified sales.

Adding up all the end use chemicals listed in the last several paragraphs we arrive at a subtotal of *at least* 6.2 MMT, and possibly as much as 8.8 MMT, of end uses not elsewhere counted, mainly antifreeze, and solvents. We think it is reasonable to split the difference (7.5 MMT). Putting it all together, organic chemical products for final consumption amounted to approximately 51.8 MMT. Granted some of the estimates and approximations we have made along the way introduce uncertainty, but we feel safe in asserting that the uncertainty is plus or minus 1 MMT. Table 7.2 shows the USITC end use data with modifications according to the discussion above.

We note again that many of the output compounds, such as alcohols, esters, ethers, ketones, and glycols are oxygenated. That is, oxygen is added at some point to a hydrocarbon base. A significant part of this oxygen is added during the production of methanol, of which US consumption in 1993 (6.8 MMT, including imports) embodied 3.3 MMT (O).[8] Additional oxygen is also needed for a number of downstream partial oxidation processes, such as production of acetaldehyde, acetic acid, acetic anhydride, acetone, ethylene and propylene oxides; synthetic ethanol, iso-propanol and butanol, acrylic acid, benzoic acid, adipic acid, terephthalic acid (TPA) and phthalic anhydride. In most of the above cases oxygen is obtained from the air, although in the case of adipic acid it is provided by nitric acid.

On reflection it is clear that most of the oxygen embodied in outputs was not embodied in inputs. (The main exceptions are detergents and cellulosics.) Based on a sample survey we did several years ago, the average oxygen content of synthetic organic products in 1988 was about 10 per cent. On this basis, we can assume that about 5 MMT of atmospheric oxygen was added by partial oxidation processes along the way.

Table 7.2   End use organic chemical products: US production and sales, 1993 (kMT)

	Production	Sales
Total counted	55337	47809
Dyes	154	140
Organic pigments	60	45
Medicinals and pharmaceuticals	184	120
Flavor and perfume materials	93	72
Rubber processing chemicals	159	139
Pesticides	644	413
Plastics and resins[a]	31917	29003
Elastomers	2621	1877
Plasticizers	963	912
Surfactants	3532	1948
Antifreeze (ethylene glycol)	2359	2250
CFCs[b]	249	212
Solvents (other than CFCs)[b]	n.a.	2200
Fuel additives	6748	5369
Lube oil and grease additives	521	510
Textile chemicals (ex. surfactants)	35	32
Miscellaneous chemicals n.e.c.	5098	2567

Notes:
[a]   Data from USITC summary Table 2.1 shown. It does not agree with data from detail Table 3.1 pp. 3–291 and pp. 3–313.
[b]   Authors' estimate. May be double counting. Not included in total sales.

Source: USITC 1993.

In summary, we have total inputs, including atmospheric oxygen, of the order of 80 MMT as compared to 51.8 MMT of salable organic products, plus 3 MMT of byproduct hydrochloric acid (HCl) as shown schematically in Figure 7.6. This translates to a mass disappearance of around 24.7 MMT, or about 31 per cent of the aggregate material inputs. This magnitude of mass loss is not as difficult to explain as it might at first seem, given the fact that many processes involve acid or alkali neutralization, resulting in simple wastes such as sodium sulfate and sodium chloride. Thus most of the sulfuric acid inputs to the sector (1.38 MMT) probably combined with sodium hydroxide to produce waste sodium sulfate: 1.38 MMT of H_2SO_4 would be neutralized by about 1.1 MMT of NaOH, generating nearly 2.5 MMT of sodium sulfate or sodium bisulfate and water, probably mostly unrecoverable.

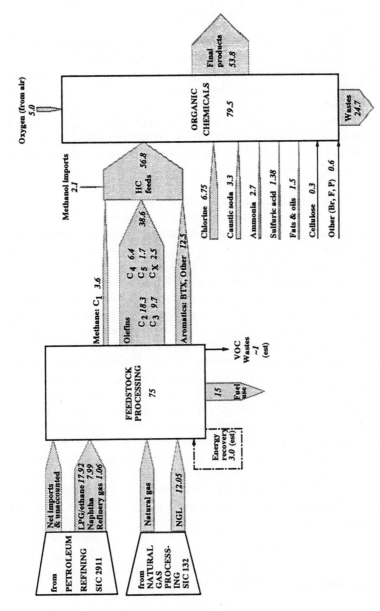

Figure 7.6   Materials balance for organic chemicals, US 1993 (MMT)

169

We have noted that (based on European data) only about 84 per cent of the 'virgin' elemental chlorine that is produced (11 MMT) is consumed within sector SIC 28; 16 per cent is consumed outside as chlorine. In addition 51 per cent 'crosses the fence' embodied in products (mainly PVC and solvents). The remainder (33 per cent) or about 3.6 MMT (Cl) – was probably lost within sector SIC 28, after having been converted to byproduct hydrochloric acid (HCl).

It is difficult to allocate the losses accurately between inorganic and organic processes. However, assuming inputs of 6.75 MMT (Cl), PVC would have accounted for 2.64 MMT (Cl) and chlorinated solvents another 0.6 MMT (Table 6.2). We postulated byproduct HCl sales of 3 MMT to other sectors (1.3 MMT to inorganics, 1.7 MMT to others) leaving 0.5 MMT, more or less, that was probably lost (as HCl) within the organic sector. The acid would have neutralized about 0.6 MMT of NaOH. These two strong acids together account for about 1.7 MMT of NaOH. The use of caustic soda in soap and detergent manufacturing has already been discussed, although this cannot account for more than 0.2 MMT of the caustic soda disappearance. This calculation implies that at least 2.5 MMT of additional caustic soda was neutralized in smaller increments by a variety of other organic and inorganic acids, including nitric acid, prussic acid (HCN), formic acid, acetic acid, carbonic acid, oxalic acid, propionic acid, acrylic acid, benzoic acid, and the fatty acids (stearic, lauric, palmitic, and so on).

The above calculation is not very plausible. It suggests that either we have overestimated the input of NaOH to the organic chemical sector, or overestimated sales of byproduct HCl outside the sector, or – more probably – both. For instance, if we cut assumed imports of NaOH (to the organic sector) by 1.1 MMT (to 3.3 MMT) and cut assumed exports of HCl (from the sector) by 1 MMT (to 2 MMT), leaving 1.5 MMT of HCl for disposal within the sector. The overall mass disappearance is practically unchanged but now only 0.5 MMT of NaOH must be accounted for by neutralization of weak acids. This result is much more realistic. Of course it has implications for the inorganic sector, which would require a new set of calculations. For the present we propose to leave the final balance for others with better access to data.

It is not important for our purposes to confirm the acid–alkali balance, or imbalance, as the case may be. The point of such an exercise has already been made: the sophisticated use of mass balances is a very effective way of identifying discrepancies and anomalies in the data, filling in omissions, and even correcting outright errors. We have illustrated all of these applications in this chapter.

While acid–alkali neutralization can potentially account for a significant amount of the mass disappearance in the synthetic organic chemicals sector (at least 6.5 and perhaps 8.5 MMT), other losses remain significant in magnitude and are less easy to explain. Another mass loss would be the dissipative use of process intermediates such as organic solvents. We noted a few paragraphs back, in connection with identifying end use products, that more than half of the organic solvents (2.4 MMT) were consumed (that is, dissipated) within the chemical industry. They were mainly used in the production of paints, pigments, adhesives and coatings. Actually, some of these solvents were probably incorporated in products. But even if all of this 2.4 MMT was lost to the air or water, we still have an unexplained mass disappearance of over 17 MMT (28 – 8.5 – 2.4).

The explanation must be related, in part, to the fact that many synthetic organic products result from a sequence of several processes, each of which might have a yield efficiency (based on inputs) of 95–98 per cent. A sequence of three to four such processes can easily account for a total carbon (or other feedstock) loss of the order of 10 per cent or 15 per cent, and perhaps more. And these losses of unreacted or partially reacted feedstocks are likely to be the wastes of most concern from an environmental perspective. But, even if 15 per cent of the input hydrocarbon mass (58 MMT more or less) were lost cumulatively in this way, the total amount would be no more than 9 MMT. In fact, we doubt that it could be more than 10 per cent (6 MMT), if that much. This would still leave us with an unexplained loss of 11 MMT.

Only one possibility remains, as far as we can see. The greater part of the mass disappearance must be feedstock (carbon) losses converted to water vapor and carbon dioxide resulting from the various oxidation processes in the industry. Several MMT of hydrocarbon feeds, including some natural gas and much of the hydrogen released by direct chlorination and oxychlorination processes, was undoubtedly consumed – in effect – as fuel to generate process heat. Yet, given the magnitudes of the various feedstock flows, it is difficult to imagine how this could account for as much as 11 MMT. A more plausible estimate would be 5 MMT. So, we are left with something of a mystery. Have we omitted a major input (for example, lime)? Have we omitted some important category of products, for which quantitative data are lacking (for example, paints or adhesives)? We simply do not know. What we do know is that the available data are sadly inadequate.

A more detailed analysis, making more intensive use of chemical process simulation models, might enable us to carry the above line of reasoning further. In fact, we believe that simulation models could enable us to estimate roughly the composition and allocation of emissions between gases vented to the atmosphere, waterborne wastes, and solids or sludges mostly disposed of on land. Such models might also enable the identification of specific opportunities to reduce overall wastes and emissions from the chemical industry. However, this would take us far beyond the scope of this chapter.

7.3   Conclusions

The synthetic organic chemical industry in 1993 consumed 56.8 MMT of hydrocarbon feedstocks, plus imported methanol. In addition, other mass inputs brought the total to 79.5 MMT, including 5 MMT of atmospheric oxygen. However final products that we can account for amounted to 54.8 MMT, including 3 MMT of byproduct hydrochloric acid.[9] Inorganic chemicals consumed within the sector included about 1.38 MMT of sulfuric acid (100 per cent); 1.5 MMT of chlorine was consumed as HCl within the sector, 3.3 MMT of caustic soda (NaOH) was used for acid neutralization within the sector, and some ammonia was also lost as unrecoverable ammonium bisulfate. It is likely that just about a quarter (6.5 MMT) of the 25 MMT difference between estimated input mass (79 MMT) and product weight (54 MMT) in the synthetic organic chemical industry results from the mutual interaction between, and neutralization of, strong acids and alkalis.

Another category of loss consists of chemical products dissipated in their final use. Detergents and cleaning agents, water softeners and chelating agents, solvents, lubricants, flocculants and flotation reagents, fuel additives, wood preservatives, fire retardants, pesticides, medicinals, paints and pigments, are all examples of such materials. Pesticides, especially, are 'instant pollutants'. The same is true of chemicals used to protect and preserve organic materials from decay, such as leather tanning chemicals and wood preservatives.

The chlorinated, brominated and fluorinated solvents constitute another especially dangerous subgroup because many of the process intermediates are toxic or carcinogenic, while some final products tend to be persistent and bio-accumulative. Some, like chlorinated biphenyls (PCBs), pesticides like DDT, and wood preservatives like pentachlorophenol (PCP), were thought to be harmless to humans and therefore safe to use. Biocides obviously have their uses, but when misused they can cause environmental damage far out of proportion to the quantities involved. The non-hydrogenated compounds such as fluorocarbons CFC-11, CFC-12 and CFC-22 are chemically inert and biologically harmless (as far as is known) but are harmful when they get into the stratosphere and release atomic chlorine when irradiated by the sun's ultra-violet light. The atomic chlorine, in turn, interacts with and catalytically destroys the stratospheric ozone layer. The presence of certain nitrogen chemicals, under some conditions, can accelerate the ozone destruction process, as occurs in the annual ozone holes.

Fertilizer chemicals, especially fixed nitrogen (as ammonia), phosphates, sulfur and potash constitute a special category, inasmuch as dissipative use cannot be simply equated to pollution. In all cases (especially nitrogen and sulfur) the natural biogeochemical cycles are accelerated, if not disrupted. Excessive fertilization – known as eutrophication – is a problem of increasing concern in rivers, lakes and coastal waters near industrial areas. Micro-organisms grow explosively until they reach a natural limit imposed by the availability of some nutrient, or oxygen. When the supply of oxygen is exhausted, there is a mass die-off and the decaying biomass continues to consume any available oxygen. The biological consequences in shallow waters with limited mechanisms for re-oxygenation can be devastating to fish and marine mammals. Another environmental problem associated with the acceleration of the nitrogen cycle is emission of nitrous oxides resulting from denitrification of nitrate fertilizers. However, about 25 per cent of fixed nitrogen, 10 per cent of phosphorus and 5 per cent of potash are used for chemical purposes other than fertilizers or animal feeds. In these cases, there is also potential for environmental toxicity. The example of cyanide (extensively used in the mining industry for gold, silver, copper and other mineral ore concentration) particularly comes to mind.

The last category of losses associated with the chemical industry consists of process losses of unreacted feedstocks (not including the acids or alkalis) or combustion wastes. We have estimated above that perhaps 0.3 MMT (2 per cent) of fixed nitrogen might be lost to the air or water in chemical conversion processes. Similarly, in the petroleum refining sector, which is the source of the hydrocarbon feedstocks for synthetic organic chemicals, losses are about 2 per cent. But the major losses in this category are undoubtedly in the synthetic organic chemical sector itself, where large mass losses remain unaccounted for. While we think that process losses probably account for 5 MMT, more or less, mass-balance arguments provide some reason to suspect that process waste and emissions due to incomplete reactions within the industry might amount to as much as 11 MMT (dry weight). Non-oxidized residuals are typically either volatile hydrocarbons in the vapor phase or heavier hydrocarbons or chlorocarbons in the aqueous phase. Our estimate, above, is obviously much larger than EPA's estimated 2 MMT of VOC emissions from the organic chemical industry. In addition, there are significant emissions of water vapor and carbon dioxide (from oxidation). A significant fraction of off-gases is used for fuel, as noted above, but some is simply flared, vented, or lost as 'fugitive emissions'.

It seems evident that the rather large estimates of 'dry' chemical wastes by EPA (USEPA 1986, 1988) cannot actually represent true dry weight. For example, EPA assigns 28.9 million tons of dry waste to the inorganic chemical sector (SIC 2812, 2819) and 49.6 million tons to the plastics and resins sector (SIC 2821). Given the very large wastes from phosphate rock processing alone, EPA's inorganic figure is clearly much too low. On the other hand, the EPA estimates for organic chemicals are probably significantly too high. These must consist largely of contaminated process water, or wet sludges. This is a very misleading measure of waste emissions, since it is relatively easy, in many cases, to reduce water-borne emissions by increased internal recycling of process water.

Opportunities for waste reduction in the chemical industry are not particularly great, as the industry is now structured. By far the greatest quantity of waste arises from processes of concentrating ores (notably phosphate rock and potash). Only substitute sources or reduced demand for chemical products could reduce these waste flows. (In fact, they will increase in future as ore grades decline.) Such opportunities as do exist are of two kinds. In the first place, process wastes are reduced if yields are improved or (even better) if new reactions are developed that skip a step in the process chain. Second, wastes are reduced *by definition* if uses can be found for them (Ayres and Ayres 1996).

Endnotes

1. We have defined the sector more broadly than the SIC definition. Our definition includes industrial organic chemicals (SIC 286) but also plastic materials and synthetic resins, synthetic rubber and synthetic fibers (SIC 282), drugs (SIC 283), soap detergents and cleaning preparations but *not* including inorganic chemicals used in such products, such as chlorinated household bleaches, ammonia used in household cleaners, sodium phosphates or methanol used for windshield cleaning fluids (SIC 284), acrylic and alkyd paints, plastic coatings (acrylic, epoxy, phenol-formaldehyde, polyurethane, vinyl), paint thinners and strippers, and so on (SIC 285), pesticides and agricultural chemicals n.e.c. (SIC 2879). We also include explosives based on organic materials, such as nitroglycerine, nitrocellulose, TNT, nitrostarch and nitrosugar.
2. The structural differences between feedstocks are somewhat important, since they bear some relationship to biological activity (including toxicity, allergenicity, carcinogenicity, mutagenicity, teratogenicity, and so on). It is increasingly suspected, for instance, that 'estrogen-like' chemicals in the environment may be responsible for long-term declines in male reproductive potential among many species, including humans. In some sense, all aromatics are more or less estrogen-like. This means that, lacking specific knowledge to the contrary, humans should be more wary of environmental exposure to small doses of aromatics than (for instance) to olefins, alcohols, fats or cellulosics. Apparently chlorinated aromatics are even more likely to be dangerous, on the average, than non-chlorinated ones.
3. See *Minerals Yearbook* 1993, 'Nonrenewable Organic Materials', Table 1. Feedstocks are defined as natural gas liquids (NGL), liquefied refinery gases (for example, LPG), dry natural gas, naphthas, other petroleum oils and still gas. The data in *Minerals Yearbook* were attributed to the US Department of Energy *Annual Energy Review* (Tables 2.6 and 3.1 and *Petroleum Supply Annual* Table 2). We find this odd, to say the least, because we presume that the IEA had access to the same USDOE publications in compiling its energy balance, yet somehow overlooked nearly 22 MMT of domestic feedstocks which were left in the 'unaccounted for' category (IEA 1995).
4. Light ends are compounds with boiling points in the range of butane (about 0°C) and below. Methane and the light alkanes (C_2–C_4) fall into this category.
5. Carbon black is used mainly for tires, of which it constitutes roughly 29 per cent by weight (Britton *et al.* 1993). Total tire production in the US for 1988 was roughly 2.2 MMT, accounting for 0.64 MMT of carbon, or 0.7 MMT of hydrocarbon feeds. There are other significant uses of carbon black, such as printing ink. On the other hand, some carbon black is made directly from natural gas.
6. Caprolactam is the monomer for nylon 6, and is entirely used for that purpose. Maleic anhydride, also derived from benzene, is an intermediate for unsaturated polyester resins

and alkyd resins, some pesticides, some oil additives and an end use as a preservative for fats and oils.

7. Chlorinated and fluorinated solvents are of special importance because of their environmental impact. The four major chlorinated solvents, and 1993 outputs, are 1,1,1 trichloroethane (205 kMT), methylene chloride (160 kMT, of which 120 kMT was destined for end uses), perchloroethylene (123 kMT) and trichloroethylene (65.7 kMT) (Swift 1995). The three principal fluorocarbons that were still produced in 1993 were CFC-11 (65 kMT), CFC-12 (168 kMT), and HCFC-22 (264 kMT) (USITC 1994). Essentially all of these were sold outside the chemical industry.

8. Not all methanol is consumed by the organic chemical industry. A significant amount is used as a solvent, especially as an automotive windshield washing liquid. We do not know how great this use is, but if each US automobile and truck utilized one liter per year, the total would come to 150 million liters/year or about 120 kMT. The actual consumption for this purpose could be greater but not enormously greater.

9. See earlier discussion of the acid–alkali balance, which suggests the strong possibility that both caustic soda inputs and hydrochloric acid sales have been overestimated by around 1MMT each. This would cut both total inputs and total product outputs by roughly the same amount; it would not change the mass disappearance, however.

8   Lost mass, wastes and toxic or hazardous emissions

8.1 Introduction

It is tempting, but not always justified, to simply equate lost mass with wastes. It is even less justified to assume that all wastes are environmentally harmful pollutants. In this chapter we hope to clarify the necessary distinctions and review the state of the statistical evidence. Our purpose here is not to assess the state of the environment as such (although we cannot avoid noting some indications).

In the remainder of this chapter we consider two types of mass flows that are important and need to be quantified better than they are. One of these mass flows is process water (which should include water used for irrigation in agriculture and drinking water consumed by livestock). At present, the mass-balance methodology cannot contribute much, although it is worth reviewing the state of the data briefly (next section). The other category is toxic and hazardous materials, where the mass balance methodology is far more relevant.

8.2 Water withdrawals and wastes

Water consumption by crops and forests is virtually undocumented, since the bulk of it comes from rainfall and/or groundwater, which are unmonitored. Water taken annually from rivers and streams for purposes of irrigation in the US amounts to roughly 200 km^3 or 200 000 MMT (since 1 m^3 = 1000 liters = 1000 kg = 1 metric ton). Much of this water is used inefficiently; it simply runs off on the surface or evaporates. That which is taken up by plants is virtually all used for evapotranspiration (that is, cooling of leaf surfaces). Clearly this mass flow dwarfs all others and, thanks to lack of data, makes it necessary to distinguish carefully between water that is involved in the photosynthesis process from water whose main function is cooling. The major environmental effect of this evaporation is, of course, to reduce earth surface temperatures relative to what they would be otherwise, and to humidify the air. In a tropical rainforest it is evapotranspiration from the leaf canopy that is the source of almost all of the rainfall. When the trees are removed the temperature rises and the rainfall decreases.

Throughout the last six chapters we have been reasonably consistent in ignoring the role of process water, with two exceptions. In the chapters on agriculture and forestry all the data refer to natural materials that contain considerable amounts of water, or to first level products that also embody water. We have had to estimate water content in these cases in order to perform mass balances. The other exception is that we have had to recognize that water (vapor) is a natural product of all combustion processes and some other chemical processes where water is released as a byproduct. Again, the application of mass balance methods requires that this water be taken into account, if only to estimate the other components of the waste stream.

On the other hand, we have purposely ignored process water and water of hydration contained in many natural minerals (for example, gypsum) and some products (such as hydrated alumina). This was done primarily because it is so difficult to account for water consumption accurately; the data on water consumption at the sectoral and subsectoral levels are extremely scarce and unreliable. But neglecting process water seems justifiable because water, as such, is environmentally neutral. The term 'wastewater' is convenient and – no doubt – inevitable. But it is inappropriate insofar as the water itself does no harm. It is merely the carrier of other wastes.

EPA, local authorities and industry associations commonly publish data on the discharge of 'wet' wastes that is virtually meaningless. An example that makes the point very clearly indeed comes from a highly touted 1987–88 survey of 176 domestic petroleum refineries by the American Petroleum Institute (API) (Bush and Levine 1992). The survey obtained responses from 115 refineries accounting for 80 per cent of domestic refining capacity. The principal result of the survey was that US refineries generated 16.1 million tons (14.6 MMT) of wet wastes in 1987 and 16.0 million tons (14.5 MMT) in 1988.

What were these wastes? It turned out that 10.2 MMT in 1987 and slightly over 10 MMT in 1988 were 'other aqueous wastes not otherwise specified' (ibid., p. 76). This single category accounted for 70 per cent of all the re- ported mass flows.[1] The rest of the list of reported wastes is only slightly less unrevealing. The next six listed items, in order of quantity reported, were 'biomass', 'spent caustics', 'DAF Float', 'API Separator sludge', 'pond sediments' and 'other inorganic wastes, not otherwise specified'. Non-aque- ous wastes were, respectively, 3.48 and 3.52 MMT in the two years, but the non-aqueous content of the wet wastes is unknown and water consumption – which would enable a calculation – is not reported. In fact, from the pub- lished data very little can be said about the chemical composition of these wastes, except perhaps biomass and spend caustics. Virtually nothing can be said about the environmental hazards involved.

Despite the absence of meaningful data, the API apparently took pride in the fact that 'these rates of waste generation represent to less than 3 per cent of total crude throughput' (Bush and Levine 1992, p. 73). Since airborne wastes such as CO_2 and VOCs – which are far greater in mass – were not counted by the survey, and most of the mass of wastes that were included in the survey was obviously process water, such a statement is absurd. Unfortunately, such pointless surveys (and meaningless statements) are still the rule, not the exception.

EPA does it too. According to EPA the pulp and paper sector (SIC 26) generated 2040 MMT of non-hazardous waste, the inorganic chemical sectors (SIC 281) generated 832 MMT; the plastics and resins sector (SIC 282) generated 164 MMT, the fertilizer/agrichemical sector (SIC 2873–79) generated 150 MMT; the petroleum refining sector (SIC 29) generated 152 MMT, the iron and steel sector (SIC 3312–3321) generated 1170 MMT, the electric power sector (SIC 4911) generated 990 MMT and so forth (USEPA 1988, 1991; Allen and Behmanesh 1992, Table II). Unfortunately, aggregated numbers like these are often used indiscriminately – for instance added together – without consideration of how these numbers were generated and how much (if any) of the mass of wastes is actually water.

For comparison, an earlier (1985) study by Science Applications Inc., sponsored by EPA (SAI 1985) estimated the 'dry' weights of waste from these sectors as follows: pulp and paper 8.6 MMT (1977); inorganic chemicals, 26.5 MMT (1979); plastics and resins manufacturing, 45 MMT (1982); fertilizer and agrichemicals, 59 MMT (1983); petroleum refining, 1.27 MMT (1983); primary iron and steel 60.2 MMT (1983) and electric power 55.7 MMT (1983) (Allen and Behmanesh 1992, Table III).

Water withdrawal and industrial use data are gathered by the US Census of Manufactures. For comparison with the EPA waste statistics noted above, it is convenient to use data from the 1983 Census. Results for mining and manufacturing are summarized in the National Water Summary 1987 (David 1987). Data are all given in units of million gallons per day (mgd). For conversion purposes, note that (in the case of water) 1 mgd = 1.379 MMT/year.

For the mining sector, total 1983 water intake was 3280 mgd. Of the intake, 523 mgd was designated as cooling water, mainly for petroleum and natural gas fractionation; 1440 mgd was designated as process water (for coal washing and flotation); the remainder of the intake was unaccounted for. The ratio of gross water use to intake for the sector was 3:1. Discharges for the whole sector were 2840 mgd, of which 1930 mgd were treated and 907 mgd were untreated. Discharges from coal mining alone were 340 mgd. The difference between intake and discharge (440 mgd) was presumably lost as water vapor (for example, from flotation ponds) or used for underground injection in the oil/gas sector.

The five biggest water users among the manufacturing industries were chemicals, paper and pulp, petroleum refining, steel, and food processing. The data given (David 1987) are inconsistent in some respects, so the following must be regarded as 'soft'.[2] The chemical industry is the largest water user. Intake was 9310 mgd, of which 7700 was for cooling purposes. Gross use was 26 400 (a reuse ratio of 2.8) and 17 000 mgd of water was recirculated, of which 15 500 was for cooling purposes. Total discharges were 8160 mgd, and consumptive use (or loss) was 1150 mgd. If it is assumed that the losses were water vapor from cooling towers, then cooling water discharges would be 7700 − 1150 = 6550 mgd, leaving process water discharges of 1610 mgd. In reality, cooling water and process water cannot be easily segregated, however, since cooling water is typically recycled several times, then used as process water before final discharge. Within the chemical industry, organic chemicals account for nearly half the discharges (3780 mgd), followed by inorganics (2080 mgd), plastics and synthetics (1070 mgd) and agricultural chemicals (556 mgd).

The paper and pulp industry is the next largest user, with gross use reported as 21 000 mgd and a recycling ratio of 3.9 (David 1987). This implies an intake level of 5400 mgd (7452 MMT). Cooling accounts for less than 30 per cent of this (approx. 1570 mgd) leaving up to 3500 mgd as process water. Discharges are not reported, but would presumably be slightly less than withdrawals, allowing for some evaporative losses. Since pulp and paper mills are mostly located in areas with ample fresh water supplies, there is little incentive to recycle cooling water. This implies that each unit of process water was recycled about 5 times before discharge into rivers and streams.

Another source reports that water requirements range from 80 to 240 metric ton (m^3) of fresh water per metric ton of paper produced (Nemerow 1995, p. 113). On this basis to produce 80 MMT of paper, water use would have been somewhere in the range of 16 000–48 000 MMT. By contrast, US EPA estimated total (that is, wet) wastes from pulp mills amounting to 2200 MMT in 1985 (USEPA 1988). Most of the chemicals lost from the process are certainly carried away in the wastewater, or the sludges from wastewater treatment. It is difficult to reconcile these figures, unless EPA underestimated total wastes and/or water use was declining very rapidly in the 1980s.[3] (Actually, the latter is not unlikely.)

Petroleum refining (SIC 29) withdrew 2100 mgd (2900 MMT), of which 91 per cent was used for cooling purposes and 9 per cent for processing (David 1987). For the petroleum industry gross use was 16 000 mgd, for a recycle ratio of 7.5. The ratio of cooling to process water is about 10:1. Wastewater discharges were therefore of the order of 260 MMT, which is not too far out of line with the EPA estimate of 152 MMT (USEPA 1988). Processing wastes are nevertheless significant. Crude oil is desalted by washing before refining. Water pollution from this process contains emulsified oil as well as salts, ammonia, sulfides and phenols.

For the steel industry (SIC 331) gross use was 16 100 mgd (22 200 MMT), with a recycle ratio of 2.5 and intake of 6470 mgd (9000 MMT) (David

1987). Of this, 3590 mgd was for cooling and 2460 mgd (3400 MMT) was for process use (for example, coke quenching, pickling). The iron and steel sector is mostly located on rivers or lakes with ample water availability, which probably explains this lavish use. (By contrast, the non-ferrous smelters and refineries are mostly located in drier parts of the country where water is much less available, and much less is used.) The USEPA estimated total non-hazardous wastes from the primary metals sector, as a whole, was 1170 MMT (USEPA 1988). This was obviously mostly water, but it still differs significantly from the Census figures. We cannot explain the difference.

As regards the food industry, gross use of 4100 mgd (5660 MMT) was reported, with a recycle ratio of 2.2 (David 1987). This implies an intake of 1850 mgd (2550 MMT), along with comparable discharges. (Discharges might actually exceed intakes, given the high water content of some foods, notably milk products.) Cooling water use is especially high for the sugar sector, but elsewhere in the industry it is not especially great.[4] It is worth noting that EPA's Office of Solid Waste Management conducted a survey (1985) which estimated total waste generation by the food processing sector (SIC 20) to be 336 MMT for the year 1985 (USEPA 1988). Evidently this includes washing and process waste water, but probably not all of it. EPA's estimate of waste discharges is only about 15 per cent of the Census figure for 1983. The two estimates can be reconciled if 85 per cent of the water intake was used for cooling purposes only.

The 1983 Census of Manufactures reported water intake by the entire mining sector (SIC 10), including coal, oil and gas, to be 3280 mgd (4500 MMT), while reported discharges were only 2840 mgd (3900 MMT) (David 1987). Of the withdrawals, 12 per cent was designated as for 'cooling' (mainly in the gas fractionation sector) and 44 per cent was designated as 'process' – mainly washing and froth flotation – while the remaining 44 per cent was unallocated. The 12 per cent figure implies that at least 700 MMT of water was used for cooling in the natural gas treatment (NGL extraction) process, but it could have been much more. Coal mining, oil and gas sectors produce much more water than they consume. EPA reported that the oil and gas sector alone produced somewhere in the neighborhood of 1800 to 2400 MMT of excess water (USEPA 1988). This presumably is included in discharges. The Census also reported that coal mines discharged 340 mgd (470 MMT) of water, including coal washing water. Based on this arithmetic, the rest of the mining sector therefore withdrew 3800 MMT and discharged 930–1530 MMT.

According to the Bureau of Mines, water used in froth flotation processes for metal and phosphate ore and concentration in 1985 was 3580 MMT (Edelstein 1987). This seems roughly consistent with the Census figures. Most of that water is discharged into ponds, whence it eventually evaporates or leaks into ground water. Clearly, a much more detailed study of water use and waste production in all sectors, but especially the mining sector, seems called for. One minimal recommendation that we would make to the statistical authorities of all countries is that much more detailed statistics on water consumption, water use by purpose, and water discharges, should be kept and published. Such statistics would greatly assist in future attempts to carry out more accurate mass flow analysis than we have been able to do in this book.

8.3   Toxic and hazardous materials and the TRI

The other category of materials that cannot invariably be analyzed by means of mass balances is toxic and hazardous materials. This is not the place for an attempt to define 'toxic' or 'hazardous'. Suffice it to say that the list of chemicals currently belonging to these categories is very long and that it changes from time to time as new evidence comes to light. The new evidence usually results in a lengthening of the list, but occasionally a chemical is removed from it.

The EPA's toxic release inventory (TRI) has become a model for Europe, if not the world. It began as a legislative response to several industrial accidents, such as the accidental release of methyl isocyanate (MIC) from a Union Carbide pesticide manufacturing facility at Bhopal, in India (December 3 1984). A few months later there was a similar (but much smaller) accident at a Union Carbide plant in West Virginia. These events, and others,[5] created public pressure for 'right to know' laws requiring industries to inform the public (through USEPA) about use and releases of toxic and hazardous chemicals. In October 1986 the US Congress passed a law, known as the Emergency Planning and Community Right-to-Know Act (EPCRA), which required manufacturers to report annually on toxic chemicals released on site or shipped off-site as waste. The Act also required EPA to compile these reports in a computerized data base, available to the public, known as the Toxic Release Inventory (TRI).

The original TRI specified 300 toxic and hazardous chemicals. (The range of coverage has been increased over time; it currently includes 650 chemicals.) However, the law on reporting applies only to manufacturers (SIC 20–39). It also exempts firms with less than 10 employees and chemicals with annual throughput/use of less than 25 000 lb (11.32 metric tons). Agriculture, mining, transportation, utilities and distribution activities are totally exempt from reporting.

Nevertheless, EPA and many environmental groups are very happy with this law. According to a recent assessment:

> Despite their initial reservations. TRI has generally proven to be positive for the business community. In many instances, top level managers had been unaware of the extent of pollution generated and its related financial costs until confronted

with TRI information. When faced with these facts for the first time, numerous firms began aggressive voluntary reduction efforts. (Hearne 1996, p. 7)

Environmental groups gleefully compile rankings of the most polluted regions or the 'dirty dozen' top toxic polluters. Oft-cited examples of industrial cleanups resulting from this publicity include BF Goodrich, which reduced toxic air emissions by 70 per cent after local citizens in Akron, Ohio became aware of the TRI data (ibid.). Monsanto is another firm that responded to the new data and subsequently became a strong public advocate of the process. It is also commonly attributed to this positive impact that many corporations (over 100 at last count) now routinely issue annual environmental reports (Hearne 1996).

Indeed, the World Bank is now using TRI data from the US manufacturing sectors to calculate international toxic intensity indexes for 80 countries for the period 1960–88 (Wheeler *et al.* 1992). These country-level toxic intensities are being used to assess development policy, trade policy and environmental regulation on a global basis. The authors confess that 'our calculation of international toxic intensity indexes from constant US-based sectoral intensities can only be defended as the best feasible procedure: actual toxic release data for other economies are unavailable' (ibid. p. 478).

The blind confidence of the World Bank econometricians in TRI is badly misplaced. Notwithstanding its undoubted beneficial effect on corporate performance (especially in the chemical industry), the real data on toxic releases is by no means available in the US. There is no reason to equate reported releases and transfers with actual emissions. In fact, to be blunt, the World Bank use of these numbers out of context – and outside the US – is totally irresponsible.

EPCRA, as passed by Congress, requires firms in the manufacturing sectors (SIC 20–39) to report only on discharges and off-site transfers of toxic or hazardous wastes. Even within the 'covered' sectors the law has major loopholes. The net effect is that coverage of actual emissions for many – perhaps most – toxic chemicals is, in fact, minimal. The Office of Technology Assessment (USOTA) of the US Congress actually estimated in 1989 that 95 per cent of the actual emissions of TRI chemicals would be missed by TRI.[6] Our own work and that of others, which we cite below, confirms this pessimistic assessment.

How then can a hazardous chemical 'disappear' from the statistics? Deliberate under-reporting is one possibility, of course. But the main explanations are as follows: (i) the chemical is released by a sector not covered by TRI, or it is released in many small increments below the minimum reporting threshold or by firms too small to be subject to reporting requirements; (ii) the chemical is included as a minor contaminant in some broader waste category[7] such as 'unspecified aqueous waste' or 'water treatment sludge' or 'incinerator ash', or even VOC, that is not broken down by component; (iii) the chemical is in 'classification limbo', for example, it is accumulating in 'temporary storage' that the firms do not choose to label as either a release or a transfer.[8]

There is also another possibility (iv), namely that the firms themselves do not really know where the substance is, how much remains in the plant, or what their process emissions are. Certainly, lacking any verification or auditing procedures, many of the questionnaires sent by EPA are answered carelessly.[9] It is widely acknowledged by industry insiders, for instance, that detailed questionnaires are often filled in by junior personnel, based on guesswork, copying from previous years, or by substituting government standards for actual numbers.

Mercury, one of the most toxic heavy metals, provides a good illustration. Mercury is used, nowadays, mostly in the electrolytic production of chlorine via the so-called mercury cell. It escapes very gradually and must be replaced. All consumption of mercury by the chlorine industry is for replacement purposes. (No new plants have been built in the US since the early 1970s.) The US Bureau of Mines publishes annual data on mercury production, consumption and major uses. The TRI publishes annual data on 'releases and transfers'. The data for the years 1987 through 1992 are shown in Table 8.1. They do not match.

Table 8.1   Where has the mercury gone?

	Mercury in SIC 2812 (Chlorine Production) USA, metric tons				
		USEPA TRI Data Base as reported by			
	USBM Minerals Yearbooks	USEPA Office of Pollution Prevention and Toxics	US Bureau of Mines		
Year	Consumption	Releases	Releases	Transfers	Total
1987	311	23.7			
1988	445	15.7			
1989	381	10.7	11.3	52.9	64.2
1990	247	11.0	11.0	58.5	69.5
1991	184	7.9	8.5	56.0	64.5
1992	209	6.3	4.5	8.7	13.2

The cumulative consumption of mercury by the US chlorine industry in the six years from 1987 through 1992 was 1777 metric tons. Virtually none was recycled. The logic of mass-balance says this mercury was lost. Yet cumulative releases reported by chlorine producers were only 75.3 metric tons, or 4.2 per cent of what was consumed. Where did the rest go? Transfers to off-site disposal only amounted to another 176 metric tons during 1989–92, even as 1021 metric tons of mercury were consumed. The discrepancy is obvious and shocking. And, it is not explained by any of the reporting exemptions. Certainly, in the case of mercury used by the chlorine producers, the problem must be either (iii) or (iv) on the above list.

Natural Resources Defense Council (NRDC) issued a report 'The Right To Know More' (Sheiman 1991), which was an exhaustive analysis of toxic emissions by sectors exempted from reporting to the TRI. Much of the material summarized in the remainder of this section is documented in that report, which was based mostly on USEPA studies. We proceed, as NRDC did, in SIC order, beginning with agriculture.

It is ironic that pesticide (and fertilizer) manufacturers must report toxic releases from manufacturing operations to TRI, whereas the uses of those chemicals in agriculture (SIC 01) – which are highly toxic – go unreported. It would be tempting to assume that all pesticides produced are used by farmers, simply equating production with emissions. However, pesticides and herbicides are also used extensively, of course, by horticulturists, golf courses, exterminators (SIC 7342) and so on. Wood preservatives are also used by the lumber industry. A significant fraction of output is exported. USEPA's Domestic Sewage Study (DSS) in 1986 reported that 600 kMT of pesticides is discharged annually to sewers (Sheiman 1991, p. 29).

Actually pesticide use by farmers was reasonably well documented by the USDA in periodic surveys. Production of pesticides has been reported, as a category, by the US International Trade Commission in its annual publication *Synthetic Organic Chemicals*, which has unfortunately been recently discontinued. Pesticides are among the most dangerous toxic chemicals, because they are often used carelessly. This has resulted in unnecessary exposure of agricultural workers, not to mention occasional episodes of poisoning of homeowners by incompetent exterminators. Over the years many deaths and illnesses have been caused by misuse of pesticides. It is worth remembering that the entire modern environmental movement began with Rachel Carson's book *Silent Spring* (1962), while the creation of TRI itself resulted in part from an accident in a pesticide plant.

The mining sector (especially non-ferrous metals) is actually the biggest source of toxic and hazardous emissions (Chapter 5). USEPA estimated in 1985 that the metal mining industry (SIC 10) produces 61 MMT of hazardous solid wastes annually, more than all other industries combined (USEPA

1985, p. 30). These wastes include wastes from acid leaching, acid mine drainage, ore beneficiation by froth flotation, heap-leaching (cyanidation), tailings impoundments, and so on. About 11 per cent of the total (6.7 MMT) was attributable to gold mining, heavily concentrated in western Montana (where the Homestake gold mines are located). Coal mining (SIC 12) was responsible for 1.2 kMT of USEPA 'priority pollutants' (ibid. p. 32), probably mostly heavy metals from coal cleaning operations that utilize froth flotation to remove pyrites.

Oil and gas extraction (SIC 13) use large quantities of toxic organic chemicals in drilling muds, and dispose of large amounts of 'produced waters' (see Chapter 4) which are usually quite contaminated. Discharges of 'priority pollutants' have been estimated at 4.35 kMT and 16.3 kMT per year, depending on the data source. Taking the midpoint of the two estimates (10.4 kMT) as a guide, releases of metals to water probably amounted to 24 kMT of barium (recall that barite is a key ingredient of drilling mud), plus 1.75 kMT of chromium, 1.6 kMT of arsenic, 0.72 kMT of zinc and 0.43 kMT of lead (USEPA 1985, p. 32). Organic discharges from drilling muds would also have included 3.9 kMT of toluene, 2.1 kMT of benzene and 2.04 kMT of phenol (ibid.). It is noteworthy that this single exempt source exceeds total barium discharges accounted for in the TRI (1988) by a factor of 1700! It also exceeds reported TRI discharges for arsenic by 450 times, for benzene by 97 times, for toluene by 33 times, for chromium by 7.5 times and for lead by 3 times.

Other exempt sectors that discharge a lot of hazardous wastes include construction (especially painting, where a lot of solvents are released), transportation and pipelines and electric power generation. For instance, the biggest sources of volatile organic compounds (VOCs), including benzene and toluene, are attributed to crude oil and gasoline loading and unloading, to and from ships, barges and tank cars, and at airports (SIC 42, 44, 45, 47). USEPA estimated that VOCs from marine cargo loading and unloading in 1988 were 59 kMT (Sheiman 1991, p. 37). Truck loading and storage tanks belonging to fuel wholesalers (SIC 517) emitted 404 kMT and gasoline service stations (SIC 554) generated 630 kMT of gasoline vapors (VOCs) in 1982, including 6.4 kMT of benzene (Sheiman 1991, p. 53). Pipelines that carry large quantities of crude oil and petroleum products also generate significant emissions, both from leaks and hydrostatic pressure tests. A 1987 study by Midwest Research Institute (MRI) for USEPA estimated that the pipeline sector (SIC 46) generated 22 kMT of non-aqueous wastes and 6.5 MMT of aqueous wastes in 1986 (Sheiman 1991, p. 38).

Waterborne polyaromatic hydrocarbons (PAHs) are largely attributable to oil spills and improper disposal of used lubricants, especially motor oil, of which a large amount is dumped or leaked onto streets and parking lots, or service stations, and subsequently washed into rivers. Transportation services (SIC 47) utilize large quantities of hydrocarbon solvents for tank car and truck cleaning and drum reconditioning, which are mostly sent to publicly owned waste treatment works (POTWs) discussed later. None of these sources are included in the TRI.

The electric power generating sector (SIC 4911) is a large emitter of heavy metals and VOCs. The former are mostly associated with fly ash from coal burning. Mostly the ash is captured by electrostatic precipitation (ESP), but some – perhaps 1 per cent – is lost to the environment. Even that small amount carries significant quantities of toxic metals, including arsenic, beryllium, chromium, manganese, and nickel. For every one of these toxic metals, it has been estimated that the electric power sector alone released more than was accounted for by the entire 1987 TRI (Sheiman 1991, p. 41). Moreover, significant quantities of arsenic and mercury are vaporized during the combustion process and emitted as vapor, thus bypassing the ESP. According to USEPA (1986), the electric power sector generates 331 kMT of hazardous wastes annually (ibid. p. 42). The gas distribution sector (SIC 492) also generated 30 kMT of hazardous waste in 1984, according to a 1985 study done for USEPA by the Midwest Research Institute (ibid.). These wastes include process wastewater and tar storage tank residues.

Fossil fuel combustion in general is estimated to be a major source of mercury emissions. EPA estimated airborne emissions of mercury from fossil fuel combustion in the US for 1988 and 1980 as 133 metric tons and 144 metric tons, respectively (OECD 1994). Certainly this source alone accounts for many times more than the total releases reported by TRI. The other major source of airborne emissions of mercury is waste incineration (because of mercury contained in batteries) which released about 22 metric tons in 1988 – also several times the total of reported TRI releases (Sheiman 1991, p. 45).

Sanitary services, including water supply (SIC 4941), sewer services (SIC 4952), and refuse disposal via landfills and incinerators (SIC 4953) are also major sources of hazardous wastes not counted in TRI. For instance, water treatment consumes several hundred thousand tons of chlorine each year in the US. One of the byproducts is chloroform – an estimated 1.9 kMT per year (Sheiman 1991, p. 42). This is five times the amount of releases associated with chloroform production in the chemical industry, which does report to TRI. There may be other hazardous wastes resulting from water treatment, such as the use of sodium phosphate water softeners, but we have no information on that subject.

Sewer services – also known as Publicly Owned Treatment Works (POTWs) – receive very large amounts of toxic and hazardous wastes from other waste generators. USEPA estimated the amount of such transfers in 1988 as 36.6 MMT (Sheiman 1991, p. 43). These included 1130 metric tons of methylene chloride, 900 metric tons of chromium compounds (for example, from electroplaters and tanners), 540 metric tons of chloroform and 450 metric tons of benzene (ibid.). A major source of toxic discharges to POTWs is industrial laundries (SIC 721). According to a 1987 study for EPA by the Midwest Research Institute, these laundries dispose of 2.45 kMT of priority pollutants and 350–400 kMT of other pollutants (mostly wastewater) into sewers (Sheiman 1991, p. 54). Dry cleaning plants (also SIC 721) also use and emit more than 120 kMT of perchlorethylene (PERC); in fact, dry cleaning is the major use of this chemical and the greater part of annual production is lost in this way. It is noteworthy that dry cleaning plants discharged about 171 times as much PERC in 1987 as producers who reported to TRI.

A different, earlier (1986) USEPA study (*The Domestic Sewage Study*, or DSS) estimated that 42–62 per cent of the input mass is biodegraded (mainly to carbon dioxide) while 14–15 per cent volatilizes to air, 8–18 per cent is discharged as relatively clean surface water and the rest is disposed of as solid sludge (USEPA 1986). Most of the heavy metals are contained in the latter fraction. The volatile pollutants from POTWs identified in that 1986 study included 1,1,1-trichloroethane – now banned under the Montreal Protocol – (2.9 kMT), methylene chloride (2 kMT), xylenes (1.6 kMT), chloroform (1.2 kMT), and trichloroethylenc (1.1 kMT) (ibid. p. 43). All except chloroform are solvents, now (or formerly) widely used in industry but also as cleaning agents in other sectors. However, it is interesting to note that USEPA studies show that POTWs are the largest source of emissions of 1,2-dichloroethane (USEPA 1986), better known as ethylene dichloride, which is an intermediate in the manufacture of vinyl chloride and PVC. POTWs are the second largest single source of trichloroethylene (ibid.). Many other chemicals are emitted in smaller quantities.

Volatile organic compounds (VOCs) are also emitted in very large amounts from landfills, incinerators, impoundments and other waste treatment facilities. In fact, USEPA estimated annual VOC emissions from this sector (SIC 4953) at 7.1 MMT in 1988 (Sheiman 1991, p. 45). Hazardous and toxic emissions to water from this sector were about 248 kMT.

8.4   Can the TRI be fixed?

The TRI has already undoubtedly served a useful purpose in raising the consciousness of the leaders of some large industrial polluters, especially in the chemical industry. It has also pointed the way to some targeted programs that might be more effective than if there had been no TRI. However, as a data base on toxicity, TRI is totally inadequate. As USOTA pointed out in 1989, it omits something like 95 per cent of the toxic and hazardous emissions. Whether the correct figure is 95 per cent or 90 per cent is irrelevant.

Moreover, as some critics have charged, the incompleteness of the reports has undoubtedly permitted some polluters to make 'phantom' reductions by changing accounting practices, reclassification, changing measurement techniques or manipulating production levels. For example, a study of 29 facilities in 1987 and 1988, where reported discharges dropped from 2.18 MMT in 1987 to 1.35 MMT a year later, discovered that almost all of the reduction was attributable to changed reporting requirements or reclassifications. For instance, ALCOA found less of a reportable chemical (Al_2O_3) and more of a non-reportable one ($Al_2(OH)_3$) by simply adding water! This simple change accounted for 82 per cent of the entire apparent reduction. Most of the rest resulted from a reclassification of Kennecott Copper to the non-reporting category. Only 4 per cent of the apparent reduction was actually due to source reductions (Poje and Horowitz 1990).

Similar phantom reductions were found by other groups (Citizens Fund 1991, 1992; Courteau and Lilienthal 1991). A study by the Research Triangle Institute ascertained that 70 per cent of reported reductions in TRI discharges through 1991 were attributed to changes in production levels, rather than source reductions (Riley *et al.* 1993). Our own study of the mercury case suggests that respondents were using accounting-sleight-of-hand to avoid reporting wastes as either discharges or transfers (Ayres 1997). Had respondents been required to make full, instead of partial, disclosure these gimmicks would not have been possible.

A related criticism of TRI in its present form is that, because it permits (indeed, encourages) accounting gimmickry it cannot measure real progress toward source reduction. In fact, there are a number of well documented examples where real progress toward source (and risk) reduction can make a firm look worse in terms of TRI. For instance, the Dupont plant at Deepwater NJ produces phosgene – a very toxic chemical (that was used in World War I as a poison gas) – as an intermediate in the production of other chemicals and plastics such as polycarbonates and polyurethanes. To minimize the risk of transportation and storage the phosgene is produced on site, in small quantities, as needed. During the year 1991 the plant produced and consumed 26.3 kMT of phosgene of which only 580 kg (0.022 per cent) was emitted. However there is a competitor, Hatco, which also used phosgene (2.27 kMT) in production, but the phosgene was shipped in from another location. Hatco claims to have released only 5 kg. Is Hatco therefore a better manager of phosgene than Dupont?[10] We doubt it.

A few years ago AT&T Bell Labs (now Lucent Technologies) announced a new process to produce arsine, one of the most toxic chemicals known (used in semiconductor manufacturing) in very small quantities, on site, as needed. This was done for exactly the same reasons – to minimize the risks associated with storage and shipping. The logic of TRI might have induced AT&T to continue to buy its toxic chemicals from outside. Hopefully, it did not. By the way, if Union Carbide India had produced MIC only in small quantities, as needed, there would have been no need for storage and the Bhopal accident would never have happened.

Finally, there is yet one more charge against TRI: its very success has encouraged people – including too many naive environmentalists and journalists – to believe that the manufacturing sectors, and especially the chemical producers, are the major polluters and therefore the major villains, letting the rest of society off the hook. This is far from the truth, and it results in major distortions of public policy (as witness its use by the World Bank). In fact, if good policy depends on good information, TRI was a major step backward.

Along with many others, we would like to see two straightforward improvements that could make a big difference. First, the TRI should be extended to the rest of the economy. In some sectors, like mining, the extension would be perfectly straightforward. Big mining companies certainly know what chemicals they use, and what wastes they generate.[11]

However, in most other sectors, where emissions result either from the *use* of chemicals (for example, farmers and dry cleaners) or from fossil fuel combustion, the users do not necessarily know exactly what chemicals they are using and consequently discharging. Moreover, many of the users are small businesses, for whom it would be an unreasonable burden to fill out detailed reporting forms even if they had the necessary information at hand. This is one of the core problems. But let it pass for the moment.

The other improvement we would like to see is the introduction of a mass balance requirement, at least for the chemical producers. In fact a structured report that properly accounted for all inputs, transformations and outflows, including end-uses – that is, a mass balance – of each toxic or hazardous chemical used in industry go a very long way toward completing the picture. There is no real need for pesticide use data to be gathered from farmers, or for solvent use data to be gathered from dry-cleaners. The mass balance principle guarantees that it is enough, in both cases, to know that the substances in question were produced and sold for use, or stored. On average, the quantity sold is the quantity used and the quantity used is the quantity discharged.

Unless the locality of the emission is important, the only important information needed for each toxic chemical, then, consists of answers to two, or at most three questions: First, how much of it is produced in the first place? Second, how much is converted into something else? Third, how much, if any, is added to stocks? The difference between production and conversion or treatment (plus additions to stock) is the amount that is dissipated into the environment. This is an absolute accounting identity. It also simplifies the problems of collecting data considerably. In fact, it means that there is no real need to ask large numbers of small businessmen to fill out forms. The major producers and distributors have all the necessary information.

Actually in the original debate in Congress about the creation of TRI, the Senate version of the bill would have required respondents to report 'the quantity of chemical substances transported to the facility, produced at the facility, and transported from the facility as wastes or products' (Hearne 1996, p. 7). Unfortunately, the House, under pressure from industry lobbyists, drafted a much weaker bill, which was the version finally passed. The final bill requires respondents to report only on release and transfer off-site as waste. Industry lobbyists also objected to the provision of the law making the data accessible to the public. Fortunately this part of the bill was retained.

However, the fact that respondents need not (and do not) report on the production, conversion or sale of toxic and hazardous chemicals is exactly what makes the resulting truncated TRI data base so misleading. It is also precisely this restrictive feature of the law that has misled the public into thinking that industry – SIC 20-39 – is the source of all toxic pollution! In this respect the industry lobbyists in defense of secrecy have actually 'shot themselves in the foot', so to speak!

8.5   Materials accounting and TRI

An illustration of both how poorly the TRI tracks some chemicals and, incidentally, how it could be repaired, was carried out by Industrial Economics Inc. for USEPA (IEI 1991). It covered 21 chemicals, or groups, among the most toxic or hazardous known. Most are produced and used in fairly large quantities, and reasonably good statistics were obtainable on imports, exports, usage as such and conversion to other chemicals. The methodology was illustrated in Figure 6.1. In several cases there were fairly large inadvertent fluxes resulting from incidental activities, such as transportation. However, in each case IEI identified all known uses, including consumption for purposes of conversion to other materials, using generally available published information, such as *Chemical Marketing Reporter.* Direct conversion losses were estimated from published or readily available process yield estimates. The results of the IEI study are summarized in Table 8.2. In each case, the TRI estimates were compared with the missing or 'unaccounted for' mass of the chemical. The differences are obviously very large, meaning that for most of these chemicals the TRI accounts for only a small percentage of the possible emissions.

One fairly obvious conclusion leaps to the eye and is worth emphasizing: TRI is most reliable in tracking emissions from chemicals that are transformed to other chemicals entirely within the chemical industry itself. Butadiene, ethylene dichloride, vinyl chloride and phosgene are good examples. On the other hand, it is least reliable in accounting for discharges of

Table 8.2   *Toxic chemicals: Materials balance estimates compared to TRI (kMT)*

Chemical	Apparent Consumption	Materials Balance Estimates of				Losses unaccounted for by TRI	TRI	
		Direct Conversion and Use Losses	Other Incidental Emissions	Total Emission Losses	TRI		metal	compounds
Benzene	7360.0	207.2	183.4	390.6	14.6	376.0		
Toluene	3071.7	361.4	984.0	1345.4	158.5	1186.9		
Xylenes, mixed	3419.2	295.2	544.2	839.4	86.5	752.9		
m-Xylene	34.6	6.9	0.2	7.1	1.6	5.5		
o-Xylene	509.6	101.6	2.6	104.2	1.3	102.9		
p-Xylene	2510.9	179.0	11.6	190.6	3.2	187.4		
Carbon tetrachloride	400.2	9.9	1.2	11.2	2.3	8.9		
Chloroform	224.8	26.5	19.9	46.4	12.2	34.2		
Methylene chloride	183.1	161.7	1.2	162.9	70.3	92.6		
Perchloroethylene	252.9	182.3	0.7	183.0	17.1	165.9		
Trichloroethylene	68.9	65.2	0.3	65.5	26.2	39.3		
1,1,1-Trichloroethane	303.4	281.5	1.6	283.1	88.1	195.1		
Methyl ethyl ketone	239.2	237.7	4.3	242.0	73.1	168.9		
Methyl isobutyl ketone	91.2	81.6	0.5	82.1	20.2	61.9		
Cadmium	3.6	3.6	1.0	4.6	0.9	3.7	0.16	0.72
Chromium	536.9	418.1	24.9	443.0	31.2	411.8	9.74	21.46
Mercury	1.6	1.3	0.3	1.6	0.1	1.5	0.13	0.01
Nickel	159.2	118.1	23.7	141.8	8.7	133.1	4.02	4.73
Cyanides	629.7	151.4	31.1	182.5	5.3	177.2		
Hydrogen cyanide	543.0	64.6	31.1	95.7	1.4	94.2		
Cyanides, other	86.8	86.8	0.0	86.9	3.9	82.9		
Total	20000.8	2890.5	1836.7	4727.2	621.6	4105.6		

Source: IEI 1991.

chemicals that are consumed as such, outside the chemical industry. Virtually all of the Persistent Organic Pollutants (POPs), for instance, fall into the latter category (Environment Canada 1995). This is also true of chlorinated solvents, for instance.

We do not argue that all of the missing mass should be classified as uncounted emissions to the environment. In the first place, IEI's estimates were based on process yield assumptions that might not be correct (although obtained from supposedly reliable industry sources). Second, market data, also from generally reliable published sources, could be inaccurate. Third, in some cases, combustible or reactive wastes such as benzene or toluene may be treated or chemically transformed (for example, by incineration) thus converting toxic emissions to less toxic ones.

Apart from statistical errors and limitations on coverage, the generic IEI methodology, and our own, are applicable to the estimation of pretreatment mass disappearance, not actual releases. Some of the difference is probably due to the presence of end-of-pipe treatment facilities, such as incinerators. On the other hand, most treatment methods merely shift a waste stream from one environmental medium to another (such as a landfill), and the waste is still a waste and should be reported as such. In the case of toxic metals, for instance, conversion to another non-hazardous form is usually impossible. Besides, discrepancies between unaccounted for missing mass and TRI releases are much too large in most cases to be explained by waste treatment.

To fill in the gaps in the picture requires some additional data that must come from companies. Current proposals to improve the TRI would call for the following additional data:

- starting inventory of the chemical
- amount brought on site
- amount produced on site
- amount consumed (chemically transformed) on site
- amount shipped off site as (or in) product
- ending inventory of the chemical

As noted already, these proposals are opposed by industry lobbyists, on various grounds.

There are three common industry objections to using a materials accounting approach. The one pushed hardest by lobbyists is cost. This would be an overwhelmingly powerful argument if the proposal was to force every small business to undertake a detailed mass balance for each toxic or hazardous chemical it uses. But we think this objection falls by the wayside, since we do not see any real need for small businesses (unless they happen to be chemical manufacturers) to fill out any forms at all. Apart from this, however, industry groups tend to exaggerate the costs. The Chemical Manufacturers Association has argued that six more questions would double the costs of TRI reporting (Hearne 1996, p. 31). But experience in New Jersey and Massachusetts, where this information is already collected routinely, does not support such a claim; on the contrary, firms spend an average of 7.5 additional hours to answer the six additional questions (Hearne 1994). This should not surprise anybody but a lobbyist – most of the work was already done in gathering the information to answer the existing questions.

Actually, there is quite good reason to believe that a company that introduces a materials accounting system internally will save money by so doing. A few firms have actually done this already, with favorable results. Examples cited include General Motors, Polaroid, Hoffman–LaRoche and Sandoz (now Novartis) (Hearne 1996, p. 29). Polaroid's voluntary Toxic Use and Waste Reduction (TUWR) program has spawned an in-house environmental accounting and reporting system (EARS). Together, the two systems have enabled Polaroid to achieve real cost reductions of $19 million over a five year period (Fatkin 1996, p. 33). The Sandoz application of materials accounting methods, at a pharmaceutical plant in New Jersey, has apparently also enabled savings of several million dollars (White *et al.* 1995). A number of firms, including Arizona Public Service, Bethlehem Steel, H.B. Fuller, and SUN, have joined with GM and Polaroid in a Coalition for Environmentally Responsible Economies (CERES) which also focusses on developing and testing materials accounting systems and disclosing the results to the public (White and Dierks 1996, p. 34).

The second standard objection to converting TRI into a materials accounting system is that publication of mass balances would tend to reveal internal operations (such as process details) that firms want to keep secret for competitive reasons. This is the 'secret ingredient' argument. This, too, is pushed hard by lobbyists. There is some (very) slight justice to the argument. For example, it is conceivable that a firm might be forced to reveal its proprietary use of some toxic or hazardous chemical, for example, as a catalyst. But, given the reporting threshold on small uses, and the fact that most plants produce a mix of products with different recipes, it is unlikely that throughput information would convey any useful information to a competitor.

This point is confirmed by experience in New Jersey and Massachusetts. Both states make it quite easy for a firm to claim confidentiality on the basis of a trade secret. Approval is automatic. Yet, in New Jersey, less than 1 per cent of companies have made this claim since 1987 (Aucott 1994–95). In 1992 the number of confidentiality requests was 24 out of about 2600 responses (ibid.).

The third objection is undoubtedly the main one. The rest of the objections are a smokescreen. As phrased by many industry spokesmen and lobbyists, there is a fear of 'possible public overreaction'. Chemical industry executives, in defending chlorine, for instance, often express the view that the public 'doesn't understand'. A skeptic might interpret this as a fear of embarrassment, or (more honestly) a fear of how Greenpeace might react. Such fears are not altogether unjustified.

But the industry position in defense of secrecy is usually presented, however, in terms of spurious concern for the public interest. A letter to EPA administrator Carol Browner signed by representatives of 40 industry associations states the issue in high flown terms:

> the goals of TRI are to provide the public [with] information so that they can make informed decisions about risk. Chemical use is not a good indicator of risk. It is not a surrogate for exposure, therefore chemical use reporting is not needed, nor is it good public policy. (cited by Hearne 1996, p. 31)

This sounds good. It was undoubtedly written by a Washington lawyer and probably not read (or understood) by very many of the senior executives of the companies belonging to the 40 groups. But let that pass. It is clever nonsense, but still nonsense. And it should be recognized as such. Of course chemical use is not a surrogate for exposure. Did anybody ever say it was? The argument for materials accounting is quite different: we need information about chemical uses in order to calculate emissions to the environment. That is what TRI was originally supposed to do, but does not do. And the reason it does not do what it was supposed to do is precisely that it does not include chemical use data.

A Dupont spokesman illustrates the industry perspective by quoting an EPA report to President Clinton, as follows:

> Dupont Corporation in Deepwater New Jersey reported TRI releases of only 1,298 pounds of phosgene in 1991. A materials accounting program indicated that, in fact, more than 58 million pounds (26.3 kMT) of phosgene were present within the facility for that same period of time. (Mongan 1996)

In reality, as Mongan notes, the 58 million pounds were not stored at all, but represented the annual production (and consumption) of the facility. Evidently the USEPA person who wrote that quoted paragraph either did not understand the New Jersey materials accounting report, or deliberately misrepresented the true situation. To many people in industry this example illustrates public misunderstanding of the chemical industry. We agree that USEPA was off-limits here. But we also think this example also illustrates the importance of materials accounting as a tool. Had the tool been used (and explained) properly there would have been no misunderstanding and Dupont would have been given the credit it actually deserves, rather than blame.

Unfortunately, to combat this alleged public misunderstanding, however, the standard industry approach seems to be to bring in public relations experts and 'spin doctors' who specialize in presenting as little data as possible in the most favorable possible light. The examples of phantom reductions, cited above, illustrate the point clearly enough. A large number of firms (over 100) now publish annual environmental reports. But too many of them talk about year-to-year reductions in environmental emissions without any supporting data on baselines, measures, assumptions or methods of calculation. They resemble the detergent advertisements that used to brag that their product washed shirts whiter than unspecified 'brand X'.

Whenever we see one of these optimistic reports written by PR people we are reminded of the fate of the US nuclear power industry. Remember? The industry spokesmen and PR people issued reassuring statements, year after year, to the effect that safety precautions were so thorough that the probability of an accident was insignificant – so small as to be not worthy of serious consideration. Then came Three Mile Island followed by Chernobyl. Nobody trusts those nuclear 'experts' any more. In fact, thanks to decades of deceptive advertising, the public does not trust industry statements very much on any subject.

To end this chapter, we would argue that materials accounting can be a real benefit to industry by helping to repair the credibility gap.

Endnotes

1. To be fair, the bulk of this category was apparently generated by only four refineries, which dispose of unprocessed aqueous wastes by direct injection into deep wells.
2. Adding the gross use figures given by David, one obtains 83 600 mgd as against her total of 92 700 mgd. Similarly, reported and imputed intake figures add up to only 25 100 mgd as against her total of 27 500 mgd. The sums for cooling water and discharges (imputed from other data given) are also significantly too low. It is possible that David's totals should have referred to the entire manufacturing sector, rather than the five largest subsectors, as stated.
3. During this decade Finnish pulp and paper mills cut their water use by 90 per cent.
4. An older source provided more (but inconsistent) detail on water consumption in the food processing sector: meat processing, SIC 201 (852 MMT); dairy processing SIC 202 (295 MMT); vegetable and fruits processing SIC 203 (3984 MMT); grain mills, SIC 204 (946 MMT); sugar mills, SIC 206 (3248 MMT) and beverages, SIC 208 (31 MMT) (Kollar and MacAuley 1980).
5. US firms were not the only ones to have had such accidents. One rather famous one was the accident that released a substantial quantity of dioxins at Seveso, Italy (1976). Another was the warehouse fire at the Sandoz agrichemicals facility in Basel, Switzerland that resulted in the release of several tons of mercury compounds into the Rhine River (1986).
6. Testimony before the Subcommittee on Superfund, Ocean and Water Protection of the Senate Committee on Environment and Public Works, May 10, 1989, quoted in Sheiman (1991).
7. One is reminded of the adage from the 1970s 'the solution to pollution is dilution'.
8. Since 1992 USEPA has tightened up its bookkeeping somewhat in regard to mercury, by prohibiting extended in-house storage of mercury-containing sludges and requiring active recovery. This solves the problem (partially) in the case of mercury, but not in general.

9.   There is one important exception: the state of New Jersey does require that the TRI questionnaires be answered in a form that is internally self-consistent (that is, based on mass balances between inputs and outputs). As a result, the New Jersey data are far more reliable than the national data.

10.   This story was taken partly from an article in *Environment* by Shelley Hearne (Hearne 1996, p. 9) and some of the data was provided by Edwin Mongan of Dupont in a letter to the same magazine (Mongan 1996, p. 31).

11.   In 1987 the Kennecott Copper mine in Utah filed a report *by mistake* (mines are exempt), reporting copper discharges alone of 29 metric tons to the air, 3.5 metric tons to water and 59 kMT to land (presumably in concentration waste). The corresponding figures for arsenic compounds were 3.5 metric tons, 0.63 metric tons and 3.75 kMT; for barium compounds 4.0 metric tons, 1.45 metric tons, and 2.56 kMT; for zinc compounds 2.2 metric tons, 1.45 metric tons and 3.13 kMT; for chromium compounds discharges were 4.3 metric tons to air, and 1.85 kMT to land; for lead compounds 5.4 metric tons to air and 1.5 kMT to land, and for cadmium 57 metric tons to land. The mine also discharged 85 metric tons of sulfuric acid to air and 12.7 metric tons to water. On this basis, this single mine was the nations eleventh largest TRI polluter.

9 Counting with dollars: From mass flow to input–output

9.1 Mass-flows: Summary of results

In this chapter we hark back to a discussion that was begun, but not followed up, in Chapter 1, namely the problem of utilizing material flow analysis (MFA) as an input to policy across the whole range from technology to economics. We have repeatedly emphasized the use of mass balances as a tool for data verification, especially in the resource and environmental context. But there are other salient reasons for tracking mass flows quantitatively. Another primary and over-arching purpose of all this effort, as the title of this chapter suggests, is to create a common framework for incorporating material flows and transformations in general equilibrium economic models.[1]

Up until now most economic models have ignored material flows (and physical constraints) altogether. But to the extent that material flows have been incorporated into economic models at all, it has been done by attaching raw material input coefficient vectors and waste emission output coefficient vectors to an input-output matrix, but with no link between them. This ad hoc approach has never been very satisfactory from a theoretical perspective. However, before discussing the economic and policy implications of our work, it is worthwhile to summarize the main results themselves. We do this in Table 9.1.

It is useful to summarize our results so far by waste category, as well as by industry. Overburden moved by mining of coal, minerals and metal ores – mostly stripping – amounts to over 7.14 billion MT, of which 5.6 billion MT was from coal mining. By contrast, topsoil loss in the US, mainly from agriculture, was 3.4 billion MT. (In addition, excavation by the road-building construction industry may move comparable amounts.) This material is merely displaced, not chemically altered. In the case of overburden removed for strip mining purposes, it can usually be replaced after the mine is exhausted, and this is increasingly being done (under pressure of regulation). The landscape is degraded for a period of decades, but if the mine is not simply abandoned but is properly refilled and graded, the land can be used again for recreational purposes or tree farming. As regards topsoil loss due to erosion, the crude data can be misleading. The figures refer to topsoil 'moved', but most of it is merely redeposited nearby or downstream. Quite a lot of displaced topsoil ends up in river deltas, such as the Nile or Mississippi. These deltas are typically very rich. (The fertility of the Nile valley has been maintained over

Table 9.1 *Summary*

SIC	SECTOR	Displaced, unchanged[a]	Free inputs from nature	Purchased non-fuel inputs	Recycled by-product inputs	Main Product Value in Billion $	MMT	Salable by-products inc. fuel	Unsalable solid wastes (dry wgt)	Gaseous, other[b]
01	Agricultural crops[c]	4117	1855	42.3	710	84.5	867.3	550		0.9
02	Livestock[c]		342	402.65		90.6	119.5	160	53.8	9
04	Timber	144.6	1059.2	5.7		13.8	261.1	57.2		
101	Iron ore	129	181	4.03		1.7	66.11		148	
10	Non-ferrous metals mining	1185	5.94		6	8.6	6.34		569.36	
12	Coal mining and cleaning	5600	878			7.9	858		20	
131	Oil and gas drilling and pumping			32		72.3	676		34	2
132	Gas separation			424		27.2	413.3	2.45		6
147	Mineral mining	110	106.8			3.0	35.5		129.5	
20	Food and kindred products, total			374.1		403.8	218.1	67.8	88.2	
201	Meat products			51.2		93.5	24.5	7.1	3	
202	Dairy			68.3		54.1	67.7	0.4		
203	Fresh and preserved vegetables and fruits			83.3		45.2	68.3		5	
204	Grain mills			48.43		49.2	45.41	2.4	2.3	
206	Sugar mills and confectionery			52.301		22.7	7.52	10.8	8.6	
207	Fats and oils			39.28		19.3	37.08	2.2	6.5	
208	Beverages			15		57.0	5.97	3.75	0.65	
24	Lumber and wood products, total			136	38.2	81.8	60.7	71	4.3	z
261	Pulp			120.6	25.4	5.5	57.6	88	13.2	
262	Paper			86.4		133.0	82.8	71	4.3	

Code	Industry									
263	Paperboard		62.3							
28	Chemicals, inorganic		232.1	5.6	16.1	81.3	99	105		
	Chemicals, organic		5	74.5	24.4		54.8	25		
2911	Petroleum refining		813.4	6	736.3		596	86.45	4	
295	Asphalt				7.7					
299	Miscellaneous petroleum and coal				6.0					
3241	Portland cement		117.2		4.0		75.1		7.3	
3312	Coking		28.43				21	8.4	3	
3312	Pig iron and steel	35.5	163.62	4	58.7		136.95	252	0.6	9
333	Non-ferrous metal smelting, refining		9		14.1		6.071	4.243	4.82	5.2
491	Electric power from coal	2460	831.22	93.8	187.3				78.4	13.8
492	Gas transmission		348				334			
xx	Fuel consumption		159	167.7					2.2	6

Notes:

a Excluding process and cooling water; including soil displaced by erosion.

b Excluding oxygen (O_2) and carbon dioxide (CO_2).

c Hay and feeds are 'main products' of agriculture, hence they are included.

d SO_2.

z Very small.

Source: Gaseous emissions data from Casler (1991).

millennia by erosion from upstream.) A much smaller amount of topsoil is actually lost permanently.

The next category of solid waste is smaller but far more harmful. It consists of concentration wastes – gangue and refuse – from mining, especially of non-ferrous metals such as copper and gold. This material is often contaminated by a variety of chemicals, some of them highly toxic (for example, sodium cyanide). It also contains significant quantities of heavy metals that cannot be economically recovered, including copper, lead, zinc, arsenic, cadmium and so forth. It is also often acidic, since most heavy metal ores are sulfides, and they are often found in combination with iron pyrites of no economic value. Coal also contains pyrites, some of which are removed by flotation or washing. When exposed to the air these sulfides oxidize and result in sulfurous acid formation and so-called acid mine wastes. Rivers in mining areas are often too acidic (not to mention other pollutants) to sustain aquatic life. Altogether, we can account for approximately 900 MMT of concentration wastes from the mining sector (SIC 10), including coal cleaning refuse and oil drilling muds, plus about 106 MMT from the chemical sector (SIC 28), mainly from phosphates. To this one might add about 78 MMT of coal ash and flue-gas desulfurization wastes from the coal-burning electric power sector (SIC 491). The total comes to 1.084 billion MT.

By contrast, the weight of solid wastes – slags – from metallurgical conversion (smelting) process amount to only 5.1 MMT, not including 19 MMT of iron/steel slag that has a number of commercial uses.

Organic wastes excluding biomass used for energy recovery purposes are estimated to be 30 MMT (plus or minus 3 MMT) for agriculture and food processing. The major uncertainty concerns wastes from sugar processing and fruit and vegetable processing. Probably half or more of this total was lost in retail shops and restaurants, not in the processing sector *per se*. In addition, the lumber sector lost 4.3 MMT as unburned waste. The wood products sector burned 22.5 MMT for fuel and the pulp sector burned 88 MMT (dry equivalent) as spent 'black liquor' for energy and chemical recovery. The pulp and paper sector discharged about 13.3 MMT of incombustible sludges from wastewater treatment, consisting mostly of salts. Gaseous combustion products constituted another very large waste stream. We estimated a total of 5925 MMT of CO_2 (of which 5880 MMT was from fossil fuel combustion) in 1993, based on fuel consumption, cement and lime. By comparison, EPA's estimate was 5095 MMT, based on 'energy use only'. It is not clear whether EPA allowed for carbon dioxide generated by fuel use within the refining sector (50 MMT), which would have resulted in about 156 MMT of CO_2. We assume that most of the difference consists of delayed emissions from non-energy uses (for example, coke, carbon electrodes, ammonia, urea and methanol synthesis, chemical feedstocks and slow oxidation of lubricating oils, asphalt, and so on). EPA also counted separately 83.96 MMT of carbon monoxide emissions, all of which are quickly oxidized to carbon dioxide in the atmosphere. This accounts for an additional 140 MMT of CO_2. However, the discrepancy is still surprisingly large (OECD 1995). Other major gaseous pollutants, estimated by EPA, include SO_2 (19.52 MMT), mostly from coal-burning power plants, NO_x (21.24 MMT, 11.6 MMT from stationary sources), about 7 MMT of particulates, of which 5.5 MMT was from stationary sources, plus 20.29 MMT of VOCs, of which 12.75 MMT were emitted by stationary sources (OECD 1995). Our methodology is not well-suited to estimating CO, NO_x, particulates or VOC emissions. We specifically identified about 9 MMT of methane losses, mainly from natural gas distribution and coal mining, but that is not a complete accounting.

It is interesting to compare the magnitudes of the various waste streams with mass flows of salable products. The largest of these was fuels, of course. Coal consumed domestically was 790 MMT; crude petroleum (about half imported) was 693 MMT and crude natural gas was 497 MMT. Fuelwood burned (including wood waste) was 167.7 MMT. Agricultural crop production was 457.3 MMT, plus about 210.5 MMT of hay and silage plus 200 MMT (roughly) of grass. Dairy and meat products amounted to 119.5 MMT, gross weight. Salable products of food processing activities added up to 285.9 MMT, of which 203 MMT was food consumed domestically. Wood products added up to 60.7 MMT, while 57.6 MMT of virgin pulp was produced. Paper was produced from a combination of pulp and recycled waste paper.

Over 2 billion MMT of chemically inert minerals – crushed stone, gravel, clay and sand – are produced each year for construction purposes, but these have little environmental impact, either in production or use, except in terms of land-use and landscape. The other major construction materials are hydraulic cements (75 MMT), bricks, tiles, plaster and glass. The latter are also chemically inert and the only environmental impact of processing is fossil fuel combustion for heat, except that calcination of limestone and other carbonates (both in cement manufacturing and otherwise) generates about 45 or 46 MMT of carbon dioxide. Crude iron output in 1993 was 48.2 MMT; steel was produced partly from crude iron and partly from recycled scrap. The total US primary production of all non-ferrous metals was 6.06 MMT in 1993. Again, finished products include a considerable amount of recycled scrap.

Chemicals constitute a more interesting category, environmentally speaking. The gross output of inorganic chemicals in 1993 was about 99 MMT, from 232 MMT of inputs (including atmospheric oxygen, nitrogen and water), not including fuel used for heat or electric power. A significant fraction of this total (58.25 MMT) consisted of fertilizers, while another 7.2 MMT or so (not including lime and kaolin) was consumed by the pulp and paper sector and 15.7 MMT went to organic chemicals production. Alumina (5.4 MMT) was smelted into aluminum. The rest (about 12.4 MMT) was divided among a suite of other industrial sectors, from mining to water treatment. Solid wastes of about 105 MMT – mainly from phosphate processing – have already been mentioned. Other identified process wastes included 22 MMT of carbon dioxide, and 6 MMT of water vapor from chemical reactions.

Actually, one major source of wastes within the chemical industry consists of ore concentration wastes. In 1993 the main solid wastes were phospho-gypsum from the 'wet process' for making superphosphate from phosphate rock (183 MMT dry weight); gangue (clay and salt) from potash concentration (9.2 MMT), 'red mud' from the Bayer process for alumina (4.6 MMT dry weight) and wastes from titanium dioxide processing (1.1 MMT). The total of these comes to 198 MMT. Waterborne wastes from chemical raw materials processing included spent brine from trona (soda ash) recovery (7.2 MMT) and chlor-alkali production (3 MMT), also dry weight. There is no way to reduce these quantities as long as primary raw materials are the source, unless uses can be found for the wastes that would reduce the need for other minerals (Ayres and Ayres 1996).

The second major category of chemical wastes consists of materials used dissipatively within the sector, or a downstream sector, and not incorporated into any long-lived product. For instance, sulfuric acid, hydrochloric acid, caustic soda and lime are all used mainly to neutralize each other. Of the 18 MMT of salt (NaCl) that is electrolytically reduced to elemental chlorine (10.9 MMT) and caustic soda (11.5 MMT), probably half of the chlorine returns to the environment quickly as sodium chloride, after some intermediate use as chlorine or hydrochloric acid and neutralization by caustic soda. Roughly half of the rest is converted eventually into calcium, magnesium, iron or some other metallic chloride by reaction with lime (actually calcium hydroxide) or the corresponding metal hydroxide ions. (The remainder is embodied in long-lived plastics, especially PVC). A relatively small percentage of dissipated chlorine is in the form of large organo-chlorine molecules, for example, from incineration of chlorinated plastics or pulp and paper bleaching waste.

Similarly, half or more of the sodium in the caustic soda returns to the environment quickly as salt, and much of the rest returns as sodium sulfate. Smaller amounts return as sodium phosphates (used for water treatment), sodium salts of fatty acids (soaps and detergents) or other soluble sodium salts (including silicates and cyanides). Most of the sodium and calcium carbonates (soda ash and limestone) give up their CO_2 content permanently to the atmosphere, and return to the environment as sulfates or chlorides.

The sulfur extracted from the environment, from underground deposits, fossil fuels or sulfide metal ores, is either converted to sulfur dioxide which escapes into the atmosphere, or is finally converted – after some intermediate use as sulfuric acid – into a calcium, sodium, magnesium, aluminum, iron or some other metallic sulfate that is dumped or dissipated. Most of the SO_2 is generated by the combustion of coal and residual oils, with a small contribution from non-ferrous smelting. However SO_2 is used as a process intermediate in a number of industries, including sulfuric acid production, sulfite pulping and beet sugar refining, and there are some losses. Fortunately, most of the wastes associated with sulfuric acid usage are insoluble sulfates that are comparatively harmless. However, environmental harm is still possible, due to the action of anaerobic bacteria in sediments that can extract the oxygen they need for metabolic purposes from nitrates (for preference) or sulfates. This process can release hydrogen sulfide (swamp gas) which is toxic.

The organic chemical sector, in turn, produced about 53.8 MMT of salable organic chemical products from 78.4 MMT of inputs, including 56.8 MMT of hydrocarbons and 14.6 MMT of inorganic chemicals, plus 1.5 MMT of fats and oils and 0.6 MMT of cellulose, plus 5 MMT of atmospheric oxygen. There was also some by-product hydrochloric acid; we estimated in Chapter 6 that 1.3 MMT of HCl was shipped back to the inorganic sector and perhaps 1.7 MMT was shipped to other users outside the chemical industry. This would account for 3 MMT (and possibly more). Of the 25 MMT of mass disappearance, slightly less than a third might be salts from the neutralization of strong acids; the remainder is difficult to explain, however.

It includes some water vapor and carbon dioxide, but there must be significant quantities of other wastes, many of which are unidentified, but not necessarily harmless. For instance, VOCs might amount to several MMT. (We have no basis for estimation.) Of the organic chemicals produced, resins used for plastics, synthetic fibers and synthetic rubber accounted for well over two-thirds. Some of these products (mainly the plastic PVC) have applications in the construction industry. But most plastics are used for products, such as packaging materials, with very short lives.

It is worthwhile pointing out yet again that process wastes are not the only source of pollution. Of the 99 MMT of inorganic chemicals and 51.8 MMT of organic chemicals produced (plus 2 MMT of byproduct HCl), virtually all was returned to the environment within a few months, either as fertilizers and pesticides or as wastes from a downstream process (such as acid neutralization) or industrial cleaning. Fertilizers certainly have environmental impacts, including emissions of ammonia and nitrous oxides, and pollution of ground water. The other end-use inorganic and organic chemicals that are produced are either consumed in some other production process (for example, bleaches, dyes, pigments, solvents, detergents, fuel additives, water softeners, antifreeze, and so on) – and then discarded in a waste stream – or they are embodied in products used by households and ultimately discarded as household wastes. In any case, except for phosphates, it is clear that consumption wastes far out-weigh production wastes as far as the chemical industry is concerned.

9.2 The link between inputs and outputs

It is time to shift gears. Setting aside conceptual, empirical and theoretical issues, there are very practical reasons for quantifying mass flows in the context of current concerns about long-run environmental threats, including climate warming. To mention just one: the notion of taxing carbon emissions by imposing a tax on hydrocarbon fuels depends on the law of conservation of mass (the first law of thermodynamics), namely the fact that each and every ton of carbon contained in the fuel ends up in the atmosphere, com-bined with oxygen, as carbon dioxide. This linkage seems almost trivially obvious to anyone trained in the physical sciences. Yet it is somewhat less than obvious to many legislators and administrators, for instance, whose education has been in the law or social sciences.

A very similar linkage exists between the sulfur content of fuels and the sulfur dioxide emitted to the atmosphere. The linkage is not nearly so simple as in the case of carbon, however, because fuel sulfur is largely recovered from gas and petroleum by the refineries and some fuel-bound sulfur is removed by coal washing and flue gas desulfurization (Chapter 4); further-more, some sulfur dioxide is also emitted by copper and other non-ferrous metal smelters (Chapter 5). However, thanks to the law of conservation of mass, the quantity of sulfur dioxide released into the atmosphere can prob-ably be assessed more accurately from available data on the sulfur content of fuels and ores, together with available data on sulfur recovery by refineries and smelters, than it could be by direct measurement. This fact would greatly facilitate the introduction of an effective tax on sulfur dioxide emissions by imposing the tax on fuels and ores instead (with a suitable rebate for elemen-tal sulfur or sulfuric acid recovery).

The mass flow analysis undertaken in this book clearly reveals some other cases where a tax on emissions could probably be accomplished more effec-tively by taxing inputs. Toxic heavy metals – especially arsenic, cadmium, chromium (for chemicals), lead and mercury – might be good examples. A stiff severance tax on copper, lead, mercury or zinc at the mine (or, equiva-lently, at the border) would strongly discourage dissipative uses and encourage more efficient recycling. This would be an excellent way to reduce dissipative uses and encourage recycling of mercury, for instance. It would also extend the life of the underground resource.[2] A severance tax on copper or zinc ore that resulted in a shift in favor of secondary production would also reduce the output of byproducts like arsenic (from copper ore) and cadmium (from zinc ore). Again, the law of conservation of mass allows a tax on production to be equivalent to a tax on emissions.[3]

Yet the link between process inputs and process outputs is by no means simple. In the case of chromium, there is very little hazard associated with metallurgical or refractory uses, where chromium is in the valence state known as Cr III. The hazard is almost entirely associated with chemical uses, especially in the form of chromic acid (the more oxidized Cr VI form), and its salts, which are used in pigments, electroplating, leather tanning and so forth. Chromium VI is one of the most toxic metals known. Clearly, it would be nearly impossible to tax only the hazardous kinds of chromium emissions, as such.

But materials flow analysis also suggests an answer. The answer in this case might be to impose the severance tax on the chemical that initiates the production sequence for all chromium chemicals, namely sodium dichromate (Chapter 6). Since there are very few producers of this chemical (perhaps only one in the US), such a tax would be quite easy to administer, and it would raise the price of chromium chemicals *vis à vis* possible alternatives. Thus, there would be no inhibition on uses of chromite ore in metallurgy (for example, for stainless steel).

In the case of nitrogen oxides (NO_x), however, there is no direct connection between inputs and outputs at all. This is because, although there is some fuel-bound nitrogen (in coal), most of the nitrogen in NO_x is derived from the air itself, and the amount generated depends on the temperature of the combustion process and the 'leanness' of the fuel–air mixture. (The more excess oxygen in the mixture the more NO_x is produced.) In other words, the emissions, in this case, depend on technical details of the combustion process. Domestic fires produce almost none, whereas steam–electric power generating plants and internal combustion engines produce quite a lot. Evidently control measures in this case must be specific to processes. (We hope to discuss process-related issues more systematically in a future third volume of this series.)

9.3 Economic inefficiencies of output (end-of-pipe) regulation

Details such as the foregoing may be of little interest, in themselves, to most policy makers. But it is obviously very important for policy makers to know if emissions of type 'X' can be estimated very accurately from a knowledge of process inputs (for example, fuel) or whether – on the contrary – only direct measurements of the emissions themselves will suffice. It is our view that EPA, and its counterpart agencies around the world, currently focus far more than is either necessary, or economically efficient, on 'end-of pipe' emissions, and treatment thereof. With this mind-set, it seems natural to base regulations on direct measurements.

Yet, natural or not, this end-of-pipe approach to regulation is inefficient in at least three different respects. First, it promotes narrow process or product specific technologies that may simply shift a waste stream from one environmental medium to another, meanwhile increasing costs for others. Emissions to air and water are typically governed on the basis of dilution (for example, parts per million), yet downstream water users often must invest heavily in treatment to remove contaminants that were legally introduced upstream. This is very questionable economics; nobody optimizes the system as a whole, only small parts of it. Yet these problems could and should have been foreseen. They are obvious consequences of conservation of mass: the wastes have to go somewhere (unless they are recycled). Second, controlling wastes at the end of the pipe promotes the use of costly and sophisticated technical means (like electrostatic precipitators or flue gas desulfurization) to capture and dispose of wastes, without attention to process alternatives that might reduce emissions at lower cost by using material inputs more efficiently or using alternative inputs. Such opportunities do frequently exist, albeit not in every case. This results in economic loss. Third, by imposing regulations only at the end of the pipe, extra costs are imposed only on final producers – who pass them on to consumers. But consumers have very little influence on the choice of technology further back in the process chain. They can only decide between products offered on the market, or on how much of a given product or service to purchase. Producers tend to argue that they produce only 'what the customer demands'. But this claim is ingenuous, to say the least. Consumers did not demand catalytic convertors or airbags (they merely want less smog and safe cars). The technology choices were made by some combination of producers and bureaucrats. The consumer would probably have better choices if a wider range of emission-reducing technologies were considered earlier in the process chain.

All of the three sources of economic inefficiency noted in the last few paragraphs arise from a persistent and widespread failure by government agencies and policy makers to recognize and exploit the implications of a basic law of physics. The fundamental law of conservation of mass applies for every chemical element in every transformation process. It provides a link between material inputs to economic processes and material outputs, including wastes. As we have pointed out repeatedly, material inputs eventually become wastes. This simple (and rather obvious) fact constitutes, in itself, a very powerful macro-level argument for minimizing resource extraction and use.

But we are making another point: the physical link between inputs and outputs also provides a basis for designing effective and economically efficient environmental policies at the micro-level. In particular, it provides a basis for minimizing waste and pollution outputs efficiently – in some cases – by taxing or otherwise regulating material inputs, rather than emissions as such. For the record, we are *not* suggesting that all end-of-pipe regulations be eliminated. Far from it. But the cases where end-of pipe regulation is the best available instrument can often be determined by systematic use of materials flow analysis (MFA). Where MFA is not sufficient, we must go to the next level of detail, which is process analysis. The example of NO_x was mentioned above; other 'byproduct' pollutants, such as dioxins, would also fall into this category.

9.4   The need for valuation

We have argued strongly for recognizing the implications of mass-balance in designing economically efficient environmental policies. We have specifically noted the potential for greater use of taxes on resource inputs as an efficient alternative (in many cases) to end-of-pipe regulation.

But, in practice, the use of taxes on mass flows as an environmental policy instrument requires several sorts of quantification. Different wastes have different environmental impacts. 'Chalk and cheese' cannot be legitimately compared without using weight factors, which are value measures. There have been a number of misguided attempts to argue that economic value is derivable from or equivalent to – or should be – to a measurable physical quantity, energy. It is not necessary to review this literature here.[4] Suffice it to say that energy has economic value. But the economic value of energy is situation dependent. It depends on its local availability in a convenient form, its price, the use to which it is put, the users preferences, and the availability of alternatives. Moreover, as we have occasion to emphasize below, the monetary value of energy (or any other commodity) is not the same as its social value.

Nor, we would add, is mass (or mass displaced) a useful measure of value. Despite recent efforts to popularize such a measure (materials intensity per unit service or MIPS[5]), it is difficult for most people to believe that a ton of overburden moved or topsoil lost by erosion is as harmful as a ton of arsenic or cadmium or Cr VI dispersed into the environment, still less a ton of dioxins. It is even harder to believe that displaced mass is equally harmful regardless of where the displacement occurs. (Gold mining is socially tolerated only because it is restricted to very remote locations.) For these reasons, it may be interesting and eye-opening to calculate the number of tons of various materials that are displaced in various countries during the production of a kilogram of strawberry yoghurt sold in Germany (von Weizsäcker *et al.* 1995). But even if strawberry yoghurt has a higher MIPS rating than (say) plain yoghurt, does that mean it is more harmful to the environment? We doubt it.

So the question remains: what tools are there to assist a policy maker or decision maker who wants to go beyond simple self-interest, irrational prejudice or untutored intuition? How does such a person decide objectively which of several alternatives (or a continuum of alternatives) is best? Or worst? It is easy to talk about optimization in multiple dimensions. But talk is cheap. At the end of the day, there is no way forward except by putting weights on the different dimensions. And that means reducing all dimensions of the problem to but a single common measure of value. And, to get quickly to the point, the name of that common measure of value is already perfectly well-known: it is dollars and cents (or whatever currency you prefer). Which is not, however, to say that the monetary measure is always right.[6]

A digression is probably inevitable at this point. Philosophers, artists, poets and some social scientists are fond of saying that money is not the measure of everything. Money cannot buy happiness, or virtue, or eternal life. True enough. Some people criticize economists for knowing the price of everything and the value of nothing. This is witty and amusing, but somewhat beside the point. But the truth is different. The truth is that money *is* our common social measure of value. The problem, of course, is that there is no objective way to put an objective social value on some things. Our main concern, of course, is valuing environmental impacts of certain mass flows. But it may help to address the fundamental problem from another direction.

For instance, many people insist that there is no legitimate or acceptable way to put a finite dollar value on human life. The implication of that assertion is that life has infinite value. But the reality is that individuals risk their own lives for the possibility of modest personal gains. And society spends lives for economic purposes. Society also spends money to save lives. But society cannot devote infinite resources to save even one life. The fact is that resources are finite. People who insist that life is priceless are simply using language carelessly. What they really mean is that they do not like markets, or economists, or they have not thought about what they do mean.

It is important to remember what a market price really means. It is by no means the value of a good for every individual. On the contrary, for some goods for some individuals, the value of the good is greater, and those individuals are willing to buy at the market price. To others, the value of the good is less than the market price and they are willing to be sellers. If buyers outnumber sellers, the price will rise. If sellers outnumber buyers, the price will fall. The market price at equilibrium is the price at which the quantity of goods on offer (the supply) is equal to the quantity wanted by buyers (demand). Things are priceless when there is no impersonal mechanism, such as a market or quasi-market to establish an objective price.

Consider once again the value of life. Each person has one and only one life. He or she can risk it. Hardly anybody would be willing to sell his or her life outright. But there are quite a lot of implicit sellers – people who are willing to take a personal risk in exchange for some gain. And of course, there are buyers – entrepreneurs who have found a way of making a profit on someone else's risk (promoters of boxing matches or motorcycle races, for instance). Some people will take large risks for very small gains, although the statistics are unreliable because most people do not really understand the risks.

Annuities are another sort of risk market. People pay out a lump sum in exchange for a lifetime income higher than the normal rate of interest on savings. The buyer of an annuity is willing to bet that he lives longer than the statistical life expectancy (otherwise he would be better off just living off his capital). The insurance company, on the other hand, is betting that the buyer will die before the capital is used up. Life insurance buyers pay out money from current income in order to provide a lump sum to protect family members from financial disaster if or when the insured person dies. In this case the insuror is betting that the payout, when it comes, will be less than the cumulative payment by the insured person. From each of these markets, a clever statistician can infer an equivalent 'value of life'.

But most people are quite risk averse in the sense of being unwilling to accept significant risks over which they have no personal control. They willingly ski off-piste, smoke cigarettes, drive cars under the influence of alcohol, experiment with narcotics, or engage in unsafe sex. But they complain bitterly if some radioactive waste from a nuclear power plant gets into the water supply, or if some dioxin is detected in the smoke from an incinerator.

The point is that there are a number of different markets which put different implicit values on human life because different groups of people are selling (that is, accepting risks for gain) and different businesses or institutions are buying (that is, offering the gain in exchange for the risk). But there is no market for involuntary risks, *by definition*. When there is no choice, to buy or not to buy, to sell or not to sell, there can be no market. Hence there can be no market price.

There are other situations, too, where exchange markets cannot exist. Exchange markets require ownership. Some public goods cannot be owned because they cannot be subdivided into discrete identifiable units. (This is called 'indivisibility'.) The atmosphere, the water in the oceans, the ozone layer, the climate and the biosphere are all examples of indivisible goods. Even if it were legally possible to have title on a cubic mile of air, you could not take possession. This means there is no way to prevent someone else from breathing it, or polluting it. Without the ability to enforce exclusive possession, nominal ownership would be meaningless. This does not mean the air has no value, of course. It only means there can be no market price.

A possible way around the difficulty is to create a market for 'rights' to breathe, or (more feasible) to pollute. Of course, there are many people who object to the very idea of rights to pollute on moral grounds. They say that everyone should have the right to breathe clean air and nobody should have the right to pollute. Unfortunately everybody also has the right to pollute, and nearly everybody does so. (When you drive your car or light a fire in your fireplace, you pollute.) So, the moral argument is inherently self-contradictory.

But it is not morality that prevents the existence of a market for rights to breathe, or rights to pollute. The problem, once again, is that even if ownership of such a right were legalized and officially exchangeable, no exchanges would occur because of the impossibility of guaranteeing exclusive possession. You might theoretically buy someone's right to pollute, but unless you can also be sure that he stops polluting, you have gained nothing. In other words, rights are meaningless, and therefore valueless, unless exclusive ownership can be enforced. And we know very well that some laws are inherently unenforceable (remember prohibition).

Yet the need for valuation remains, even when exchange markets cannot provide unique price information. What other possibilities remain? For the remainder of this chapter we restrict ourselves to the narrower (but still very difficult) problem of setting values on material flows and environmental consequences thereof.

9.5   Economic measures of value

We have emphasized the need for valuation, so far, in the context of market prices or substitutes thereof. Market prices, of course, reflect *marginal* values, meaning the dollar value of the last unit of commodity or service exchanged. It is possible, of course, to construct an aggregate value measure by simply multiplying price times quantity. This procedure is so commonplace that it is often taken for granted.[7]

Clearly the marginal price of an asset is useful to know, but it must be used with care. For an economist, the marginal price is a point where two imaginary curves cross (Figure 9.1). These two curves are known as the *marginal demand curve* and the *marginal supply curve*. The marginal demand curve is a declining function showing the price at which the next (marginal) unit could be sold in the market. It reflects the fact that a few consumers are willing to pay a high price, but that to sell greater quantities the price must fall.

The marginal supply curve, by contrast, is an increasing function of price. It reflects one of the most basic axioms of economics: namely, that the higher the market price, the more producers will offer goods for sale, that is, the greater the supply will be. At some price there is a marginal consumer and a marginal producer who are, by assumption, indifferent. The available supply will match the total demand (where the two curves intersect) and the market will clear. Anticipating subsequent discussion, we note that the supply curve is applicable to a good that is produced by market actors who must consume

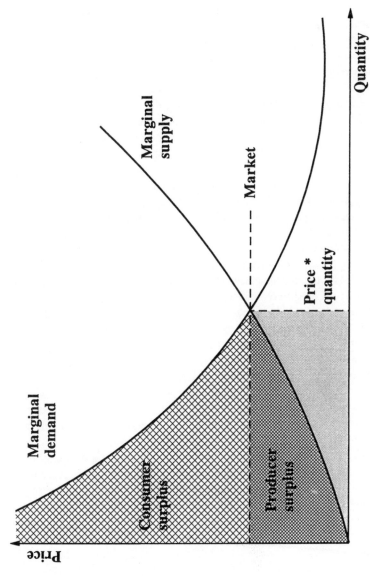

Figure 9.1   Price times quantity versus social value in open (economic) systems

labor, capital and raw materials. We need to be careful about extending this notion beyond the market realm.

Unfortunately, we seldom have reliable information about the shapes (that is, the slopes) of these curves except very near the point of intersection. In the case of the supply curve, it is usually safe to assume that the supply will be zero at a price corresponding to the lowest possible unit cost of production (but that is not zero, in general). At least two points on the supply curve are therefore known, and the slope near the intersection can often be estimated from either statistical or engineering information. But in the case of the demand curve we only know the point of intersection and perhaps the nearby slope. It is normally assumed that the demand curve approaches zero asymptotically as the supply becomes very large. This is a rather important caveat, as will be seen.

However, suppose for purposes of argument that the demand curve, in particular, is given. Then we can define three different measures of aggregate value. First of all is the marginal price times quantity measure. It is represented by the rectangular shaded area in Figure 9.1. Next is the triangular cross-hatched (and shaded) area under the horizontal (price) line and above the increasing cost curve. This is known as producer surplus, since it represents the sum total of profits of all producers in the market. This may not be obvious, at first glance, to people who did not take a course in economics. But remember that we are imagining a large number of producers with different internal costs, ranked in increasing order of cost. So the actual selling price is a lot higher than the price at which the lowest cost producer was willing to sell. The difference is profit.

Similarly, some consumers were willing to pay a lot more than the actual market price. The difference between what the non-marginal consumer was willing to pay and what the consumer actually paid is the surplus value of the product to that consumer. The sum total of all such surpluses is the sail-shaped cross-hatched area below the horizontal price line in Figure 9.1. This is the consumer surplus. The total theoretical aggregate value of a commodity or service is the sum of producer and consumer surplus, that is, the total cross-hatched area. It is easy to draw a demand curve and a supply curve such that this cross-hatched area looks equal – or nearly equal – to the shaded area. This is often done in economics textbooks. However, in reality this would rarely be true.

In fact, when the commodity or service in question is a necessity for life (food or drinking water, for instance) the demand curve may become vertical at a point on the horizontal axis representing the minimum quantity required for survival. In such a case the area under the demand curve becomes infinite and the consumer surplus also become infinite. This creates some conceptual difficulties which make the consumer surplus measure difficult to use in practice.

However, the price times quantity measure – the rectangular shaded area – also introduces conceptual difficulties in some cases. Note that market prices depend on the shape of the supply curve. For man-made products this curve is a function of production technology and invested capital (which, in turn, can also depend on past demand). But for natural and environmental resources other determinants are sometimes more important.

In cases where the available supply in terms of flow rate (quantity per unit time) is far in excess of any current level of utilization, the result is a near-zero price, reflecting only collection and distribution costs. In the nineteenth century fuelwood was free for the cutting in America. Colonists wanted land for plowing, not trees. Much of the original Appalachian forest was cleared by burning – as the Amazonian and Indonesian forests are being cleared today. It was very nearly the case for crude oil in Texas around the turn of the century, for natural gas during much of this century, and again for oil in Saudi Arabia much more recently. The oil and gas were so plentiful and so near the surface that the price to final consumers in early days was essentially all value added by processors and distributors, with very little 'rent' going to actual resource owners. Of course, the rent component of the price rises over time as the resource becomes scarcer, even though the costs of discovery and extraction are rising also.

But the point of the example is that the availability of petroleum products in very large quantities at very low prices – thanks to nature's generosity – made large scale mechanization of industry and agriculture possible. Large-scale mechanization, in turn, has enabled more petroleum and gas resources to be discovered and exploited, keeping the price low. During the whole of the twentieth century, it can be argued that the social value (consumer plus producer surplus) of petroleum and gas has been extremely large in comparison with the price times quantity measure. Indeed, it is arguable that the two measures depend inversely on price, at least in the short run. If a vast new discovery (for instance) should lower the price by lowering the supply curve, the consumer surplus, which dominates the aggregate social value, would probably rise. The losers would be the owners of current reserves.

This situation constitutes a very fundamental problem when it comes to pricing environmental assets. The standard picture of a declining demand curve and a rising supply curve is applicable to the case where it makes sense to extrapolate (at least conceptually) to an asymptotic limit of indefinitely increasing demand. It is not a priori absurd to imagine a world awash in still more and cheaper oil and gas. (That is, unless we remember that more hydrocarbons also means more carbon dioxide, VOCs, low-level ozone, SO_2 and NO_x.) But how must we modify the picture if demand does *not* increase without limit? The case of forests was mentioned a few paragraphs back. In the case of forests, there can be too much as well as too little. In short, there is an optimum amount of forest. The same is true of rainfall. That situation can be generalized.

In fact, the local supply of a commodity can be so great that the local market value of an additional increment is negative, not positive. Take the case of an environmental service: rainfall. People living in a dry area would generally be willing to pay something for a bit more rain – or an irrigation canal. But, people living in a rain forest would generally prefer less rain. People living in an area that is adapted to a dry climate, such as the western slope of the Andes, regard a year of extraordinary rainfall (like *El Niño*) as a disaster, even though the same amount of rain is quite normal in Indonesia, where its absence is the disaster. In terms of our standard picture, the demand curve is certainly high and positive for small levels of rainfall, and it decreases as the rainfall increases toward some optimal level (depending on the location). But for still larger levels of rainfall the demand drops to zero. Beyond that the demand becomes increasingly negative.

This same characteristic pattern applies to many environmental parameters. For instance, if the amount of oxygen in the atmosphere were reduced, it would be like living at a higher altitude. Breathing would be harder and would require more energy. Our hearts would have to work harder to pump blood. People – and animals – with breathing problems and heart trouble would suffer. If the atmospheric oxygen level were higher than it is aerobic organisms would grow faster but they would also die younger, because though oxygen is necessary for life it is also toxic.[8] Also, forest fires would start more easily, as James Lovelock has pointed out.[9]

The same pattern holds for global temperature: according to the latest scientific assessment of the Intergovernmental Panel on Climate Change (IPCC) higher average temperatures would lead to sea level rise, ecological disruption and increased storminess (IPCC 1995). Lower global temperatures (in time) would be accompanied by glaciation, sea level fall, and also ecological disruption. (In fact any departure from current norms in either direction would cause ecological disturbance.) It is not difficult to think of other examples of situations where there is a natural balance between too little and too much. Surely it applies to acidity. If the rainfall becomes more acid than historical equilibrium, the alkaline buffering capacity of the soil is used up, land vegetation suffers, toxic heavy metals in soils and sediments are mobilized, and lakes become inhospitable to fish. Almost certainly this pattern also applies to macro-nutrients such as nitrogen, sulfur, phosphorus, and potassium as well as to micro-nutrients like calcium, copper, iron, magnesium, selenium and zinc.

It is reasonable to assume that these parameters do not respond to a market of any kind. In particular, rainfall, carbon dioxide, oxygen, stratospheric ozone, and global temperature are produced by non-economic agents. There is no economic cost of production, but the supply is limited. The supply curve is thus a vertical line. The 'shadow price' is the intersection of the declining demand curve and the vertical supply line.[10] Imagine that we start at a point far away from the optimum, for example, at zero rainfall and very high – even infinite – shadow price. As the supply increases the marginal value of the next increment of supply drops, until finally the local rainfall matches to local demand (that is, the level to which the local fauna and flora have adapted). Marginal demand falls to zero. So far, there is no contradiction. Rainfall (or fresh water from any source) has a positive shadow price as long as the supply is below the optimum. But, the shadow price of rainfall declines as the optimum supply is approached from below.

Now suppose it is the year of *El Niño*; the rainfall supply in normally dry places (like Peru and Somalia) rises still more. In those places the market wants more sunshine and less rain. Demand for rain drops below zero, demand for flood insurance and houseboats rises. The shadow price of rainfall becomes negative. Obviously this picture of prices declining as supply increases is inconsistent with a smoothly rising aggregate supply curve for rainfall, although it is perfectly consistent with a single rising supply curve for irrigation water or drinking water at any given location. The two situations differ in that irrigation water or drinking water are produced by humans and are assumed to have no negative consequences or spillovers (pun not unintended!) whereas excess rainfall does.

A further implication of this argument is this: *the optimum supply of rainfall must coincide with a 'shadow price' of exactly zero.* This statement also applies to rainforests, acidity, humidity, global temperature, carbon dioxide, oxygen, stratospheric ozone, and other environmental parameters that have resulted from an evolutionary process of adaptation. When the supply is a little below optimum, the market would like more and would pay a positive price for another increment. When the supply is greater than optimum, the market wants less and would pay to have less, not more. Incidentally, the price times quantity measure also approaches zero from above when the resource is undersupplied, and becomes negative when the resource is oversupplied. But presumably nobody would argue that the social value of rainfall must be zero, just because the shadow price is zero at the point of optimum supply. On the contrary, this is the point where the social value is maximum (Figure 9.2).

This rule also applies in situations where the substance in question is economically beneficial but also toxic or hazardous to the environment if dispersed in excessive quantities. The term 'excessive' is relative, of course. Nitrogen, phosphorus, and sulfur, for instance, can probably be dispersed into the environment in somewhat greater than natural quantities without adverse effects. This may be true of carbon dioxide (disregarding the greenhouse

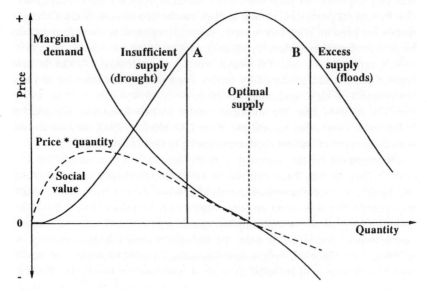

Figure 9.2 Price times quantity versus social value in closed (balanced) systems

effect) and stratospheric ozone too. This does not mean there is no point at which the marginal value of an additional increment is negative, only that the optimum – for human purposes – is probably somewhat above the present level.

Some purists might argue that there should be no emissions of any toxic substance to the environment. However, this is probably also simplistic. Since all materials that are extracted from the environment are eventually converted into wastes – it is only a question of time – this rule would prohibit all economic use of virtually all heavy metals, including such useful ones as chromium, copper, lead, mercury, nickel, tin and zinc. It would also rule out all chemical uses of chlorine, bromine and fluorine. (Greenpeace advocates the total elimination of chlorine, for instance, Thornton 1991, 1993.) In these cases the optimum level of mobilization may well be less than the present level, but it is unlikely to be zero.

A more sensible rule might be to try to define a 'maximum safe dose' or 'exposure limit'. This approach is also problematic, however, because the so-called maximum exposure limit is often set by public health authorities at levels much lower than the lowest exposure level at which any adverse health effects are seen on rodents (for instance). Such levels, in turn, may have little relevance for humans. Another approach is to identify an environmental 'carrying capacity' for such substances, based on typical levels of mobilization by natural processes, insofar as they can be determined. Thus all heavy metals are present in surface waters, in some locations, without measurable harm to the biosphere. Mercury vapor is emitted to the atmosphere in significant quantities by natural weathering and volcanos. Quite a few organochlorines are produced by marine organisms, and dispersed into the environment in large quantities (Gribble 1992, 1994; Gribble *et al.* 1995; Euro Chlor 1994). Even the notorious dioxins are now known to be produced in forest fires and other natural processes (Wormgoor 1994); they have even been discovered in ancient sediments (Rappe in Gribble *et al.* 1995).

The argument for the 'carrying capacity' approach is that humankind and other higher species have evolved in an environment that contains these substances, in trace amounts. Nevertheless, when natural background levels are exceeded by significant amounts, they can be considered as toxins. The optimum level of use or consumption can then be equated with the level of harmlessness, that is at, or near, the average natural background level of mobilization. (Since this level is quite variable, for most toxic substances, the highest safe level is likely to be an order of magnitude or two higher than the average.)

To conclude this rather long discussion, there are a number of situations where a monetary shadow price for an environmental parameter or resource flux, times a quantity, is *not* a reasonable proxy for net rent (consumer plus producer surplus) and thus not an acceptable proxy for the social value of that resource flux. The reason is that the optimum level of the parameter or flux necessarily corresponds with zero shadow price. In general this problem arises in cases where the resource flux has an optimal level resulting from evolutionary adaptation. This conclusion holds regardless of whether the shadow price is actually zero or not, or whether it can be estimated independently in the absence of a real market.

9.6   Monetization in MFA

In view of the foregoing discussion, the realm of applicability of the price times quantity measure, can be defined, in principle, as the locus of situations having three characteristics: (1) There is a quantifiable mass flow with an increasing cost curve; (2) there are, or could be, efficient markets for these mass flows, and (3) there is no significant economic damage cost or penalty associated with excess consumption. The first two criteria apply to normal commodities. The third criterion is the surprise. Basically, it requires that the material is not toxic or hazardous at any reasonable level of mobilization.

For normal commodities there is not a great deal more to be said. Input–output tables are constructed, in the first place, from mass flows and prices.

We summarized the major mass flows discussed in previous chapters of this book in Table 9.1 along with corresponding sales and value-added figures. The interesting questions that are suggested by this table, of course, are: what value should be assigned to the mass flows from the environment (inputs) and mass flows to the environment (waste emissions)?

The boundaries of the realm defined by conditions (1) and (2) are not completely clear in practice. There are some who appear to believe that the realm of actual or potential monetary valuation encompasses virtually everything. Among so-called libertarians it is a matter of doctrine that legal ownership is the key: that where markets are imperfect, the universal solution is privatization. Privatization (it is argued) would create property rights in environmental amenities and services and allow free exchange markets to determine the 'right prices' for those amenities and services. The problem of enforcement is also assumed to be privatizable, through resort to the courts: when someone is abusing your property rights, you sue.

Undoubtedly there is some room to create effective markets where none now exist. One example, which makes the point quite effectively, is the creation a few years ago of an auction market for sulfur dioxide emission rights for electrical utilities in the US. The experience also demonstrates a key point that deserves emphasis: prior to the creation of this market, industry experts estimated the likely cost of a single sulfur dioxide emission 'right' to be $700. This was based on inflated estimates of the engineering cost of reducing emissions. In fact, the latest trades have established a price of only $70 per unit, a mere 10 per cent of the original estimate. From this experience and others, it is clear that engineering cost estimates, when performed by interested parties, are likely to be very wide of the mark. (We make this point, because – as will be seen – one of the more popular approaches for estimating the marginal economic damages of pollution is to use 'cost of control' as a surrogate for actual damage.)

On reflection, there are few materials that fully meet the third requirement. Even milk and aspirin can be dangerous in excess. However, looking at the matter like a reasonable man-in-the-street (the sort of person the law assumes juries to consist of) we can assume that everything meets the tests unless it is specifically excluded.

Other economists are willing to concede that there are fundamental limits to the potential domain of exchange markets, and therefore to direct monetization. The difficulties arise where environmental services – or rights of access to them – *cannot* be contained, quantified or exchanged for one reason or another. Some environmental services are inherently not divisible into discrete portions. Climate and biodiversity are examples. Others, such as intangible rights (for example, of access to common property resources, or emission rights) may be inherently unenforceable – or excessively costly to enforce – and therefore of no value to owners. Nobody will buy for money in a market what he can simply take and use without cost or penalty.

Having said this, the question remains: how can we monetize the value of services derived from mass flows that satisfy criteria (1) and (3) but not (2) above? The nineteenth century German chemist Leibig pointed out that every natural system is limited by the availability of some chemical nutrient, or by moisture, temperature or sunlight (Leibig's Law). The limiting factor is the only one such that an additional increment of it will increase the productivity of the system. In principle it is the only one, in any given case, that has a positive shadow price.[11] However, if the 'missing' factor is added in excess amount, some other factor will then be the limiting one. In agriculture the usual strategy is to add enough of the cheaper nutrients (N, P, K, S, Ca) such that the final limitation will be imposed by water, temperature or sunlight. Supplementary irrigation water is often added, also, during periods of peak evapo-transpiration (mid-summer). Thus, on an average basis, all of these are likely to have positive shadow prices in most agricultural areas.

It follows that mass flows in the US agricultural system with significant positive monetary value include plant nutrients from topsoil, fossil groundwater used for irrigation, and (possibly) atmosphere-derived nutrients such as carbon dioxide, sulfur oxide and nitrogen oxides (bearing in mind that acidic inputs from the atmosphere must be compensated by alkaline inputs that are extracted from the ground, usually lime or limestone). Natural rainfall in summer would also qualify in most agricultural areas.

Oxygen from the atmosphere clearly does not qualify. For reasons sketched previously, its shadow price must be set at zero, since it is presumably already at its optimal level.

It is tempting to argue that the shadow monetary values of these plant nutrients, and the natural rainfall in summer, can be estimated roughly on the basis of the market value (per unit mass) of fertilizers and water that are purchased on the market. This is a good test of the method. According to recent estimates (Figure 2.2) natural processes provide 70 per cent of fixed nitrogen and nearly 60 per cent of phosphorus to US agriculture. Farmers in 1993 spent over $15 billion on agricultural chemicals (including pesticides) (USDA 1996, Table 562). Thus, it would appear that fertilizers from natural recycling processes were 'worth' something like $30 billion, more or less, at these prices.

In the case of irrigation water it is more difficult to obtain a good number, since it is well known that water prices actually paid by farmers are heavily subsidized at levels far below prices paid by industrial or urban users. Unfortunately we have no reliable data on either prices or quantities. Farmers expenditures for irrigation water are included with 'miscellaneous expenses' along with repair and maintenance of farm machinery, electric power, insurance, management costs, veterinary services for livestock, and fees of various kinds. These costs amounted to $42.7 billion in 1993 (USDA 1996), of which irrigation water could hardly have been more than a small fraction.

The value of carbon dioxide as a nutrient for crop plants (and forests) is probably positive, since there appears to be a small but reasonably well documented carbon-eutrophication effect. This means that increasing the CO_2 level increases plant growth slightly. Hence, in view of Leibig's law, the shadow price of carbon dioxide for agriculture is non-zero and positive. However, whatever the number is, it would presumably be a small subtraction from the much larger negative value of (excessive) carbon dioxide emissions due to sea-level rise, increased weather variability (droughts, floods, storminess), increased risk of disease and pest outbreaks, and so on (See Figure 9.2).

With regard to many other biologically active materials, including nutrients like fixed nitrogen and sulfur and where they are not wanted (for example, in ground water, lakes and streams and coastal–estuarine zones), as well as heavy metals and many chemicals, criterion (3) does not apply. These are substances now being mobilized and dispersed to the environment in excess of carrying capacity. These are materials that are economically beneficial in quantities below the optimum level of consumption and/or the carrying capacity of the earth (or local area) for that substance. But they are hazardous in quantities that exceed the optimum consumption level and/or the carrying capacity. In such cases the shadow price is currently negative. In other words, society can increase its welfare by generating (or, at any rate, dissipating) less of these substances. This may or may not be accomplished by paying to reduce the emissions. Since markets do not exist for pollutants, as such, the cost of control is sometimes used as a surrogate. However, there are a host of practical difficulties.

In some respects, health-related costs are the easiest to assess, if 'costs' are interpreted as days lost from work, or days spent in hospital. (The thorny issue of putting a monetary value on human life is hard to avoid, in an honest assessment, but nevertheless it is usually avoided.) Unfortunately, most EPA work on marginal damage analysis in this area has almost entirely been based on extrapolated health benefits (costs avoided) that are based on questionable assumptions about mortality from low-level exposures that are strongly challenged by some critics.

As an illustration of the problems of this approach, we refer to a life cycle analysis (LCA) of packaging materials based largely on EPA data (and partially sponsored by EPA) that was undertaken by the Tellus Institute (1992). The Tellus study undertook to construct a 'pollutant price', based on a reasonably consistent methodology, for a large number of toxic and carcinogenic elements and compounds. The analysis for toxic materials was based on a

Massachusetts study of the cost of control of lead pollution, but only for two sources of lead pollution, namely secondary lead smelters and lead painted window sills. (Cost of control, in the latter case, was equated with the cost of removing the paint.) The other toxic materials were then compared with lead on the basis of some index of relative hazard or toxicity, as compared to lead (that is, a scoring model). Tellus used two of the several possible measures of potency, namely the maximum safe (that is, reference dose) or RD, and a measure of relative carcinogenicity. The end result was a table of pollutant prices (see Table 9.2).

This table should not be taken too seriously. The available data are simply not good enough. It is, at best, an illustration of what current data and methods can achieve. But it is certainly very misleading in some respects. For instance, it should be noted that the cost for chromium, (not in the table, but determined by Tellus, using the same method), turns out to be a meager $4/ kg. It is unclear where that particular number came from, but it is suspiciously low. We recall the point made earlier, that chromium has two valence states (III) and (VI), and that the latter form (for example, as chromic acid or its salts) is one of the most toxic of all metals, certainly comparable to arsenic.[12]

EPA estimates of monetary damage in other areas have been prepared using different criteria for different regulatory programs. Thus, in the case of so-called 'criteria air pollutants' (those that have been regulated) the rather sneaky assumption was made in earlier EPA studies that the marginal cost of damage is the same as the marginal cost of control. The logic underlying this equation is dubious and many external reviewers and critics disagree strongly. Indeed, a number of studies have suggested that control costs far exceed health benefits, for some regulations, while being far less than benefits in other cases.

One of the few economists to undertake the necessary effort to review the evidence is Robert Repetto of World Resources Institute (WRI). Repetto's work is mainly concerned with redefining 'productivity' at the industry to properly reflect progress in reducing pollution (Repetto 1990; Repetto *et al.* 1996). However, the WRI work builds on EPA data and provides a relatively authoritative overview of the environmental damages associated with some major air and water pollutants.

We present, in Table 9.3 a collection of monetary estimates of the marginal damages caused by the emission of one metric ton of the major atmospheric pollutants of global importance. The range of values, estimated by different methodologies, using different data, speaks for itself of the magnitude of the uncertainties.

Table 9.2   Estimated costs of pollution ($/kg)

Pollutant	Pollutant price ($)
CO	0.93
NO_x	8.00
Particulates	12.89
SO_x	12.94
Zinc	24
Benzene	55
Copper	132
Pentachlorophenol	165
Vanadium	705
Nickel	921
Silver	1 646
Selenium	1 646
1,3 Butadiene	3 418
Lead	3 526
Carbon tetrachloride	3 650
Vinyl chloride	4 368
Beryllium	4 576
Hexachlorobenzene	4 604
4,4 DDT	4 937
1,3 Dichloropropane	8 399
Nitrobenzene	9 874
Cadmium	10 729
Antimony	12 342
Lindane	16 457
Mercury	16 457
PAHs	21 837
Arsenic	49 938
Thallium	70 528
2,3,7,8 TCDD	284 824 615

Source: Tellus 1992.

9.7   Conclusions

The main conclusions to be drawn from this book have all been stated before. They can be recapitulated in many pages or a few words. To try the reader's patience as little as possible, we can reduce the message to a pair of Aristotelian syllogisms. The major premise of the first one is that decision makers – both public and private – need reliable quantitative information to make good

Table 9.3 Estimates of relative damage potential of specified pollutants and toxic substances

Source		1993 dollars per metric ton				
Marginal damage estimate[a]		CO	VOC and CO	NO$_x$	SO$_x$	Particulates
Repetto *et al.* 1996, p. 24		0.8	1148	661	758	2509
Repetto 1990				199	552	2209
Elkins and Russel 1985			1148		1151	2764
USBPA 1988	West of Cascades			678	2761	1181
	East of Cascades			53	310	128
ORNL and	Knoxville				42	2523
RFF 1992[b]	Four Corners				4	230
NY State	Rural I			645	501	2291
Externalities	Rural II			696	523	3136
Study[c]	Suburban			645	573	5514
(Rowe *et al.* 1995)	Urban			788	859	31363
Northern State	Urban	1.2		226	99	3385
Power (Banzhaf	Rural	0.2		18	12	467
1995)	Metropolitan fringe	0.8		60	51	1605
EPRI (Koomey	Rural PA/WV			108	745	
1990)[d]	Suburban NY				1971	
NPC (Wang *et*	Las Vegas Valley			169		1092
al. 1994)	Outside			138		154

		CO	PAH	NO$_x$	SO$_x$	Particulates
Environmental Load Index[e]		35.5	64350	28.6	13.1	1.0
(Steen and Ryding 1993)		CO$_2$	Ethylene	N$_2$O	BOD	COD
		11.7	129.7	926.8	0.26	0.21

Notes:
[a] Marginal Damage Estimates here are all shown in Repetto *et al.* 1996, pp. 23–4 Tables 2.1 and 2.2. The original units (1987 dollars) have been converted to 1993 dollars using a conversion factor of 0.786 1993$ per 1987$.
[b] Coal fired plants.
[c] Central estimates for Natural Gas Combination Cycle facility.
[d] Best estimate.
[d] Original units for the Environmental Load Index were 1993 ECUs per kg. These have been converted to 1993 dollars per metric ton using a conversion factor of 1.32 dollars per ECU.

decisions. The minor premise is that available information is often inconsistent and unreliable, while reliable quantitative information is scarce. We have demonstrated this proposition with numerous examples of faulty and inconsistent data, although the problems with the toxic release inventory (TRI) discussed in the last chapter are probably enough to make the point. It follows that decision making, being based on flawed data, is often flawed.

The second syllogism is equally simple. The major premise is a 'no regrets' proposition: if a simple method of data verification is available that would improve the quality of information available for decision making, it should be used. The minor premise is that the mass-balance methodology is both simple to use, at least in principle, and widely applicable. (It is, in fact, a straightforward generalization of the idea of double-entry bookkeeping.) The conclusion is that the mass-balance method should be used systematically by all data gathering and compiling agencies.

Why has it not happened? The answer is, probably, that it requires a top-down 'systems' view to see what needs to be done, whereas most statistical databases have evolved rather haphazardly from administrative beginnings. In most cases nobody was really in charge. Certainly, nobody was in charge of designing a system for national statistical data, taken as a whole. This makes it difficult to change things.

We agree that the applications illustrated in this book may not always have seemed simple or straightforward. This is partly because the necessary linkage between the outputs of one sector or process and inputs to another sector or process is not always obvious to someone who is not intimately familiar with the subject (or both subjects). Moreover, the data are often gathered by variable means from disparate sources, presented in inconsistent units and published in very different places. For us this has been a kind of detective story. However, most of these problems for the pioneer need be solved only once. Those who follow will have a much easier task. Eventually the data gathering, processing and compilation procedures can be reduced to protocols and formulae.

However, let someone else write the textbook.

Endnotes

1. This has been a long-term goal of mine (RUA) since the idea of such a model was first suggested by my colleague, Allen Kneese (Ayres and Kneese 1969; Kneese *et al.* 1970).
2. However, these issues are complex. Secondary lead smelters are also significant emitters, and an increase in recycling without a parallel improvement in the efficiency of the recycling technology might lead to increased levels of exposure to lead, at least in some locations.
3. Actually, a tax on primary production would be considerably more effective. A tax on (say) arsenic emissions would be nearly impossible to administer, since the only large-scale emitters are copper smelters, but most emissions result from dissipative uses. Moreover, even if the tax were imposed on the arsenic content of products rather than on emissions *per se* it would discriminate unfairly against easily recycled products (such as gallium arsenide semiconductors) in contrast to herbicides and wood preservatives. Moreover, only final users of such products would make technological choices. If, for example, a tax on arsenic resulted in a higher price and reduced usage for arsenic-based wood preservatives, the total quantity of arsenic mobilized by copper mining would be unaffected, and if arsenic could not be recovered and sold it would most likely end up in mine waste. Meanwhile, the alternative for arsenic-based wood preservatives might be pentachlorophenol (which was formerly used) or some other chemical with equally bad environmental impacts.

4. Actually, the energy theory of value is seldom made explicit, since it is too easy to demolish (for example, Huettner 1976). Actually, we ourselves argue elsewhere that a more fundamental measure, sometimes called 'exergy' (but also given other names, such as potential useful work, or even 'potential entropy') may also have utility as the best available *physical* measure for comparing quantities of different kinds of natural resource inputs (for example, wood, coal, copper ore, and so on) and waste emissions (for example, SO_x, VOC) to a given environmental medium, on a common scale. However, the use of such a measure can be justified only in cases where monetary measures are unavailable or clearly inappropriate, as where there exists an optimum level of supply (see later discussion and Figure 9.2).

5. See, for instance, Schmidt-Bleek (1994).

6. Some philosophers will jump in here and argue that it is elitist (or worse) for any individual to put himself above the market by arguing that this or that market price is wrong. Of course, it is possible to be fairly objective about noting the existence of market failures, but we acknowledge that there is an inevitable element of bias in going further to quantify the correction. On the other hand, to pretend that the market is always objective, even when it is not, is just another form of bias – in favor of those who benefit from the market failure (that is, the status quo).

7. For instance, in the *Statistical Abstract of the United States 1995* (US Bureau of the Census) there is a table (Table 1099) purporting to show the value of all farm land and buildings in the year 1992 ($687 billion). But, of course this number is calculated by extrapolating from actual (that is, marginal) farm and land sales, by district. It is essentially the product of the marginal price of farmland times the total quantity of land in farms. Similarly, when the *Economic Report of the President* (CEA 1996) estimated national wealth (until recently) by calculating the value of land (as above) plus the market value of financial assets (that is, stocks and bonds) the same approximation is involved. Yet if more than a tiny fraction of stockholders attempted to realize their financial wealth at the same time, the market would crash and much of this wealth would literally disappear.

8. Aging is largely due to progressive oxygen damage to chromosomes. So-called aging inhibitors are anti-oxidants like vitamins A, C, E and selenium.

9. 'Our present atmosphere, with an oxygen level of 21 percent is at the safe upper limit for life. Even a small increase in concentration would greatly add to the danger of fires. The probability of a forest fire being ignited by a lightning flash increases by 70 percent for each 1 percent rise in oxygen concentration above the present level. Above 25 percent very little of our land vegetation could survive the raging conflagrations which would destroy tropical rainforests and Arctic tundra alike' (Lovelock 1988, pp. 70–71).

10. The 'shadow price' is an imaginary price at which exchanges would take place if there were a market. One can say a good deal about such prices, even though they are (by definition) not empirically observable. In some models they can be computed.

11. This is a standard result of optimization under linear constraints.

12. In Sweden, chromium is regarded as the most hazardous of all pollutants in the environment, by a fairly large margin (Tukker *et al.* 1996).

References

Adriaanse, Albert, Stefan Bringezu, Allen Hammond, Yuichi Moriguchi, Eric Rodenburg, Donald Rogich and Hemut Schütz (1997), *Resource Flows: The Material Basis of Industrial Economies*, Washington, DC: World Resources Institute, with Wuppertal Institute, Germany, National Ministry of Housing, Netherlands and National Institute for Environmental Studies, Japan.

Allen, David T. and Nasrin Behmanesh (1992), 'Non-hazardous waste generation', *Hazardous Waste and Hazardous Materials*, **9**(1), Winter, 91–6.

Altenpohl, Dieter (1982), *Aluminum Viewed from Within*, Dusseldorf: Aluminium-Verlag.

Altenpohl, Dieter (1997), Personal communication, Zurich, Switzerland.

Aucott, Michael (1994–95), 'Releases versus throughput: why the TRI fails to account for chemicals entering the environment and how it could be improved', *Pollution Prevention Review*, Winter, 59–84.

Axtell, Robert (1993), Personal communication, Washington, DC: Brookings Institution.

Ayres, Robert U. (1989a), 'Industrial metabolism and global change', *International Social Science Journal*, **121**, Paris: UNESCO.

Ayres, Robert U. (1989b), 'Industrial metabolism', in: Jesse Ausubel and Hedy E. Sladovich (eds), *Technology and Environment*, Washington, DC: National Academy Press.

Ayres, Robert U. (1997), 'The life cycle of chlorine: Part I; chlorine production and the chlorine–mercury connection', *Journal of Industrial Ecology*, **I**(1).

Ayres, Robert U. and Leslie W. Ayres (1996), *Industrial Ecology: Closing the Materials Cycle*, Aldershot, UK: Edward Elgar.

Ayres, Robert U. and Leslie W. Ayres (1997), 'The life cycle of chlorine: Part II; conversion processes and use in the European chemical industry', *Journal of Industrial Ecology*, **I**(2).

Ayres, Robert U. and Allan V. Kneese (1969), 'Production, consumption and externalities', *American Economic Review*, June.

Ayres, Robert U. and Allan V. Kneese (1989), 'Externalities: economics and thermodynamics' in: F. Archibugi and P. Nijkamp (eds), *Economy and Ecology: Towards Sustainable Development*, Netherlands: Kluwer Academic Publishers.

Ayres, Robert U. and Udo E. Simonis (eds) (1994), *Industrial Metabolism; Restructuring for Sustainable Development*, Tokyo: United Nations University Press

Banzhaf, Spencer (1995), Data estimates (unpublished), May.

Barns, David and J.A. Edmonds (1990), *An Evaluation of the Relationship Between the Production and Use of Energy and Atmospheric Methane Emissions*, Washington, DC: United States Department of Energy, Office of Energy Research, April.

Billen, Gilles, Francine Toussaint, Philippe Peeters, Marc Sapir, Anne Steenhout and Jean-Pierre Vanderborght (1983), *L'écosystème Belgique: Essai d'écologie industrielle*, Brussels, Belgium: Centre de Recherce et d'Information Socio-Politiques (CRISP).

Bonneville Power Authority (1988).

Britton, F.E.K. *et al.* (1993), *New Developments in Tire Technology*, Paris: EcoPlan International.

Brown, Lester R. and Edward C. Wolf (1984), *Soil Erosion: Quiet Crisis in the World Economy*, Worldwatch Paper (60), Washington, DC: Worldwatch Institute.

Burkle, J.O. (1980), 'Primary lead industry', in: *Industrial Process Profiles for Industrial Use*, Chapter 27, Industrial Environmental Research Laboratory, United States Department of Commerce, Cincinnati OH.

Bush, Barbara L. and Gail Levine (1992), 'The generation and management of wastes and secondary materials in the petroleum refining industry: 1987–1988', *Hazardous Waste and Hazardous Materials*, **9**(1), Winter, 73–84.

Chemical and Engineering News (CEN) (1995), 'Production by the US chemical industry', *Chemical and Engineering News*, June 29.

Chemical and Engineering News (CEN) (1996), 'Production by the US chemical industry', *Chemical and Engineering News*, June 29.

Carson, R. (1962), *Silent Spring*, Boston: Houghton Mifflin Co.

Casler, Stephen D. (1991), *Fuel Combustion and Pollution Emissions: Disaggregated Estimates for the US Economy*, Department of Economics, Allegheny College, Meadville PA, June.

Citizens Fund (1991), *Manufacturing Pollution: A Survey of the Nation's Toxic Polluters*, Washington, DC, July.

Citizens Fund (1992), *Manufacturing Pollution*, Washington, DC, August.

Council of Economic Advisors (CEA) (1996), *Economic Report of the President Together with the Annual Report of the Council of Economic Advisors*, Washington, DC: United States Government Printing Office.

Courteau, J.B. and N. Lilienthal (1991), *Toward a More Informed Public: Recommendations for Improving the Toxics Release Inventory*, New York: INFORM.

Crutzen, Paul J. (1976), *The Nitrogen Cycle and Stratospheric Ozone*, Nitrogen Research Review Conference, United States National Academy of Sciences, Fort Collins, CO, October 12–13.

Crutzen, Paul J., I. Aselmann and W. Seiler (1986), 'Methane production by domestic animals, wild ruminants, other herbivorous fauna, and humans', *Tellus*, **38B**, 271–84.

Darr, David (1994), United States Department of Agriculture, Personal Communication.

David, Elizabeth L. (1987), 'Manufacturing and mining water use in the United States, 1954–83', in: *National Water Summary 1987 – Water Supply and Use: 81–92*, US Geological Survey, Reston, VA, Water-Supply Paper 2350.

Deevey, E.C. (1970), 'Mineral cycles', *Scientific American*, **223**, 148–58.

Dones, R., S. Hirschberg and I. Knoepfel (1994), *Greenhouse Gas Emission Inventory Based on Full Energy Chain Analysis*, IAEA Workshop on Full Energy Chain Assessment of Greenhouse Gas Emission Factors for Nuclear and Other Energy Sources, International Atomic Energy Agency, Beijing, China, October 4–7, 1994.

Dones, R., U. Gantner, S. Hirschberg, G. Doka and I. Knoepfel (1996), *Environmental Inventories for Future Electricity Supply Systems for Switzerland*, Villigen, Switzerland: Paul Scherrer Institut, February.

Douglas, Ian and Nigel Lawson (undated), *An Earth Science Approach to Materials Flows Generated by Urbanization and Mining*, Manchester, UK: School of Geography, University of Manchester.

Edelstein, Daniel (1987), 'Froth flotation in the United States, 1985', *Mineral Industry Surveys*, Washington, DC: United States Bureau of Mines. January 13.

Edelstein, Daniel (1993), 'Froth flotation in the United States, 1991', *Mineral Industry Surveys*, Washington, DC: United States Bureau of Mines, September 20.

Ehrenfeld, John and Nicholas Gertler (1997), 'Industrial ecology in practice: the evolution of interdependence at Kalundborg', *Journal of Industrial Ecology*, **1**(1), Winter, 67–79.

Elkins, Charles L. and M. Russell (1985), *Guidelines for Cost-Effectiveness of New Source Performance Standards*, Washington, DC: United States Environmental Protection Agency, September 11.

Environment Canada (1995), Ottawa, *Personal Communication*.

Euro Chlor (1994), *Halogenated Organic Compounds in the Environment*, COC (94/2), Brussels, Belgium: Euro Chlor, March.

Fatkin, Harry (1996), 'Comment on Hearne's "Tracking Toxics"', *Environment*, **38**(6), July/August, 31–3.

Frischknecht, R., P. Hofstetter, I. Knoepfel, R. Dones and E. Zollinger (1994), *Okobilanzen für Energiesyteme* (Ecobalances for Energy Systems), Zurich: Laboratory for Energy Systems, Swiss Federal Institute of Technology (LESIETH).

Gaines, Linda L. (1980), *Energy and Material Flows in the Copper Industry*, Technical Memo, Argonne, IL: Argonne National Laboratory.

Gaines, L.L. and S.Y. Shen (1980), *Energy and Materials Flows in the Production of Olefins and Their Derivatives*, Argonne, IL: Argonne National Laboratory, August.

Gaines, L.L. and A.M. Wolsky (1981), *Energy and Materials Flows in Petroleum Refining*, Technical Report, Argonne, IL: Argonne National Laboratory.

Georgescu-Roegen, Nicholas (1971), *The Entropy Law and the Economic Process*, Cambridge, MA: Harvard University Press.

Graf, G.E. (1924), *Erdol, Erdolkapitalismus, und Erdolpolitik*, Jena, Germany: Urania-Verlag GmbH.

Gribble, Gordon W. (1992), 'Naturally occurring organohalogen compounds: A survey', *Journal of Natural Products*, **55**(10), 1353–95.

Gribble, Gordon W. (1994), 'The natural production of chlorinated compounds', *Environmental Science and Technology*, **28**(7), 310a–19a.

Gribble, Gordon W., Robert M. Moore, David B. Harper, Anders Grimvall, Gunilla Asplund, Ed W.B. de Leer, Christian Grøn, German Müller, Christopher Rappe and William C. Keene (1995), *The Natural Chemistry of Chlorine in the Environment: An Overview by A Panel of Independent Scientists*, Brussels, Belgium: Euro Chlor.

Guelorget, Yves, V. Julien and Paul M. Weaver (1993), *A Life Cycle Analysis of Automobiles Tires in France*, Working Paper (93/67/EPS), Fontainebleau, France: INSEAD.

Hall, E.H., W.H. Hanna, L.D. Reed, J. Varga Jr., D.N. Williams, K.E. Wilkes, B.E. Johnson, W.J. Mueller, E.J. Bradbury and W.J. Frederick (1975), *Evaluation of the Theoretical Potential for Energy Conservation in Seven Basic Industries*, Columbus, Ohio: Battelle Columbus Laboratories.

Hearne, Shelley A. (1994), *Potential Modifications to the US EPA Toxics Release Inventory to Better Assess Pollution Prevention*, PhD Thesis, New York: Columbia University.

Hearne, Shelley A. (1996), 'Tracking toxics: chemical use and the public's "Right-to- Know"', *Environment*, **38**(6), July/August, 4–34.

Holmbom, Bjarne (1991), *Chlorine Bleaching of Pulp: Technology and Chemistry, Environmental and Health Effects, Regulations and Communication*, Case Study, Turku/Abo, Finland: Abo Akademi.

Howard, James L. (1997), *US Timber Production, Trade, Consumption, and Price Statistics 1965–1994*, Miscellaneous Publication, Madison, WI: Forest Products Laboratory, United States Department of Agriculture Forest Service.

Huettner, David A. (1976), 'Net energy analysis: an economic assessment', *Science*, April 9, 101–4.

Industrial Economics, Incorporated (1991), *Materials Balance Profiles for 33/50 Chemicals*, Cambridge, MA.

Intergovernmental Panel on Climate Change (IPCC) (1995), 'The science of climate change: contribution of working group I', in: *Second Assessment Report of the Intergovernmental Panel On Climate Change*, Cambridge, UK: Cambridge University Press.

International Bank for Reconstruction and Development (IBRD) (1980), *Environmental Considerations in the Pulp and Paper Industry*, Washington, DC: IBRD, December.

International Energy Agency (1995), *Energy Statistics of OECD Countries 1992–1993*, Paris: OECD.

Kneese, Allen V., Robert U. Ayres and Ralph d'Arge (1970), *Aspects of Environmental Economics: A Materials Balance Approach*, Baltimore, MD: Johns Hopkins University Press.

Kollar, K.L. and P. MacAuley (1980), 'Water requirements for industrial development', *Journal of the American Water Works Association*, **72**(1).

Koomey, Jonathan (1990), *Comparative Analysis of Monetary Estimates of External Environmental Costs Associated with Combustion of Fossil Fuels*, Energy Analysis Program, Applied Science Division, Lawrence Berkeley Laboratory, University of California, Berkeley, CA.

LeBel, Phillip G. (1982), *Energy Economics and Technology*, Baltimore, MD: The Johns Hopkins University Press.

Lovelock, James E. (1988), *The Ages of Gaia: A Biography of Our Living Earth*, London: Oxford University Press.

Lowenheim, Frederick A. and Marguerite K. Moran (1975), *Faith, Keyes, and Clark's 'Industrial Chemicals'*, New York: Wiley-Interscience, 4th edition.

Manzone, R. (1993), *PVC: Life Cycle and Perspectives*, COMMET Advanced Course, Urbino, Italy.

Management Institute for Environment and Business (MEB) (undated), c. 1995, *Competitive Implications of Environmental Regulation: A Study of Six Industries*, for the United States Environmental Protection Agency, Washington DC.

McGannon, H.E. (ed.) (1971), *The Making, Shaping and Treating of Steel*, Pittsburgh, PA: United States Steel Corporation.

H.M. Mittelhauser Corporation (1979), *Energy/Material Flows Associated with Cyclic Petrochemicals*, Technical Report (ANLCNSV-TM-56), Downers Grove, IL: H.M. Mittelhauser Corporation.

Mongan, Edward (1996), 'Comment on Hearne's "Tracking Toxics"', *Environment*, **38**(6), July/August, 30–31.

Nemerow, Nelson L. (1995), *Zero Pollution for Industry: Waste Minimization Through Industrial Complexes*, New York: John Wiley and Sons.

Nicolis, Gregoire and Ilya Prigogine (1977), *Self-Organization in Non-Equilibrium Systems*, New York: Wiley-Interscience.

Nriagu, Jerome O. (1990), 'Global metal pollution', *Environment*, **32**(7), 7–32.

Oak Ridge National Laboratory and Resources for the Future (1992), *US-EC Fuel Cycle Study: Background Document to the Approach and Issues*, Washington, DC: Oak Ridge National Laboratory and Resources for the Future, November 1992. (Prepared for the United State Department of Energy).

Obernberger, Ingwald (1994), *Characterization and Utilization of Wood Ashes*, Technical Paper, Institute of Chemical Engineering, Technical University, Graz, Austria.

Organization for Economic Cooperation and Development (OECD) (1994), *The OECD Jobs Study: Evidence and Explanations*, Paris: OECD.

Organization for Economic Cooperation and Development (OECD) (1995), *OECD Environment Data Compendium 1995*, Paris: OECD.

Poje, Gerald V. and Daniel M. Horowitz (1990), *Phantom Reductions: Tracking Toxic Trends*, Washington, DC: National Wildlife Federation.

Repetto, Robert (1990), *The Concept and Measurement of Environmental Productivity: An Exploratory Study of the Electric Power Industry*, Towards 2000: Environment, Technology and the New Century (Symposium), World Resources Institute and the OECD, Annapolis, MD, June 1990. (Background Paper.)

Repetto, Robert, Dale Rothman, Paul Faeth and Duncan Austin (1996), *Has Environmental Protection Really Reduced Productivity Growth? We Need Unbiased Measures*, Washington, DC: World Resources Institute.

Riley, G., J. Warren and R. Baker (1993), *Assessment of Changes in Reported TRI Releases and Transfers Between 1989 and 1990*, Research Triangle Park, NC: Center for Economics Research, Research Triangle Institute.

Rogner, Hans-Holger (1987), 'Energy in the world: the present situation and future options', in: Proceedings of the 17th International Congress of Refrigeration, August 24–28, 1987.

Roodman, David Malin (1996), *Paying the Piper: Subsidies, Politics and the Environment*, Worldwatch Paper (133), Washington, DC: Worldwatch Institute.

Roskill Information Services Ltd. (1991), *The Economics of Silicon and Ferrosilicon*, London: Roskill Information Services Ltd., 7th edition.

Roskill Information Services Ltd. (1992), *The Economics of Bromine 1992*, London: Roskill Information Services Ltd., 6th edition.

Roskill Information Services Ltd. (1993), *The Economics of Chromium 1993*, London: Roskill Information Services Ltd., 8th edition.

Rowe, Robert *et al.* (1995), *The New York Environmental Externalities Study:*

Summary of Approach and Results, Workshop on the External Costs of Energy, Brussels, Belgium, January 30–31, 1995.

Schlesinger, William H. and Anne E. Hartley (1992), 'A Global Budget for Atmospheric NH₃', *Biogeochemistry*, **15**, 191–211.

Schlesinger, William H. (1991), *Biogeochemistry; An Analysis of Global Change*, New York: Academic Press.

Schmidt-Bleek, Friedrich (1994), *Wieviel Umwelt braucht der mensch? MIPS, Das Mass für Ökolologisches Wirtschaften*, Berlin: Birkhauser Verlag, in German.

Science Applications International Corporation (SAI) (1985), *Summary of Data on Industrial Nonhazardous Waste Disposal Practices*, EPA Contract (68-01-7050), Washington, DC.

Sheiman, Deborah A. (1991), *The Right to Know More*, Washington, DC: NRDC.

Shreve, R. Norris (1956), *The Chemical Process Industries*, New York: McGraw-Hill Book Company.

Sittig, M. (1977), *Pulp and Paper Manufacture, Energy Conservation and Pollution Prevention*, Park Ridge, NJ: Noyes Data Corporation.

Smil, Vaclav (1993), *Nutrient Flows in Agriculture* (unpublished).

Stanford Research Institute (SRI) (1989), *Chemical Economics Handbook*, Menlo Park, CA: SRI International.

Stanford Research Institute (SRI) (annual), *PEP Yearbook*, Menlo Park, CA: SRI International.

Steen, Bengt and Sten-Olof Ryding (1993), *The EPS Enviro-Accounting Method*, AFR-Report 11, Swedish Waste Research Council for a Low-Waste, Ecocyclic Society, Stockholm.

Subak, Susan, Paul Raskin and David von Hippel (1992), *National Greenhouse Gas Accounts: Current Anthropogenic Sources and Sinks*, Report, Stockholm Environmental Institute, Boston, MA.

Swift, T. Kevin (1995), *Chlorine and Its Major End Uses*, Washington, DC: Chemical Manufacturers Association (CMA).

Tellus Institute (1992), *CSG/Tellus Packaging Study: Inventory of Material and Energy Use and Air and Water Emissions from the Production of Packaging Materials*, Boston, MA: Tellus Institute.

Thiemens, Mark H. and William C. Trogler (1991), 'Nylon production: an unknown source of atmospheric nitrous oxide', *Science*, **251**, 932–4.

Thornton, Joe (1991), *The Product is the Poison: The Case for Chlorine Phase-Out*, Washington, DC: Greenpeace.

Thornton, Joe (1993), *Chlorine, Human Health and the Environment*, Washington, DC: Greenpeace.

Tukker, A., R. Kleijn, L. van Oers and E.R.W. Smeets (1996), *A PVC Sub-*

stance *Flow Analysis for Sweden*, Research Report (STB/96/48–1), TNO-STB, Apeldoorn, Netherlands.

Ulrich, Alice H. (1990), *US Timber Production, Trade, Consumption and Price Statistics 1960–88*, Washington, DC: Forest Service, United States Department of Agriculture.

United Nations Environment Programme – Industry and Environment (1991), *Environmental Aspects of Selected Non-Ferrous Metals (Cu, Ni, Pb, Zn, Au) Ore Mining: A Technical Guide*, Industry and Environment Program Activity Center, Paris: UNEP.

United Nations Statistical Office (1993), *Industrial Statistics Yearbook: Commodity Production Statistics 1991*, Vol. II, New York: United Nations.

United States Bureau of the Census (1991), *Statistical Abstract of the United States: 1991*, Washington, DC: United States Government Printing Office, 111th edition.

United States Bureau of the Census (1993), *Statistical Abstract of the United States: 1993*, Washington, DC: United States Government Printing Office, 113th edition.

United States Bureau of the Census (1995), *Statistical Abstract of the United States: 1995*, Washington, DC: United States Government Printing Office, 115th edition.

United States Bureau of Mines (USBM) (1985), *Mineral Facts and Problems*, Washington, DC: United States Government Printing Office.

United States Bureau of Mines (USBM) (1994), *Mineral Commodity Summaries*, Washington, DC: United States Bureau of Mines.

United States Bureau of Mines (annual), *Minerals Yearbook: Volume I; Metals and Minerals*, Washington, DC: United States Government Printing Office.

United States Congress Office of Technology Assessment (USOTA) (1984), *Wood Use: US Competitiveness and Technology; Vol II – Technical Report*, Washington, DC: United States Congress Office of Technology Assessment.

United States Congress Office of Technology Assessment (USOTA) (1992), *Managing Industrial Solid Wastes from Manufacturing, Mining, Oil and Gas Production, and Utility Coal Combustion*, Washington, DC: United States Congress Office of Technology Assessment.

United States Department of Agriculture (1991), *Agricultural Statistics*, Washington, DC: United States Government Printing Office.

United States Department of Agriculture (1992), *Agricultural Statistics*, Washington, DC: United States Government Printing Office.

United States Department of Agriculture; National Agricultural Statistics Service (1996), *Agricultural Statistics: 1995–96*, Washington, DC: United States Government Printing Office.

United States Department of Commerce International Trade Administration (1988), *Overview on the Use and Storage of Coal Combustion Ash in the United States*, Discussion Paper, United States Department of Commerce, Washington, DC.

United States Department of Commerce (1992), *Current Industrial Reports: Inorganic Chemicals*, Washington, DC: United States Department of Commerce.

United States Environmental Protection Agency (USEPA) (1985), *Compilation of Air Pollution Emission Factors, Volume I: Stationary Point and Area Sources*, Research Triangle Park, NC: United States Environmental Protection Agency.

United States Environmental Protection Agency Office of Solid Waste (USEPA) (1986), *Waste Minimization Issues and Options*, Washington, DC: United States Environmental Protection Agency Office of Solid Waste.

United States Environmental Protection Agency (USEPA) (1988), *Solid Waste Disposal in the United States*, Washington, DC: United States Environmental Protection Agency.

United States Environmental Protection Agency Office of Solid Waste (USEPA) (1991), *1987 National Biennial Report of Hazardous Waste Treatment, Storage and Disposal Facilities Regulated Under RCRA*, Washington, DC: United States Environmental Protection Agency Office of Solid Waste.

United States International Trade Commission (USITC) (annual), *Synthetic Organic Chemicals 19xx*, Washington, DC: United States Government Printing Office.

USOMB (1987), *Standard Industrial Classification Manual 1987*, Office of Management and Budget, Executive Office of the President, Washington, DC: National Technical Information Service (NTIS), Springfield, Va. #PB-87-100012.

van Liere, J. (1995), *Source to Service: Triple-E Concept in Energy Chains*, Arnhem, Netherlands: KEMA.

van Ost, Hendrik (1997), United States Geological Survey, Personal Communication, Autumn.

Vellinga, Pier, Frans Berkhout and Joyeeta Gupta (eds) (1998), *Managing a Material World: Perspectives in Industrial Ecology*, Dordrecht, Netherlands: Kluwer Academic Publishers.

Von Weizsäcker, Ernst Ulrich, Amory B. Lovins and L. Hunter Lovins (1997), *Factor Four: Doubling Wealth, Halving Resource Use*, London: Earthscan.

Wang, M.Q., D.J. Santini and S.A. Warinner (1994), *Methods of Valuing Air Pollution and Estimated Monetary Values of Air Pollutants in Various Regions*, Center for Transportation Research, Energy Systems Division, Argonne National Laboratory, Chicago.

Wheeler, D., Mala Hettige and P. Norton (1993), *Industrial Pollution Projection System*, Washington, DC: World Bank Paper.

White, Allen L. and Angela Dierks (1996), 'Comment on Hearne's "Tracking Toxics"', *Environment*, **38**(6), July/August, 33–4.

White, Allen L., D.E. Savage and Angela Dierks (1995), 'Environmental accounting: principles for sustainable enterprise', in: *Technical Applications in the Pulp and Paper Industry* (TAPPI) **2**, 949–58. Proceedings of the TAPPI International Environmental Conference, Atlanta, GA, May 7–10,1995.

World Energy Council (WEC) (1992), *1992 Survey of Energy Resources*, World Energy Council.

Wormgoor, J.W. (1994), *Sources of Dioxin Emissions into the Air in Western Europe*, TNO Institute of Environmental and Energy Technology, Apeldoorn, Netherlands.

Index